Maria Mitchell, Life, Letters, and Journals

By

Maria Mitchell

Published by Forgotten Books 2012

Originally Published 1896

PIBN 1000291607

MARIA MITCHELL

LIFE, LETTERS, AND JOURNALS

COMPILED BY

PHEBE MITCHELL KENDALL

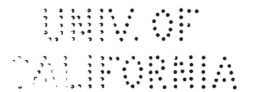

ILLUSTRATED

BOSTON
LEE AND SHEPARD PUBLISHERS
10 MILK STREET
1896

COPYRIGHT, 1896, BY LEE AND SHEPARD

MARIA MITCHELL

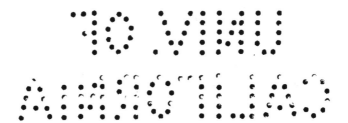

PRESS OF
Rockwell and Churchill
BOSTON U.S.A.

CONTENTS

CHAPTER I

CHAPTER VII

CHAPTER VIII

CHAPTER IX

CHAPTER X

MARIA MITCHELL

CHAPTER I

BIRTH — PARENTS   HOME SURROUNDINGS AND EARLY LIFE

MARIA MITCHELL was born on the island of Nantucket, Mass., Aug. 1, 1818. She was the third child of William and Lydia [Coleman] Mitchell.

Her ancestors, on both sides, were Quakers for many generations; and it was in consequence of the intolerance of the early Puritans that these ancestors had been obliged to flee from the State of Massachusetts, and to settle upon this island, which, at that time, belonged to the State of New York.

For many years the Quakers, or Friends, as they called themselves, formed much the larger part of the inhabitants of Nantucket, and thus were enabled to crystallize, as it were, their own ideas of what family and social life should be; and although in course of time many " world's people " swooped down and helped to swell the number of islanders, they still continued to hold their own methods, and to bring up their children in accordance with their own conceptions of " Divine light."

Mr. and Mrs. Mitchell were married during the war of 1812; the former lacking one week of being twenty-one years' old, and the latter being a few months over twenty.

The people of Nantucket by their situation endured many hardships during this period; their ships were upon the sea a prey to privateers, and communication with the mainland was exposed to the same danger, so that it was difficult to obtain such necessaries of life as the island could not furnish. There were still to be seen, a few years ago, the marks left on the moors, where fields of corn and potatoes had been planted in that trying time.

So the young couple began their housekeeping in a very simple way. Mr. Mitchell used to describe it as being very delightful; it was noticed that Mrs. Mitchell never expressed herself on the subject, — it was she, probably, who had the planning to do, to make a little money go a great way, and to have everything smooth and serene when her husband came home.

Mrs. Mitchell was a woman of strong character, very dignified, honest almost to an extreme, and perfectly self-controlled where control was necessary. She possessed very strong affections, but her self-control was such that she was undemonstrative.

She kept a close watch over her children, was clear-headed, knew their every fault and every merit, and was an indefatigable worker. It was she who looked out for the education of the children and saw what their capacities were.

Mr. Mitchell was a man of great suavity and gentleness; if left to himself he would never have denied a single request made to him by one of his children. His first impulse was to gratify every desire of their hearts, and if it had not been for the clear head of the mother, who took care that the household should be managed wisely and economically, the results might have been disastrous. The father had wisdom enough to perceive this, and when a child came to him, and in a very pathetic and winning way proffered some request for an unusual indulgence, he generally replied, "Yes, if mother thinks best."

Mr. Mitchell was very fond of bright colors; as they were excluded from the dress of Friends, he indulged himself wherever it was possible. If he were buying books, and there was a variety of binding, he always chose the copies with red covers. Even the wooden framework of the reflecting telescope which he used was painted a brilliant red. He liked a gay carpet on the floor, and the walls of the family sitting-room in the house on Vestal street were covered with paper resplendent with bunches of pink roses. Suspended by a cord from the ceiling in the centre of this room was a glass ball, filled with water, used by Mr. Mitchell in his experiments on polarization of light, flashing its dancing rainbows about the room.

At the back of this house was a little garden, full of gay flowers: so that if the garb of the young Mitchells was rather sombre, the setting was bright and cheerful, and the life in the home was healthy and wide-awake. When the hilarity became excessive the mother would put in her little check, from time to time, and the father

would try to look as he ought to, but he evidently
enjoyed the whole.

As Mr. Mitchell was kind and indulgent to his children, so he was the sympathetic friend and counsellor
of many in trouble who came to him for help or
advice. As he took his daily walk to the little farm
about a mile out of town, where, for an hour or two
he enjoyed being a farmer, the people would come
to their doors to speak to him as he passed, and the
little children would run up to him to be patted on
the head.

He treated animals in the same way. He generally
kept a horse. His children complained that although
the horse was good when it was bought, yet as Mr.
Mitchell never allowed it to be struck with a whip, nor
urged to go at other than a very gentle trot, the horse
became thoroughly demoralized, and was no more fit to
drive than an old cow!

There was everything in the home which could amuse
and instruct children. The eldest daughter was very
handy at all sorts of entertaining occupations; she had
a delicate sense of the artistic, and was quite skilful
with her pencil.

The present kindergarten system in its practice is
almost identical with the home as it appeared in the first
half of this century, among enlightened people. There
is hardly any kind of handiwork done in the kindergarten that was not done in the Mitchell family, and in
other families of their acquaintance. The girls learned
to sew and cook, just as they learned to read, — as
a matter of habit rather than of instruction. They

learned how to make their own clothes, by making their dolls' clothes, — and the dolls themselves were frequently home-made, the eldest sister painting the faces much more prettily than those obtained at the shops; and there was a great delight in gratifying the fancy, by dressing the dolls, not in Quaker garb, but in all of the most brilliant colors and stylish shapes worn by the ultra-fashionable.

There were always plenty of books, and besides those in the house there was the Atheneum Library, which, although not a free library, was very inexpensive to the shareholders.

There was another very striking difference between that epoch and the present. The children of that day were taught to value a book and to take excellent care of it; as an instance it may be mentioned that one copy of Colburn's "Algebra" was used by eight children in the Mitchell family, one after the other. The eldest daughter's name was written on the inside of the cover; seven more names followed in the order of their ages, as the book descended.

With regard to their reading, the mother examined every book that came into the house. Of course there were not so many books published then as now, and the same books were read over and over. Miss Edgeworth's stories became part of their very lives, and Young's "Night Thoughts," and the poems of Cowper and Bloomfield were conspicuous objects on the bookshelves of most houses in those days. Mr. Mitchell was very apt, while observing the heavens in the evening, to quote from one or the other of these poets, or

from the Bible. " An undevout astronomer is mad " was
one of his favorite quotations.

Among the poems which Maria learned in her childhood, and which was repeatedly upon her lips all
through her life, was, " The spacious firmament on
high." In her latter years if she had a sudden fright
which threatened to take away her senses she would test
her mental condition by repeating that poem; it is
needless to say that she always remembered it, and her
nerves instantly relapsed into their natural condition.

The lives of Maria Mitchell and her numerous
brothers and sisters were passed in simplicity and with
an entire absence of anything exciting or abnormal.

The education of their children is enjoined upon the
parents by the " Discipline," and in those days at least
the parents did not give up all the responsibility in that
line to the teachers. In Maria Mitchell's childhood the
children of a family sat around the table in the evenings
and studied their lessons for the next day, — the parents
or the older children assisting the younger if the lessons
were too difficult. The children attended school five
days in the week, — six hours in the day, — and their
only vacation was four weeks in the summer, generally
in August.

The idea that children over-studied and injured their
health was never promulgated in that family, nor indeed
in that community; it seems to be a notion of the
present half-century.

Maria's first teacher was a lady for whom she always
felt the warmest affection, and in her diary, written in
her later years, occurs this allusion to her:

"I count in my life, outside of family relatives, three aids given me on my journey; they are prominent to me: the woman who first made the study-book charming; the man who sent me the first hundred dollars I ever saw, to buy books with; and another noble woman, through whose efforts I became the owner of a telescope; and of these, the first was the greatest."

As a little girl, Maria was not a brilliant scholar; she was shy and slow; but later, under her father's tuition, she developed very rapidly.

After the close of the war of 1812, when business was resumed and the town restored to its normal prosperity, Mr. Mitchell taught school, — at first as master of a public school, and afterwards in a private school of his own. Maria attended both of these schools.

Mr. Mitchell's pupils speak of him as a most inspiring teacher, and he always spoke of his experiences in that capacity as very happy.

When her father gave up teaching, Maria was put under the instruction of Mr. Cyrus Peirce, afterwards principal of the first normal school started in the United States.

Mr. Peirce took a great interest in Maria, especially in developing her taste for mathematical study, for which she early showed a remarkable talent.

The books which she studied at the age of seventeen, as we know by the date of the notes, were Bridge's "Conic Sections," Hutton's "Mathematics," and Bowditch's "Navigator." At that time Prof. Benjamin Peirce had not published his "Explanations of the Navigator and Almanac," so that Maria was obliged to consult many scientific books and reports before she could herself construct the astronomical tables.

Mr. Mitchell, on relinquishing school-teaching, was appointed cashier of the Pacific Bank; but although he gave up teaching, he by no means gave up studying his favorite science, astronomy, and Maria was his willing helper at all times.

Mr. Mitchell from his early youth was an enthusiastic student of astronomy, at a time, too, when very little attention was given to that study in this country. His evenings, when pleasant, were spent in observing the heavens, and to the children, accustomed to seeing such observations going on, the important study in the world seemed to be astronomy. One by one, as they became old enough, they were drafted into the service of counting seconds by the chronometer, during the observations.

Some of them took an interest in the thing itself, and others considered it rather stupid work, but they all drank in so much of this atmosphere, that if any one had asked a little child in this family, "Who was the greatest man that ever lived?" the answer would have come promptly, " Herschel."

Maria very early learned the use of the sextant. The chronometers of all the whale ships were brought to Mr. Mitchell, on their return from a voyage, to be " rated," as it was called. For this purpose he used the sextant, and the observations were made in the little back yard of the Vestal-street home.

There was also a clumsy reflecting telescope made on the Herschelian plan, but of very great simplicity, which was put up on fine nights in the same back yard, when the neighbors used to flock in to look at the moon. Afterwards Mr. Mitchell bought a small Dolland telescope, which thereafter, as long as she lived, his daughter used for " sweeping " purposes.

After their removal to the bank building there were added to these an " altitude and azimuth circle," loaned to Mr. Mitchell by West Point Academy, and two transit instruments. A little observatory for the use of the first was placed on the roof of the bank building, and two small buildings were erected in the yard for the transits. There was also a much larger and finer telescope loaned by the Coast Survey, for which service Mr. Mitchell made observations.

At the time when Maria Mitchell showed a decided taste for the study of astronomy there was no school in the world where she could be taught higher mathematics and astronomy. Harvard College, at that time, had no telescope better than the one which her father was using, and no observatory except the little octagonal projection to the old mansion in Cambridge occupied by the late Dr. A. P. Peabody.

However, every one will admit that no school nor institution is better for a child than the home, with an enthusiastic parent for a teacher.

At the time of the annular eclipse of the sun in 1831 the totality was central at Nantucket. The window was taken out of the parlor on Vestal street, the telescope, the little Dolland, mounted in front of it, and with Maria by his side counting the seconds the father observed the eclipse. Maria was then twelve years old.

At sixteen Miss Mitchell left Mr. Peirce's schoc 's a pupil, but was retained as assistant teacher; she on relinquished that position and opened a private s ool on Traders' Lane. This school too she gave up for the position of librarian of the Nantucket Atheneum, which office she held for nearly twenty years.

This library was open only in the afternoon, and on Saturday evening. The visitors were comparatively few in the afternoon, so that Miss Mitchell had ample leisure for study, — an opportunity of which she made the most. Her visitors in the afternoon were elderly men of leisure, who enjoyed talking with so bright a girl on their favorite hobbies. When they talked Miss Mitchell closed her book and took up her knitting, for she was never idle. With some of these visitors the friendship was kept up for years.

It was in this library that she found La Place's " Mecanique Celeste," translated by her father's friend, Dr. Bowditch; she also read the " Theoria Motus," of Gauss, in its original Latin form. In her capacity as librarian Miss Mitchell to a large extent controlled the reading of the young people in the town. Many of them on arriving at mature years have expressed their gratitude for the direction in which their reading was turned by her advice.

Miss Mitchell always had a special friendship for young girls and boys. Many of these intimacies grew out of the acquaintance made at the library, — the young girls made her their confidante and went to her for sympathy and advice. The boys, as they grew up, and went away to sea, perhaps, always remembered her, and made a point, when they returned in their vacations, of coming to tell their experiences to such a sympathetic listener.

"April 18, 1855. A young sailor boy came to see me to-day. It pleases me to have these lads seek me on their return from their first voyage, and tell me how much they have learned about navigation. They always say, with pride, 'I can take a lunar, Miss Mitchell, and work it up!'

"This boy I had known only as a boy, but he has suddenly become a man and seems to be full of intelligence. He will go once more as a sailor, he says, and then try for the position of second mate. He looked as if he had been a good boy and would make a good man.

"He said that he had been ill so much that he had been kept out of temptation; but that the forecastle of a ship was no place for improvement of mind or morals. He said the captain with whom he came home asked him if he knew me, because he had heard of me. I was glad to find that the captain was a man of intelligence and had been kind to the boy."

Miss Mitchell was an inveterate reader. She devoured books on all subjects. If she saw that boys were eagerly reading a certain book she immediately read it; if it were harmless she encouraged them to read it; if otherwise, she had a convenient way of *losing* the book. In November, when the trustees made their annual examination, the book appeared upon the shelf, but the next day after it was again lost. At this time Nantucket was a thriving, busy town. The

whale-fishery was a very profitable business, and the
town was one of the wealthiest in the State.   There
was a good deal of social and literary life.   In a Friend's
family neither music nor dancing was allowed.

Mr. and Mrs. Mitchell were by no means narrow sectarians, but they believed it to be best to conform to
the rules of Friends as laid down in the "Discipline."
George Fox himself, the founder of the society, had
blown a blast against music, and especially instrumental
music in churches.   It will be remembered that the
Methodists have but recently yielded to the popular
demand in this respect, and have especially favored
congregational singing.

It is most likely that George Fox had no ear for
music himself, and thus entailed upon his followers an
obligation from which they are but now freeing themselves.

There was plenty of singing in the Mitchell family,
and the parents liked it, especially the father, who, when
he sat down in the evening with the children, would say,
"Now sing something."   But there could be no instruction in singing; the children sang the songs that they
picked up from their playmates.

However, one of the daughters bought a piano, and
Maria's purse opened to help that cause along.   It
would not have been proper for Mr. Mitchell to help
pay for it, but he took a great interest in it, nevertheless.
So indeed did the mother, but she took care not to
express herself outwardly.

The piano was kept in a neighboring building not too
far off to be heard from the house.   Maria had no ear

for music herself, but she was always to be depended upon to take the lead in an emergency, so the sisters put their heads together and decided that the piano must be brought into the house. When they had made all the preparations the father and mother were invited to take tea with their married daughter, who lived in another part of the town and had been let into the secret.

The piano was duly removed and placed in an upper room called the "hall," where Mr. Mitchell kept the chronometers, where the family sewing was done, and where the larger part of the books were kept, — a beautiful room, overlooking "the square," and a great gathering-place for all their young friends. When the piano was put in place, the sisters awaited the coming of the parents. Maria stationed herself at the foot of the stairs, ready to meet them as they entered the front door; another, half-way between, was to give the signal to a third, who was seated at the piano. The footsteps were heard at the door, the signal was given; a lively tune was started, and Maria confronted the parents as they entered.

" What's that? " was the exclamation.

" Well," said Maria, soothingly, " we've had the piano brought over."

" Why, of all things ! " exclaimed the mother.

The father laid down his hat, walked immediately upstairs, entered the hall, and said, " Come, daughter, play something lively ! "

So that was all.

But that was not all for Mr. Mitchell; he had broken

the rules accepted by the Friends, and it was necessary for some notice to be taken of it, so a dear old Friend and neighbor came to deal with him. Now, to be "under dealings," as it is called, was a very serious matter, — to be spoken of only under the breath, in a half whisper.

" I hear that thee has a piano in thy house," said the old Friend.

" Yes, my daughters have," was the reply.

" But it is in thy house," pursued the Friend.

" Yes; but my home is my children's home as well as mine," said Mr. Mitchell, " and I propose that they shall not be obliged to go away from home for their pleasures. I don't play on the piano."

It so happened that Mr. Mitchell held the property of the " monthly meeting " in his hands at the time, and it was a very improper thing for the accredited agent of the society to be " under dealings," as Mr. Mitchell gently suggested.

This the Friend had not thought of, and so he said, " Well, William, perhaps we'd better say no more about it."

When the father came home after this interview he could not keep it to himself. If it had been the mother who was interviewed she would have kept it a profound secret, — because she would not have liked to have her children get any fun out of the proceedings of the old Friend. But Mr. Mitchell told the story in his quiet way, the daughters enjoyed it, and declared that the piano was placed upon a firm foothold by this proceeding. The news spread abroad, and several other young

Quaker girls eagerly seized the occasion to gratify their musical longings in the same direction.[1]

Few women with scientific tastes had the advantages which surrounded Miss Mitchell in her own home. Her father was acquainted with the most prominent scientific men in the country, and in his hospitable home at Nantucket she met many persons of distinction in literature and science.

She cared but little for general society, and had always to be coaxed to go into company. Later in life, however, she was much more socially inclined, and took pleasure in making and receiving visits. She could neither dance nor sing, but in all amusements which require quickness and a ready wit she was very happy. She was very fond of children, and knew how to amuse them and to take care of them. As she had half a dozen younger brothers and sisters, she had ample opportunity to make herself useful.

She was a capital story-teller, and always had a story on hand to divert a wayward child, or to soothe the little sister who was lying awake, and afraid of the dark. She wrote a great many little stories, printed them with a pen, and bound them in pretty covers. Most of them were destroyed long ago.

Maria took her part in all the household work. She knew how to do everything that has to be done in a large family where but one servant is kept, and she did everything thoroughly. If she swept a room it became

---

[1] It is pleasant to note that this objection to music among Friends is a thing of the past, and that the Friends' School at Providence, R.I., which is under the control of the " New England Yearly Meeting of Friends," has music in its regular curriculum.

clean. She might not rearrange the different articles of furniture in the most artistic manner, but everything would be clean, and there would be nothing left crooked. If a chair was to be placed, it would be parallel to something; she was exceedingly sensitive to a line out of the perpendicular, and could detect the slightest deviation from that rule. She had also a sensitive eye in the matter of color, and felt any lack of harmony in the colors worn by those about her.

Maria was always ready to "bear the brunt," and could at any time be coaxed by the younger children to do the things which they found difficult or disagreeable.

The two youngest children in the family were delicate, and the special care of the youngest sister devolved upon Maria, who knew how to be a good nurse as well as a good playfellow. She was especially careful of a timid child; she herself was timid, and, throughout her life, could never witness a thunder-storm with any calmness.

On one of those occasions so common in an American household, when the one servant suddenly takes her leave, or is summarily dismissed, Miss Mitchell describes her part of the family duties:

"Oct. 21, 1854. This morning I arose at six, having been half asleep only for some hours, fearing that I might not be up in time to get breakfast, a task which I had volunteered to do the preceding evening. It was but half light, and I made a hasty toilet. I made a fire very quickly, prepared the coffee, baked the graham bread, toasted white bread, trimmed the solar lamp, and made another fire in the dining-room before seven o'clock.

" I always thought that servant-girls had an easy time of it, and I still think so. I really found an hour too long for all this, and when I rang the bell at seven for breakfast I had been waiting fifteen minutes for the clock to strike.

" I went to the Atheneum at 9.30, and having decided that I would take the Newark and Cambridge places of the comet, and work them up, I did so, getting to the three equations before I went home to dinner at 12.30. I omitted the corrections of parallax and aberrations, not intending to get more than a rough approximation. I find to my sorrow that they do not agree with those from my own observations. I shall look over them again next week.

" At noon I ran around and did up several errands, dined, and was back again at my post by 1.30. Then I looked over my morning's work, — I can find no mistake. I have worn myself thin trying to find out about this comet, and I know very little now in the matter.

" I saw, in looking over Cooper, elements of a comet of 1825 which resemble what I get out for this, from my own observations, but I cannot rely upon my own.

" I saw also, to-day, in the 'Monthly Notices,' a plan for measuring the light of stars by degrees of illumination, — an idea which had occurred to me long ago, but which I have not practised.

" October 23. Yesterday I was again reminded of the remark which Mrs. Stowe makes about the variety of occupations which an American woman pursues.

" She says it is this, added to the cares and anxieties,

which keeps them so much behind the daughters of England in personal beauty.

"And to-day I was amused at reading that one of her party objected to the introduction of waxed floors into American housekeeping, because she could seem to see herself down on her knees doing the waxing.

"But of yesterday. I was up before six, made the fire in the kitchen, and made coffee. Then I set the table in the dining-room, and made the fire there. Toasted bread and trimmed lamps. Rang the breakfast bell at seven. After breakfast, made my bed, and 'put up' the room. Then I came down to the Atheneum and looked over my comet computations till noon. Before dinner I did some tatting, and made seven button-holes for K. I dressed and then dined. Came back again to the Atheneum at 1.30, and looked over another set of computations, which took me until four o'clock. I was pretty tired by that time, and rested by reading 'Cosmos.' Lizzie E. came in, and I gossiped for half an hour. I went home to tea, and that over, I made a loaf of bread. Then I went up to my room and read through (partly writing) two exercises in German, which took me thirty-five minutes.

"It was stormy, and I had no observing to do, so I sat down to my tatting. Lizzie E. came in and I took a new lesson in tatting, so as to make the pearl-edged. I made about half a yard during the evening. At a little after nine I went home with Lizzie, and carried a letter to the post-office. I had kept steadily at work for sixteen hours when I went to bed."

CHAPTER II

1847-1854

MISS MITCHELL'S COMET — EXTRACTS FROM DIARY — THE COMET

MISS MITCHELL spent every clear evening on the house-top "sweeping" the heavens.

No matter how many guests there might be in the parlor, Miss Mitchell would slip out, don her regimentals as she called them, and, lantern in hand, mount to the roof.

On the evening of Oct. 1, 1847, there was a party of invited guests at the Mitchell home. As usual, Maria slipped out, ran up to the telescope, and soon returned to the parlor and told her father that she thought she saw a comet. Mr. Mitchell hurried upstairs, stationed himself at the telescope, and as soon as he looked at the object pointed out by his daughter declared it to be a comet. Miss Mitchell, with her usual caution, advised him to say nothing about it until they had observed it long enough to be tolerably sure. But Mr. Mitchell immediately wrote to Professor Bond, at Cambridge, announcing the discovery. On account of stormy weather, the mails did not leave Nantucket until October 3.

- Frederick VI., King of Denmark, had offered, Dec. 17, 1831, a gold medal of the value of twenty ducats to the first discoverer of a telescopic comet. The regulations, as revised and amended, were republished, in April, 1840, in the "Astronomische Nachrichten."

When this comet was discovered, the king who had offered the medal was dead. The son, Frederick VII., who had succeeded him, had not the interest in science which belonged to his father, but he was prevailed upon to carry out his father's designs in this particular case.

The same comet had been seen by Father de Vico at Rome, on October 3, at 7.30 P.M., and this fact was immediately communicated by him to Professor Schumacher, at Altona. On the 7th of October, at 9.20 P.M., the comet was observed by Mr. W. R. Dawes, at Kent, England, and on the 11th it was seen by Madame Rümker, the wife of the director of the observatory at Hamburg.

The following letter from the younger Bond will show the cordial relations existing between the observatory at Cambridge and the smaller station at Nantucket:

CAMBRIDGE, Oct. 20, 1847.

DEAR MARIA: There! I think that is a very amiable beginning, considering the way in which I have been treated by you! If you are going to find any more comets, can you not wait till they are announced by the proper authorities? At least, don't kidnap another such as this last was.

If my object were to make you fear and tremble, I should tell you that on the evening of the 30th I was sweeping within a few degrees of your prize. I merely throw out the hint for what it is worth.

It has been very interesting to watch the motion of this comet among the stars with the great refractor; we could almost see it move.

An account of its passage over the star mentioned by your father when he was here, would make an interesting notice for one of the foreign journals, which we would readily forward. . . .

[Here follow Mr. Bond's observations.]

Respectfully,

Your obedient servant,

G. P. BOND.

Hon. Edward Everett, who at that time was president of Harvard College, took a great interest in the matter, and immediately opened a correspondence with the proper authorities, and sent a notice of the discovery to the " Astronomische Nachrichten."

The priority of Miss Mitchell's discovery was immediately admitted throughout Europe.

The King of Denmark very promptly referred the matter to Professor Schumacher, who reported in favor of granting the medal to Miss Mitchell, and the medal was duly struck off and forwarded to Mr. Everett.

Among European astronomers who urged Miss Mitchell's claim was Admiral Smyth, whom she knew through his " Celestial Cycle," and who later, on her visit to England, became a warm personal friend. Madame Rümker, also, sent congratulations.

Mr. Everett announced the receipt of the medal to Miss Mitchell in the following letter:

CAMBRIDGE, March 29, 1849.

MY DEAR MISS MITCHELL: I have the pleasure to inform you that your medal arrived by the last steamer; it reached me by mail, yesterday afternoon.

I went to Boston this morning, hoping to find you at the Adams House, to put it into your own hand.

As your return to Nantucket prevented this, I, of course, retain it, subject to your orders, not liking to take the risk again of its transmission by mail.

Having it in this way in my hand, I have taken the liberty to show it to some friends, such as W. C. Bond, Professor Peirce, the editors of the " Transcript," and the members of my family, — which I hope you will pardon.

I remain, my dear Miss Mitchell, with great regard,

Very faithfully yours,

EDWARD EVERETT.[1]

In 1848 Miss Mitchell was elected to membership by the " American Academy of Arts and Sciences," unanimously; she was the first and only woman ever admitted. In the diploma the printed word " Fellow" is erased, and the words " Honorary Member " inserted by Dr. Asa Gray, who signed the document as secretary. Some years later, however, her name is found in the list of Fellows of this Academy, also of the American Institute and of the American Association for the Advancement of Science. For many years she attended the annual conventions of this last-mentioned association, in which she took great interest.

The extract below refers to one of these meetings, probably that of 1855:

"August 23. It is really amusing to find one's self lionized in a city where one has visited quietly for years; to see the doors of fashionable mansions open wide to receive you, which never opened before. I suspect that the whole corps of science laughs in its sleeves at the farce.

---

[1] See Appendix.

"The leaders make it pay pretty well. My friend Professor Bache makes the occasions the opportunities for working sundry little wheels, pulleys, and levers; the result of all which is that he gets his enormous appropriations of $400,000 out of Congress, every winter, for the maintenance of the United States Coast Survey.

"For a few days Science reigns supreme, — we are fêted and complimented to the top of our bent, and although complimenters and complimented must feel that it is only a sort of theatrical performance, for a few days and over, one does enjoy acting the part of greatness for a while! I was tired after three days of it, and glad to take the cars and run away.

"The descent into a commoner was rather sudden. I went alone to Boston, and when I reached out my free pass, the conductor read it through and handed it back, saying in a gruff voice, ' It's worth nothing; a dollar and a quarter to Boston.' Think what a downfall! the night before, and

> ' One blast upon my bugle horn
> Were worth a hundred men ! '

Now one man alone was my dependence, and that man looked very much inclined to put me out of the car for attempting to pass a ticket that in his eyes was valueless. Of course I took it quietly, and paid the money, merely remarking, ' You will pass a hundred persons on this road in a few days on these same tickets.'

"When I look back on the paper read at this meeting by Mr. J in his uncouth manner, I think when a man is thoroughly in earnest, how careless he is of mere *words!*"

In 1849 Miss Mitchell was asked by the late Admiral
Davis, who had just taken charge of the American
Nautical Almanac, to act as computer for that work, — a
proposition to which she gladly assented, and for nine-
teen years she held that position in addition to her
other duties. This, of course, made a very desirable
increase to her income, but not necessarily to her ex-
penses. The tables of the planet Venus were assigned
to her. In this year, too, she was employed by Professor Bache, of the United States Coast Survey, in the
work of an astronomical party at Mount Independence,
Maine.

"1853. I was told that Miss Dix wished to see me,
and I called upon her. It was dusk, and I did not at
once see her; her voice was low, not particularly
sweet, but very gentle. She told me that she had heard
Professor Henry speak of me, and that Professor Henry
was one of her best friends, the truest man she knew.
When the lights were brought in I looked at her. She
must be past fifty, she is rather small, dresses indif-
ferently, has good features in general, but indifferent
eyes. She does not brighten up in countenance in
conversing. She is so successful that I suppose there
must be a hidden fire somewhere, for heat is a motive
power, and her cold manners could never move Legis-
latures. I saw some outburst of fire when Mrs. Hale's
book was spoken of. It seems Mrs. Hale wrote to her
for permission to publish a notice of her, and was
decidedly refused; another letter met with the same
answer, yet she wrote a 'Life,' which Miss Dix says
is utterly false.

" In her general sympathy for suffering humanity, Miss Dix seems neglectful of the individual interest. She has no family connection but a brother, has never had sisters, and she seemed to take little interest in the persons whom she met. I was surprised at her feeling any desire to see me. She is not strikingly interesting in conversation, because she is so grave, so cold, and so quiet. I asked her if she did not become at times weary and discouraged; and she said, wearied, but not discouraged, for she had met with nothing but success. There is evidently a strong will which carries all before it, not like the sweep of the hurricane, but like the slow, steady, and powerful march of the molten lava.

" It is sad to see a woman sacrificing the ties of the affections even to do good. I have no doubt Miss Dix does much good, but a woman needs a home and the love of other women at least, if she lives without that of man."

The following entry was made many years after : —

" August, 1871. I have just seen Miss Dix again, having met her only once for a few minutes in all the eighteen years. She listened to a story of mine about some girls in need, and then astonished me by an offer she made me."

" Feb. 15, 1853. I think Dr. Hall [in his ' Life of Mary Ware '] does wrong when he attempts to encourage the use of the *needle*. It seems to me that the needle is the chain of woman, and has fettered her more than the laws of the country.

" Once emancipate her from the ' stitch, stitch, stitch,' the industry of which would be commendable if it served any purpose except the gratification of her vanity, and she would have time for studies which would engross as the needle never can. I would as soon put a girl alone into a closet to meditate as give her only the society of her needle. The art of sewing, so far as men learn it, is well enough; that is, to enable a person to *take the stitches*, and, if necessary, to make her own garments in a strong manner; but the dressmaker should no more be a universal character than the carpenter. Suppose every man should feel it is his duty to do his own mechanical work of *all* kinds, would society be benefited? would the work be well done? Yet a woman is expected to know how to do all kinds of sewing, all kinds of cooking, all kinds of any *woman's* work, and the consequence is that life is passed in learning these only, while the universe of truth beyond remains unentered.

"May 11, 1853. I could not help thinking of Esther [a much-loved cousin who had recently died] a few evenings since when I was observing. A meteor flashed upon me suddenly, very bright, very short-lived; it seemed to me that it was sent for me especially, for it greeted me almost the first instant I looked up, and was gone in a second, — it was as fleeting and as beautiful as the smile upon Esther's face the last time I saw her. I thought when I talked with her about death that, though she could not come to me visibly, she might be able to influence my feelings; but it cannot be, for my faith has been weaker than ever since she died, and my fears have been greater."

A few pages farther on in the diary appears this poem:

" ESTHER

"Living, the hearts of all around
  Sought hers as slaves a throne ;
Dying, the reason first we found —
  The fulness of her own.

" She gave unconsciously the while
  A wealth we all might share —
To me the memory of the smile
  That last I saw her wear.

" Earth lost from out its meagre store
  A bright and precious stone ;
Heaven could not be so rich before,
  But it has richer grown."

"Sept. 19, 1853. I am surprised to find the verse which I picked up somewhere and have always admired —

 " 'Oh, reader, had you in your mind
  Such stores as silent thought can bring,
 Oh, gentle reader, you would find
  A tale in everything ' —

belonging to Wordsworth and to one of Wordsworth's simple, I am almost ready to say *silly*, poems. I am in doubt what to think of Wordsworth. I should be ashamed of some of his poems if I had written them myself, and yet there are points of great beauty, and lines which once in the mind will not leave it.

"Oct. 31, 1853. People have to learn sometimes not only how much the heart, but how much the head, can bear. My letter came from Cambridge [the Harvard

Observatory], and I had some work to do over. It was a wearyful job, but by dint of shutting myself up all day I did manage to get through with it. The good of my travelling showed itself then, when I was too tired to read, to listen, or to talk; for the beautiful scenery of the West was with me in the evening, instead of the tedious columns of logarithms. It is a blessed thing that these pictures keep in the mind and come out at the needful hour. I did not call them, but they seemed to come forth as a regulator for my tired brain, as if they had been set sentinel-like to watch a proper time to appear.

"November, 1853. There is said to be no up or down in creation, but I think the *world* must be *low*, for people who keep themselves constantly before it do a great deal of stooping!

"Dec. 8, 1853. Last night we had the first meeting of the class in elocution. It was very pleasant, but my deficiency of ear was never more apparent to myself. We had exercises in the ascending scale, and I practised after I came home, with the family as audience. H. says my ear is competent only to vulgar hearing, and I cannot appreciate nice distinctions. . . . I am sure that I shall never say that if I had been properly educated I should have made a singer, a dancer, or a painter — I should have failed less, perhaps, in the last. . . . Coloring I might have been good in, for I do think my eyes are better than those of any one I know.

"Feb. 18, 1854. If I should make out a calendar by my feelings of fatigue, I should say there were six Saturdays in the week and one Sunday.

" Mr. —— somewhat ridicules my plan of reading Milton with a view to his astronomy, but I have found it very pleasant, and have certainly a juster idea of Milton's variety of greatness than I had before. I have filled several sheets with my annotations on the ' Paradise Lost,' which I may find useful if I should ever be obliged to teach, either as a schoolma'am or a lecturer.[1]

" March 2, 1854. I ' swept' last night two hours, by three periods. It was a grand night — not a breath of air, not a fringe of a cloud, all clear, all beautiful. I really enjoy that kind of work, but my back soon becomes tired, long before the cold chills me. I saw two nebulæ in Leo with which I was not familiar, and that repaid me for the time. I am always the better for open-air breathing, and was certainly meant for the wandering life of the Indian.

" Sept. 12, 1854. I am just through with a summer, and a summer is to me always a trying ordeal. I have determined not to spend so much time at the Atheneum another season, but to put some one in my place who shall see the strange faces and hear the strange talk.

" How much talk there is about religion! Giles[2] I like the best, for he seems, like myself, to have no settled views, and to be religious only in feeling. He says he has no piety, but a great sense of infinity.

" Yesterday I had a Shaker visitor, and to-day a Catholic; and the more I see and hear, the less do I

---

[1] This paper has been printed since Miss Mitchell's death in " Poet-lore," June–July, 1894.

[2] Rev. Henry Giles.

care about church doctrines. The Catholic, a priest, I
have known as an Atheneum visitor for some time. He
talked to-day, on my asking him some questions, and
talked better than I expected. He is plainly full of
intelligence, full of enthusiasm for his religion, and,
I suspect, full of bigotry. I do not believe he will die
a Catholic priest. A young man of his temperament
must find it hard to live without family ties, and I shall
expect to hear, if I ever hear of him again, that some
good little Irish girl has made him forget his vows.

"My visitors, in other respects, have been of the average sort. Four women have been delighted to make
my acquaintance — three men have thought themselves in the presence of a superior being; one offered
me twenty-five cents because I reached him the key of
the museum. One woman has opened a correspondence with me, and several have told me that they knew
friends of mine; two have spoken of me in small letters to small newspapers; one said he didn't see me,
and one said he did! I have become hardened to all;
neither compliment nor quarter-dollar rouses any emo-
tion. My fit of humility, which has troubled me all
summer, is shaken, however, by the first cool breeze of
autumn and the first walk taken without perspiration.

"Sept. 22, 1854. On the evening of the 18th, while
'sweeping,' there came into the field the two nebulæ
in Ursa Major, which I have known for many a year,
but which to my surprise now appeared to be three.
The upper one, as seen from an inverting telescope,
appeared double-headed, like one near the Dolphin,
but much more decided than that, the space between the

two heads being very plainly discernible and subtend-
ing a decided angle. The bright part of this object
was clearly the old nebula — but what was the append-
age? Had the nebula suddenly changed? Was it a
comet, or was it merely a very fine night? Father
decided at once for the comet; I hesitated, with my
usual cowardice, and forbade his giving it a notice in
the newspaper.

"I watched it from 8.30 to 11.30 almost without
cessation, and was quite sure at 11.30 that its position
had changed with regard to the neighboring stars. I
counted its distance from the known nebula several
times, but the whole affair was difficult, for there were
flying clouds, and sometimes the nebula and comet
were too indistinct to be definitely seen.

"The 19th was cloudy and the 20th the same, with
the variety of occasional breaks, through which I saw
the nebula, but not the comet.

"On the 21st came a circular, and behold Mr. Van
Arsdale had seen it on the 13th, but had not been sure
of it until the 15th, on account of the clouds.

"I was too well pleased with having really made the
discovery to care because I was not first.

"Let the Dutchman have the reward of his sturdier
frame and steadier nerves!

"Especially could I be a Christian because the 13th
was cloudy, and more especially because I dreaded the
responsibility of making the computations, *nolens
volens*, which I must have done to be able to call it
mine. . . .

"I made observations for three hours last night, and

am almost ill to-day from fatigue; still I have worked all day, trying to reduce the places, and mean to work hard again to-night.

"Sept. 25, 1854. I began to recompute for the comet, with observations of Cambridge and Washington, to-day. I have had a fit of despondency in consequence of being obliged to renounce my own observations as too rough for use. The best that can be said of my life so far is that it has been industrious, and the best that can be said of me is that I have not pretended to what I was not. `

"October 10. As soon as I had run through the computations roughly for the comet, so as to make up my mind that by my own observations (which were very wrong) the Perihelion was passed, and nothing more to be hoped for from observations, I seized upon a pleasant day and went to the Cape for an excursion. We went to Yarmouth, Sandwich, and Plymouth, enjoying the novelty of the new car-route. It really seemed like railway travelling on our own island, so much sand and so flat a country.

" The little towns, too, seemed quaint and odd, and the old gray cottages looked as if they belonged to the last century, and were waked from a long nap by the railway whistle. .

" I thought Sandwich a beautiful, and Plymouth an interesting, town. I would fain have gone off into some poetical quotation, such as ' The breaking waves dashed high' or 'The Pilgrim fathers, where are they?' but K., who had been there before, desired me not to be absurd, but to step quietly on to the half-buried rock and quietly off. Younger sisters know a deal, so I did as I was bidden to do, and it was just as well not to make myself hoarse without an appreciative audience.

"I liked the picture by Sargent in Pilgrim Hall, but seeing Plymouth on a mild, sunny day, with everything looking bright and pleasant, it was difficult to conceive of the landing of the Pilgrims as an event, or that the settling of such a charming spot required any heroism.

"The picture, of course, represents the dreariness of winter, and my feelings were moved by the chilled appearance of the little children, and the pathetic countenance of little Peregrine White, who, considering that he was born in the harbor, is wonderfully grown up before they are welcomed by Samoset. According to history little Peregrine was born about December 6 and Samoset met them about March 16; so he was three months old, but he is plainly a forward child, for he looks up very knowingly. Such a child had immortality thrust upon him from his birth. It must have had a deadening influence upon him to know that he was a marked man whether he did anything worthy of mark or not. He does not seem to have made any figure after his entrance into the world, though he must have created a great sensation when he came.

"October 17. I have just gone over my comet computations again, and it is humiliating to perceive how very little more I know than I did seven years ago when I first did this kind of work. To be sure, I have only once in the time computed a parabolic orbit; but it seems to me that I know no more in general. I think I am a little better thinker, that I take things less upon trust, but at the same time I trust myself much less. The world of learning is so broad, and the human soul is so limited in power! We reach forth and strain every nerve, but we seize only a bit of the curtain that hides the infinite from us.

"Will it really unroll to us at some future time? Aside from the gratification of the affections in another world, that of the intellect must be great if it is enlarged and its desires are the same.

"Nov. 24, 1854. Yesterday James Freeman Clarke, the biographer of Margaret Fuller, came into the Atheneum. It was plain that he came to see me and not the institution. . . . He rushed into talk at once, mostly on people, and asked me about my astronomical labors. As it was a kind of flattery, I repaid it in kind by asking him about Margaret Fuller. He said she did not strike any one as a person of intellect or as a student, for all her faculties were kept so much abreast that none had prominence. I wanted to ask if she was a lovable person, but I did not think he would be an unbiassed judge, she was so much attached to him.

"Dec. 5, 1854. The love of one's own sex is precious, for it is neither provoked by vanity nor retained by flattery; it is genuine and sincere. I am grateful that I have had much of this in my life.

"The comet looked in upon us on the 29th. It made a twilight call, looking sunny and bright, as if it had just warmed itself in the equinoctial rays. A boy on the street called my attention to it, but I found on hurrying home that father had already seen it, and had ranged it behind buildings so as to get a rough position.

" It was piping cold, but we went to work in good earnest that night, and the next night on which we could see it, which was not until April.

" I was dreadfully busy, and a host of little annoyances crowded upon me. I had a good star near it in the field of my comet-seeker, but *what* star?

" On that rested everything, and I could not be sure even from the catalogue, for the comet and the star were so much in the twilight that I could get no good neighboring stars. We called it Θ Arietes, or 707.

" Then came a waxing moon, and we waxed weary in trying to trace the fainter and fainter comet in the mists of twilight and the glare of moonlight.

" Next I broke a screw of my instrument, and found that no screw of that description could be bought in the town.

" I started off to find a man who could make one, and engaged him to do so the next day. The next day was Fast Day; all the world fasted, at least from labor.

" However, the screw was made, and it fitted nicely. The clouds cleared, and we were likely to have a good night. I put up my instrument, but scarcely had the screw-driver touched the new screw than out it flew from its socket, rolled along the floor of the ' walk,' dropped quietly through a crack into the gutter of the house-roof. I heard it click, and felt very much like using language unbecoming to a woman's mouth.

" I put my eye down to the crack, but could not see it. There was but one thing to be done, — the floor-boards must come up. I got a hatchet, but could do nothing.

I called father; he brought a crowbar and pried up the board, then crawled under it and found the screw. I took good care not to lose it a second time.

" The instrument was fairly mounted when the clouds mounted to keep it company, and the comet and I again parted.

" In all observations, the blowing out of a light by a gust of wind is a very common and very annoying accident; but I once met with a much worse one, for I dropped a chronometer, and it rolled out of its box on to the ground. We picked it up in a great panic, but it had not even altered its rate, as we found by later observations.

" The glaring eyes of the cat, who nightly visited me, were at one time very annoying, and a man who climbed up a fence and spoke to me, in the stillness of the small hours, fairly shook not only my equanimity, but the pencil which I held in my hand. He was quite innocent of any intention to do me harm, but he gave me a great fright.

" The spiders and bugs which swarm in my observing-houses I have rather an attachment for, but they must not crawl over my recording-paper. Rats are my abhorrence, and I learned with pleasure that some poison had been placed under the transit-house.

" One gets attached (if the term may be used) to certain midnight apparitions. The Aurora Borealis is always a pleasant companion; a meteor seems to come like a messenger from departed spirits; and the blossoming of trees in the moonlight becomes a sight looked for with pleasure.

·ʻ Aside from the study of astronomy, there is the same enjoyment in a night upon the housetop, with the stars, as in the midst of other grand scenery; there is the same subdued quiet and grateful seriousness; a calm to the troubled spirit, and a hope to the desponding.

" Even astronomers who are as well cared for as are those of Cambridge have their annoyances, and even men as skilled as they are make blunders.

" I have known one of the Bonds,[1] with great effort, turn that huge telescope down to the horizon to make an observation upon a blazing comet seen there, and when he had found it in his glass, find also that it was not a comet, but the nebula of Andromeda, a cluster of stars on which he had spent much time, and which he had made a special object of study.

" Dec. 26, 1854. They were wonderful men, the early astronomers. That was a great conception, which now seems to us so simple, that the earth turns upon its axis, and a still greater one that it revolves about the sun (to show this last was worth a man's lifetime, and it really almost cost the life of Galileo). Somehow we are ready to think that they had a wider field than we for speculation, that truth being all unknown it was easier to take the first step in its paths. But is the region of truth limited? Is it not infinite? . . . We know a few things which were once hidden, and being known they seem easy; but there are the flashings of the Northern Lights — ' Across the lift they start and shift;' there is the conical zodiacal beam

---

[1] Of the Harvard College Observatory.

seen so beautifully in the early evenings of spring and the early mornings of autumn; there are the startling comets, whose use is all unknown; there are the brightening and flickering variable stars, whose cause is all unknown; and the meteoric showers — and for all of these the reasons are as clear as for the succession of day and night; they lie just beyond the daily mist of our minds, but our eyes have not yet pierced through it."

CHAPTER III

1855-1857

EXTRACTS FROM DIARY — RACHEL — EMERSON — A HARD
WINTER

"JAN. 1, 1855. I put some wires into my little transit
this morning. I dreaded it so much, when I found yesterday that it must be done, that it disturbed my sleep.
It was much easier than I expected. I took out the
little collimating screws first, then I drew out the tube,
and in that I found a brass plate screwed on the diaphragm which contained the lines. I was at first a
little puzzled to know which screws held this diaphragm
in its place, and, as I was very anxious not to unscrew
the wrong ones, I took time to consider and found I
need turn only two. Then out slipped the little plate
with its three wires where five should have been, two
having been broken. As I did not know how to manage a spider's web, I took the hairs from my own head,
taking care to pick out white ones because I have no
black ones to spare. I put in the two, after first stretching
them over pasteboard, by sticking them with sealing-
wax dissolved in alcohol into the little grooved lines
which I found. When I had, with great labor, adjusted
these, as I thought, firmly, I perceived that some of the
wax was on the hairs and would make them yet coarser,
and they were already too coarse; so I washed my little

camel's-hair brush which I had been using, and began
to wash them with clear alcohol. Almost at once I
washed out another wire and soon another and another.
I went to work patiently and put in the five perpendicular ones besides the horizontal one, which, like the
others, had frizzled up and appeared to melt away.
With another hour's labor I got in the five, when a rude
motion raised them all again and I began over. Just at
one o'clock I had got them all in again. I attempted
then to put the diaphragm back into its place. The
sealing-wax was not dry, and with a little jar I sent the
wires all agog. This time they did not come out of
the little grooved lines into which they were put, and I
hastened to take out the brass plate and set them in
parallel lines. I gave up then for the day, but, as they
looked well and were certainly in firmly, I did not consider that I had made an entire failure. I thought it
nice ladylike work to manage such slight threads and
turn such delicate screws; but fine as are the hairs of
one's head, I shall seek something finer, for I can see
how clumsy they will appear when I get on the eyepiece
and magnify their imperfections. They look parallel now
to the eye, but with a magnifying power a very little
crook will seem a billowy wave, and a faint star will hide
itself in one of the yawning abysses.

" January 15. Finding the hairs which I had put into
my instrument not only too coarse, but variable and
disposed to curl themselves up at a change of weather,
I wrote to George Bond to ask him how I should procure spider lines. He replied that the web from
cocoons should be used, and that I should find it

difficult at this time of year to get at them. I remembered at once that I had seen two in the library room of the Atheneum, which I had carefully refrained from disturbing. I found them perfect, and unrolled them. . . . Fearing that I might not succeed in managing them, I procured some hairs from C.'s head. C. being not quite a year old, his hair is remarkably fine and sufficiently long. . . . I made the perpendicular wires of the spider's webs, breaking them and doing the work over again a great many times. . . . I at length got all in, crossing the five perpendicular ones with a horizontal one from C.'s spinning-wheel. . . . After twenty-four hours' exposure to the weather, I looked at them. The spider-webs had not changed, they were plainly used to a chill and made to endure changes of temperature; but C.'s hair, which had never felt a cold greater than that of the nursery, nor a change more decided than from his mother's arms to his father's, had knotted up into a decided curl! — *N.B.* C. may expect ringlets.

"January 22. Horace Greeley, in an article in a recent number of the 'Tribune,' says that the fund left by Smithson is spent by the regents of that institution in publishing books which no publisher would undertake and which do no good to anybody. Now in our little town of Nantucket, with our little Atheneum, these volumes are in constant demand. . . .

"I do not suppose that such works as those issued by the Smithsonian regents are appreciated by all who turn them over, but the ignorant learn that such things exist; they perceive that a higher cultivation than theirs is in the world, and they are stimulated to strive after greater excellence. So I steadily advocate, in purchasing books for the Atheneum, the lifting of the people. 'Let us buy, not such books as the people want, but books just above their wants, and they will reach up to take what is put out for them.'

"Sept. 10, 1855. To know what one ought to do is certainly the hardest thing in life. 'Doing' is comparatively easy; but there are no laws for your individual case — yours is one of a myriad.

" There are laws of right and wrong in general, but they do not seem to bear upon any particular case.

" In chess-playing you can refer to rules of movement, for the chess-men are few, and the positions in which they may be placed, numerous as they are, have a limit.

" But is there any limit to the different positions of human beings around you? Is there any limit to the peculiarities of circumstances?

" Here a man, however much of a copyist he may be by nature, comes down to simple originality, unless he blindly follows the advice of some friend; for there is no precedent in anything exactly like his case; he must decide for himself, and must take the step alone; and fearfully, cautiously, and distrustingly must we all take many of our steps, for we see but a little way at best, and we can foresee nothing at all.

"September 13. I read this morning an article in ' Putnam's Magazine,' on Rachel. I have been much interested in this woman as a genius, though I am pained by the accounts of her career in point of morals, and I

am wearied with the glitter of her jewelry. Night puts
on a jewelled robe which few admire, compared with
the admiration for marketable jewelry. The New York
' Tribune ' descends to the rating of the value of those
worn by her, and it is the prominent point, or rather
it makes the multitude of prominent points, when she is
spoken of.

"The writer in ' Putnam ' does not go into these
small matters, but he attempts a criticism on acting, to
which I am not entirely a convert. He maintains that
if an actor should really show a character in such light
that we could not tell the impersonation from the
reality, the stage would lose its interest. I do not
think so. We should draw back, of course, from physical suffering; but yet we should be charmed to suppose
anything real, which we had desired to see. If we felt
that we really met Cardinal Wolsey or Henry VIII. in
his days of glory, would it not be a lifelong memory
to us, very different from the effect of the stage, and if
for a few moments we really *felt* that we had met them,
would it not lift us into a new kind of being?

"What would we not give to see Julius Cæsar and the
soothsayer, just as they stood in Rome as Shakspere
represents them? Why, we travel hundreds of miles
to see the places noted for the doings of these old
Romans; and if we could be made to believe that we
met one of the smaller men, even, of that day, our
ecstasy would be unbounded. 'A tin pan so painted
as to deceive is atrocious,' says this writer. Of course,
for we are not interested in a tin pan; but give us a
portrait of Shakspere or Milton so that we shall feel

that we have met them, and I see no atrocity in the matter. We honor the homes of these men, and we joy in the hope of seeing them. What would be beyond seeing them in life?

"October 31. I saw Rachel in 'Phedre' and in 'Adrienne.' I had previously asked a friend if I, in my ignorance of acting, and in my inability to tell good from poor, should really perceive a marked difference between Rachel and her aids. She thought I should. I did indeed! In 'Phedre,' which I first saw, she was not aided at all by her troupe; they were evidently ill at ease in the Greek dress and in Greek manners; while she had assimilated herself to the whole. It is founded on the play of Euripides, and even to Rachel the passion which she represents as Phedre must have been too strange to be natural. Hippolytus refuses the love which Phedre offers after a long struggle with herself, and this gives cause for the violent bursts in which Rachel shows her power. It was an outburst of passion of which I have no conception, and I felt as if I saw a new order of being; not a woman, but a per-sonified passion. The vehemence and strength were wonderful. It was in parts very touching. There was as fine an opportunity for Aricia to show some power as for Phedre, but the automaton who repre-sented Aricia had no power to show. Œnon, whom I took to be the sister Sarah, was something of an actress, but her part was so hateful that no one could applaud her. I felt in reading 'Phedre,' and in hear-ing it, that it was a play of high order, and that I learned some little philosophy from some of its senti-

ments; but for 'Adrienne' I have a contempt. The
play was written by Scribe specially for Rachel, and
the French acting was better done by the other performers than the Greek. I have always disliked to see
death represented on the stage. Rachel's representa-
tion was awful! I could not take my eyes from the
scene, and I held my breath in horror; the death was
so much to the life. It is said that she changes color.
I do not know that she does, but it looked like a
ghastly hue that came over her pale face.

" I was displeased at the constant standing. Neither
as Greeks nor as Frenchmen did they sit at all; only
when dying did Rachel need a chair. They made love
standing, they told long stories standing, they took
snuff in that position, hat in hand, and Rachel fainted
upon the breast of some friend from the same fatiguing
attitude.

" The audience to hear 'Adrienne' was very fine.
The Unitarian clergymen and the divinity students
seemed to have turned out.

" Most of the two thousand listeners followed with the
book, and when the last word was uttered on the French
page, over turned the two thousand leaves, sounding
like a shower of rain. The applause was never very
great; it is said that Rachel feels this as a Boston
peculiarity, but she ought also to feel the compliment
of so large an audience in a city where foreigners are so
few and the population so small compared to that of
New York.

"Nov. 14, 1855. Last night I heard Emerson give a
lecture. I pity the reporter who attempts to give it to

the world. I began to listen with a determination to remember it in order, but it was without method, or order, or system. It was like a beam of light moving in the undulatory waves, meeting with occasional meteors in its path; it was exceedingly captivating. It surprised me that there was not only no commonplace thought, but there was no commonplace expression. If he quoted, he quoted from what we had not read; if he told an anecdote, it was one that had not reached us. At the outset he was very severe upon the science of the age. He said that inventors and discoverers helped themselves very much, but they did not help the rest of the world; that a great man was felt to the centre of the Copernican system; that a botanist dried his plants, but the plants had their revenge and dried the botanist; that a naturalist bottled up reptiles, but in return the man was bottled up.

"There was a pitiful truth in all this, but there are glorious exceptions. Professor Peirce is anything but a formula, though he deals in formulæ.

"The lecture turned at length upon beauty, and it was evident that personal beauty had made Emerson its slave many a time, and I suppose every heart in the house admitted the truth of his words. . . .

"It was evident that Mr. Emerson was not at ease, for he declared that good manners were more than beauty of face, and good expression better than good features. He mentioned that Sir Philip Sydney was not handsome, though the boast of English society; and he spoke of the astonishing beauty of the Duchess of Hamilton, to see whom hundreds collected when she took a ride. I think in these cases there is something besides beauty; there was rank in that of the Duchess, in the case of Sydney there was no need of beauty at all.

"Dec. 16, 1855. All along this year I have felt that it was a hard year — the hardest of my life. And I have kept enumerating to myself my many trials; to-day it suddenly occurred to me that my blessings were much more numerous. If mother's illness was a sore affliction, her recovery is a great blessing; and even the illness itself has its bright side, for we have joyed in showing her how much we prize her continued life. If I have lost some friends by death, I have not lost all. If I have worked harder than I felt that I could bear, how much better is that than not to have as much work as I wanted to do. I have earned more money than in any preceding year; I have studied less, but have observed more, than I did last year. I have saved more money than ever before, hoping for Europe in 1856." . . .

Miss Mitchell from her earliest childhood had had a great desire to travel in Europe. She received a very small salary for her services in the Atheneum, but small as it was she laid by a little every year.

She dressed very simply and spent as little as possible on herself — which was also true of her later years. She took a little journey every year, and could always have little presents ready for the birthdays and Christmas days, and for the necessary books which could not be found in the Atheneum library, and which she felt that she ought to own herself, — all this on a salary which an ordinary school-girl in these days would think too meagre to supply her with dress alone.

In this family the children were not ashamed to say,
" I can't afford it," and were taught that nothing was
cheap that they could not pay for — a lesson that has
been valuable to them all their lives.

" .   .   . 1855. Deacon Greeley, of Boston, urged my
going to Boston and giving some lectures to get money.
I told him I could not think of it just now, as I wanted
to go to Europe. ' On what money? ' said he. ' What
I have earned,' I replied. ' Bless me! ' said he; ' am
I talking to a capitalist? What a mistake I have
made.' "

During the time of the prosperity of the town, the
winters were very sociable and lively; but when the
inhabitants began to leave for more favorable opportunities for getting a livelihood, the change was felt
very seriously, especially in the case of an exceptionally
stormy winter. Here is an extract showing how Miss
Mitchell and her family lived during one of these
winters:

" Jan. 22, 1857. Hard winters are becoming the
order of things. Winter before last was hard, last
winter was harder, and this surpasses all winters known
before.

" We have been frozen into our island now since the
6th. No one cared much about it for the first two or
three days; the sleighing was good, and all the world
was out trying their horses on Main street — the race-
course of the world. Day after day passed, and the
thermometer sank to a lower point, and the winds
rose to a higher, and sleighing became uncomfortable;
and even the dullest man longs for the cheer of a

newspaper. The 'Nantucket Inquirer' came out for awhile, but at length it had nothing to tell and nothing to inquire about, and so kept its peace.

" After about a week a vessel was seen off Siasconset, and boarded by a pilot. Her captain said he would go anywhere and take anybody, as all he wanted was a harbor. Two men whose business would suffer if they remained at home took passage in her, and with the pilot, Patterson, she left in good weather and was seen off Chatham at night. It was hoped that Patterson would return and bring at least a few newspapers, but no more is known' of them. Our postmaster thought he was not allowed to send the mails by such a conveyance.

" Yesterday we got up quite an excitement because a large steamship was seen near the Haul-over. She set a flag for a pilot, and was boarded. It was found that she was out of course, twenty days from Glasgow, bound to New York. " What the European news is we do not yet know, but it is plain that we are nearer to Europe than to Hyannis. Christians as we are, I am afraid we were all sorry that she did not come ashore. We women revelled in the idea of the rich silks she would probably throw upon the beach, and the men thought a good job would be made by steamboat companies and wreck agents.

" Last night the weather was so mild that a plan was made for cutting out the steamboat; all the Irishmen in town were ordered to be on the harbor with axes, shovels, and saws at seven this morning. The poor fellows were exulting in the prospect of a job, but they

are sadly balked, for this morning at seven a hard
storm was raging — snow and a good north-west wind.
What has become of the English steamer no one knows,
but the wind blows off shore, so she will not come any
nearer to us.

"Inside of the house we amuse ourselves in various
ways. F.'s family and ours form a club meeting three
times a week, and writing 'machine poetry' in great
quantities. Occasionally something very droll puts us
in a roar of laughter. F., E., and K. are, I think,
rather the smartest, though Mr. M. has written rather
the best of all. At the next meeting, each of us is to
produce a sonnet on a subject which we draw by lot.
I have written mine and tried to be droll. K. has written hers and is serious.

"I am sadly tried by this state of things. I cannot
hear from Cambridge (the Nautical Almanac office),
and am out of work; it is cloudy most of the time, and
I cannot observe; and I had fixed upon just this time
for taking a journey. My trunk has been half packed
for a month.

"January 23. Foreseeing that the thermometer would
show a very low point last night, we sat up until near
midnight, when it stood one and one-half below zero.
The stars shone brightly, and the wind blew freshly
from west north-west.

"This morning the wind is the same, and the mercury stood at six and one-half below zero at seven
o'clock, and now at ten A.M. is not above zero. The
Coffin School dismissed its scholars. Miss F. suffered
much from the exposure on her way to school.

" The ' Inquirer' came out this morning, giving the news from Europe brought by the steamer which lies off 'Sconset. No coal has yet been carried to the steamer, the carts which started for 'Sconset being obliged to return.

" There are about seven hundred barrels of flour in town ; it is admitted that fresh meat is getting scarce ; the streets are almost impassable from the snow-drifts.

" K. and I have hit upon a plan for killing time. We are learning poetry — she takes twenty lines of Goldsmith's ' Traveller,' and I twenty lines of the ' Deserted Village.' It will take us twenty days to learn the whole, and we hope to be stopped in our course by the opening of the harbor. Considering that K. has a fiance from whom she cannot hear a word, she carries herself very amicably towards mankind. She is making herself a pair of shoes, which look very well ; I have made myself a morning-dress since we were closed in.

" Last night I took my first lesson in whist-playing. I learned in one evening to know the king, queen, and jack apart, and to understand what my partner meant when she winked at me.

" The worst of this condition of things is that we shall bear the marks of it all our lives. We are now sixteen daily papers behind the rest of the world, and in those sixteen papers are items known to all the people in all the cities, which will never be known to us. How prices have fluctuated in that time we shall not know — what houses have burned down, what robberies have been committed. When the papers do

come, each of us will rush for the latest dates ; the news
of two weeks ago is now history, and no one reads history, especially the history of one's own country.

"I bought a copy of 'Aurora Leigh' just before
the freezing up, and I have been careful, as it is the
only copy on the island, to circulate it freely.   It must
have been a pleasant visitor in the four or five households which it has entered.   We have had Dr. Kane's
book and now have the 'Japan Expedition.'

"The intellectual suffering will, I think, be all.   I
have no fear of scarcity of provisions or fuel.   There
are old houses enough to burn.   Fresh meat is rather
scarce because the English steamer required so much
victualling.   We have a barrel of pork and a barrel of
flour in the house, and father has chickens enough to
keep us a good while.

"There are said to be some families who are in a
good deal of suffering, for whom the Howard Society is
on the lookout.   Mother gives very freely to Bridget,
who has four children to support with only the labor of
her hands.

"The Coffin School has been suspended one day on
account of the heaviest storm, and the Unitarian church
has had but one service.   No great damage has been
done by the gales.   My observing-seat came thunder-
ing down the roof one evening about ten o'clock, but
all the world understood its cry of 'Stand from
under,' and no one was hurt.   Several windows were
blown in at midnight, and houses shook so that vases
fell from the mantelpieces.

"The last snow drifted so that the sleighing was

difficult, and at present the storm is so smothering that few are out. A. has been out to school every day, and I have not failed to go out into the air once a day to take a short walk.

" January 24. We left the mercury one below zero when we went to bed last night, and it was at zero when we rose this morning. But it rises rapidly, and now, at eleven A.M., it is as high as fifteen. The weather is still and beautiful; the English steamer is still safe at her moorings.

" Our little club met last night, each with a sonnet. I did the best I could with a very bad subject. K. and E. rather carried the honors away, but Mr. J. M.'s was very taking. Our ' crambo ' playing was rather dull, all of us having exhausted ourselves on the sonnets. We seem to have settled ourselves quietly into a tone of resignation in regard to the weather; we know that we cannot ' get out,' any more than Sterne's Starling, and we know that it is best not to fret.

" The subject which I have drawn for the next poem is ' Sunrise,' about which I know very little. K. and I continue to learn twenty lines of poetry a day, and I do not find it unpleasant, though the ' Deserted Village ' is rather monotonous.

" We hear of no suffering in town for fuel or provisions, and I think we could stand a three months' siege without much inconvenience as far as the physicals are concerned.

" January 26. The ice continues, and the cold. The weather is beautiful, and with the thermometer at fourteen I swept with the telescope an hour and a half last

night, comfortably.   The English steamer will get off
to-morrow.   It is said that they burned their cabin
doors last night to keep their water hot.   Many people
go out to see her; she lies off 'Sconset, about half a
mile from shore.   We have sent letters by her which,
I hope, may relieve anxiety.

"K. bought a backgammon board to-day.   Clifford
[the little nephew] came in and spent the morning.

"January 29.   We have had now two days of warm
weather, but there is yet no hope of getting our steamboat off.   Day before yesterday we went to 'Sconset to
see the English steamer.   She lay so near the shore
that we could hear the orders given, and see the people
on board.   When we went down the bank the boats
were just pushing from the shore, with bags of coal.
They could not go directly to the ship, but rowed some
distance along shore to the north, and then falling into
the ice drifted with it back to the ship.   When they
reached her a rope was thrown to them, and they made
fast and the coal was raised.   We watched them
through a glass, and saw a woman leaning over the
side of the ship.   The steamer left at five o'clock that
day.

"It was worth the trouble of a ride to 'Sconset to see
the masses of snow on the road.   The road had been
cleared for the coal-carts, and we drove through a narrow path, cut in deep snow-banks far above our heads,
sometimes for the length of three or four sleighs.   We
could not, of course, turn out for other sleighs, and
there was much waiting on this account.   Then, too,
the road was much gullied, and we rocked in the sleigh

as we would on shipboard, with the bounding over hillocks of snow and ice.

" Now, all is changed : the roads are slushy, and the water stands in deep pools all over the streets. There is a dense fog, very little wind, and that from the east. The thermometer above thirty-six.

" [Mails arrived February 3, and our steamboat left February 5.] "

CHAPTER IV

1857

SOUTHERN TOUR

IN 1857 Miss Mitchell made a tour in the South, having under her charge the young daughter of a Western banker.

"March 2, 1857. I left Meadville this morning at six o'clock, in a stage-coach for Erie. I had, early in life, a love for staging, but it is fast dying out. Nine hours over a rough road are enough to root out the most passionate love of that kind.

"Our stage was well filled, but in spite of the solid base we occasionally found ourselves bumping up against the roof or falling forward upon our opposite neighbors.

"Stage-coaches are, I believe, always the arena for political debate. To-day we were all on one side, all Buchanan men, and yet all anti-slavery. It seemed reasonable, as they said, that the South should cease to push the slave question in regard to Kansas, now that it has elected its President.

"When I took the stage out to Meadville on the 'mud-road,' it was filled with Fremont men, and they seemed to me more able men, though they were no younger and no more cultivated.

"March 5. I believe any one might travel from

Maine to Georgia and be perfectly ignorant of the route, and yet be well taken care of, mainly from the good-nature in every one.

"I found from Nantucket to Chicago more attention than I desired. I had a short seat in one of the cars, through the night. I did not think it large enough for two, and so coiled myself up and went to sleep. There were men standing all around. Once one of them came along and said something about there being room for him on my seat. Another man said, 'She's asleep, don't disturb her.' I was too selfish to offer the half of a short seat, and too tired to reason about the man's being, possibly, more tired than I.

"I was invariably offered the seat near the window that I might lean against the side of the car, and one gentleman threw his shawl across my knees to keep me warm (I was suffering with heat at the time!). Another, seeing me going to Chicago alone, warned me to beware of the impositions of hack-drivers; telling me that I must pay two dollars if I did not make a bargain beforehand. I found it true, for I paid one dollar for going a few steps only.

"One peculiarity in travelling from East to West is, that you lose the old men. In the cars in New England you see white-headed men, and I kept one in the train up to New York, and one of grayish-tinted hair as far as Erie; but after Cleveland, no man was over forty years old.

"For hundreds of miles the prairie land stretches on the Illinois Central Railroad between Chicago and St. Louis. It may be pleasant in summer, but it is a dreary waste in winter. The space is too broad and too uniform to have beauty. The girdle of trees would be pretty, doubtless, if seen near, but in the distance and in winter it is only a black border to a brown plain.

" The State of Illinois must be capitally adapted to railroads on account of this level, and but little danger can threaten a train from running off of the track, as it might run on the soil nearly as well as on the rails.

" Our engine was uncoupled, and had gone on for nearly half a mile without the cars before the conductor perceived it.

" The time from Chicago to St. Louis is called fifteen hours and a quarter; we made it twenty-three.

" If the prairie land is good farming-land, Illinois is destined to be a great State. If its people will think less of the dollar and more of the refinements of social life and the culture of the mind, it may become the great State of the Union yet.

" March 12. Planter's Hotel, St. Louis. We visited Mercantile Hall and the Library. The lecture-room is very spacious and very pretty. No gallery hides the frescoed walls, and no painful economy has been made of the space on the floor.

" 13th. I begin to perceive the commerce of St. Louis. We went upon the levee this morning, and for miles the edge was bordered with the pipes of steamboats, standing like a picket-fence. Then we came to the wholesale streets, and saw the immense stores for dry-goods and crockery.

" To-day I have heard of a scientific association called the ' Scientific Academy of St. Louis,' which is about a year old, and which is about to publish a volume of transactions, containing an account of an artesian well, and of some inscriptions just sent home from Nineveh, which Mr. Gust. Seyffarth has deciphered.

" Mr. Seyffarth must be a remarkable man; he has translated a great many inscriptions, and is said to surpass Champollion. He has published a work on Egyptian astronomy, but no copy is in this country.

" Dr. Pope, who called on me, and with whom I was much pleased, told me of all these things. Western men are so proud of their cities that they spare no pains to make a person from the Eastern States understand the resources, and hopes, and plans of their part of the land.

" Rev. Dr. Eliot I have not seen. He is about to establish a university here, for which he has already $100,000, and the academic part is already in a state of activity.

" Rev. Mr. Staples tells me that Dr. Eliot puts his hands into the pockets of his parishioners, who are rich, up to the elbows.

" Altogether, St. Louis is a growing place, and the West has a large hand and a strong grasp.

" Doctor Seyffarth is a man of more than sixty years, gray-haired, healthy-looking, and pleasant in manners. He has spent long years of labor in deciphering the inscriptions found upon ancient pillars, Egpytian and Arabic, dating five thousand years before Christ. I asked him if he found the observations continuous, and he said that he did not, but that they seem to be astrological pictures of the configuration of the planets, and to have been made at the birth of princes.

" He has just been reading the slabs sent from Nine-

veh by Mr. Marsh; their date is only about five hundred years B.C.

"Mr. Seyffarth's published works amount to seventy,
and he was surprised to find a whole set of them in the
Astor Library in New York.

"March 19. We came on board of the steamer
'Magnolia,' this morning, in great spirits. We were a
little late, and Miss S. rushed on board as if she had
only New Orleans in view. I followed a little more
slowly, and the brigadier-general came after, in a sober
and dignified manner.

"We were scarcely on board when the plank was
pulled in, and a few minutes passed and we were afloat
on the Mississippi river. Miss S. and myself were the
only lady passengers; we had, therefore, the whole
range of staterooms from which to choose. Each
could have a stateroom to herself, and we talked in
admiration of the pleasant times we should have, watching the scenery from the stateroom windows, or from
the saloon, reading, etc.

"We started off finely. I, who had been used only
to the rough waters of the Atlantic coast, was surprised
at the steady gliding of the boat. I saw nothing of the
mingling of the waters of the Missouri and the Mississippi of which I had been told. Perhaps I needed
somebody to point out the difference.

"The two banks of the river were at first much alike,
but after a few hours the left bank became more hilly,
and at intervals presented bluffs and rocks, rude and
irregular in shape, which we imagined to be ruins of
some old castle.

" At intervals, too, we passed steamers going up to St. Louis, all laden with passengers. We exulted in our majestic march over the waters. I thought it the very perfection of travelling, and wished that all my family and all my friends were on board.

" I wondered at the stupidity of the rest of the world, and thought that they ought all to leave the marts of business, to step from the desk, the counting-room, and the workshop on board the ' Magnolia,' and go down the length of the ' Father of Waters.'

" And so they would, I suppose, but for sand-bars. Here we are five hours out, and fast aground ! We were just at dinner, the captain making himself agree-able, the dinner showing itself to be good, when a peculiar motion of the boat made the captain heave a sigh — he had been heaving the lead all the morning. ' Ah,' he said, ' just what I feared ; we've got to one of those bad places, and we are rubbing the bottom.'

" I asked very innocently if we must wait for the tide, and was informed that there was no tide felt on this part of the river. Miss S. turned a little pale, and showed a loss of appetite. I was a little bit moved, but kept it to myself and ate on.

" As soon as dinner was over, we went out to look at the prospect of affairs. We were close into the land, and could be put on shore any minute ; the captain had sent round a little boat to sound the waters, and the report brought back was of shallow water just ahead of us, but more on the right and left.

" While we stood on deck a small boat passed, and a

sailor very gleefully called out the soundings as he threw the lead, ' Eight and a half-nine.'

" But we are still high and dry now at two o'clock P.M. They are shaking the steamer, and making efforts to move her. They say if she gets over this, there is no worse place for her to meet.

" I asked the captain of what the bottom is composed, and he says, ' Of mud, rocks, snags, and everything.'

" He is now moving very cautiously, and the boat has an unpleasant tremulous motion.

" March 20. Latitude about thirty-eight degrees. We are just where we stopped at noon yesterday — there is no change, and of course no event. One of our crew killed a 'possum yesterday, and another boat stopped near us this morning, and seems likely to lie as long as we do on the sand-bar.

" We read Shakspere this morning after breakfast, and then betook ourselves to the wheel-house to look at the scenery again. While there a little colored boy came to us bearing a waiter of oranges, and telling us that the captain sent them with his compliments. We ate them greedily, because we had nothing else to do.

" 21st. Still the sand-bar. No hope of getting off. We heard the pilot hail a steamboat which was going up to St. Louis, and tell them to send on a lighter, and I suppose we must wait for that. . . . It is my private opinion that this great boat will not get off at all, but will lie here until she petrifies. . . .

" March 24. We left the ' Magnolia ' after four days and four hours upon the sand-bar near Turkey island, upon seeing the 'Woodruff' approach. We left in a little rowboat, and it seemed at first as if we could not overtake the steamer; but the captain saw us and slackened his speed.

"Miss S. and I clutched hands in a little terror as our small boat seemed likely to run under the great steamer, but our oarsmen knew their duty and we were safely put on board of the 'Woodruff.'

"March 25. We stopped at Cairo at eight o'clock this morning. Mr. S. went on shore and brought newspapers on board. The Cairo paper I do not think of high order. I saw no mention in it of the detention of the 'Magnolia'!

"March 26. Yesterday we count as a day of events. It began to look sunny on the banks, especially on the Kentucky side, and Miss S. and I saw cherry-blossoms. We remembered the eclipse, and Mr. S. having brought with him a piece of broken glass from one of the windows of the 'Magnolia,' I smoked it over a piece of candle which I had brought from Room No. 22 of the Planter's House at St. Louis, and we prepared to see the eclipse.

"I expected to see the moon on at five o'clock and twenty minutes, but as I had no time I could not tell when to look for it.

"It was not on at that time by my watch, but in ten minutes after was so far on that I think my time cannot be much wrong.

"It was a little cloudy, so that we saw the sun only 'all flecked with bars,' and caught sight of the phenomenon at intervals.

"We were at a coal-landing at the time, and not far from Madrid. The boat stopped so long to take in an immense pile of corn-bags that our passengers went on shore — such of them as could climb the slippery bank.

"When we saw them coming back laden with peach-blossoms, and saw the little children dressing their hats with them, we were seized with a longing for them, and Mr. S. offered to go and get us some; we begged to go too, but he objected.

"We were really envious of his good luck when we saw him jump into a country wagon, drawn by oxen which trotted off like horses, and, waving his handkerchief to us, ride off in great glee. He came back with an armful of peach-tree branches. Whose orchard he robbed at our instigation I cannot say. A little girl, the daughter of the captain, pulled some blossoms open, and showed us that the fruit germs were not dead, but would have become peaches if we had not coveted them.

"The 25th was also our first night steam-boating. After passing Cairo the river is considered safe for night travel, and the boat started on her way at 8.30 P.M. We had been out about half an hour when a lady who was playing cards threw down her cards and rushed with a shriek to her stateroom. I perceived then that there had been a peculiar motion to the boat and that it suddenly stopped. We found that one of the paddle-wheels was caught in a snag, but there was no harm done. It made us a little nervous, but we slept well enough after it.

"When I look out upon the river, I wonder that boats are not continually snagged. Little trees are sticking up on all sides, and sometimes we seem to be going over a meadow and pushing among rushes.

"A yawl, which was sent out yesterday to sound, was snagged by a stump which was high out of water; probably they were carried on to it by a current. The little boat whirled round and round, and the men were plainly frightened, for they dropped their oars and clutched the sides of the boat. They got control, however, in a few minutes, and had the jeers of the men left on the steamer for their pains.

"March 30. We stopped at Natchez before breakfast this morning, and, having half an hour, we took a carriage and drove through the city. It was like driving through a succession of gardens: roses were hanging over the fences in the richest profusion, and the arbor-vitæ was ornamenting every little nook, and adorning every cottage.

"Natchez stands on a high bluff, very romantic in appearance; jagged and rugged, as if volcanoes had been at work in a time long past, for tall trees grew in the ravines.

"Most of our lady passengers are, like ourselves, on a tour of pleasure; six of them go with us to the St. Charles Hotel. Some are from Keokuk, Ia., and I think I like these the best. One young lady goes ashore to spend some time on a plantation, as a governess. She looks feeble, and we all pity her.

"To-day we pass among plantations on both sides of the river. We begin to see the live-oak — a noble tree.

The foliage is so thick and dark that I have learned to
know it by its color. The magnolia trees, too, are becoming fragrant.

"March 31. We are at length in New Orleans, and
up three flights at the St. Charles, in a dark room.

"The peculiarities of the city dawn upon me very
slowly. I first noticed the showy dress of the children,
then the turbaned heads of the black women in the
streets, and next the bouquet-selling boys with their
French phrases.

"April 3. This morning we went to a slave market.
It looked on first entrance like an intelligence office.
Men, women, and children were seated on long
benches parallel with each other. All rose at our
entrance, and continued standing while we were there.
We were told by the traders to walk up and down the
passage between them, and talk with them as we liked.
As Mr. S. passed the men, several lifted their hands
and said, 'Here's the boy that will suit you; I can do
any kind of work.' Some advertised themselves with
a good deal of tact. One woman pulled at my shawl
and asked me to buy her. I told her that I was not
a housekeeper. 'Not married?' she asked. — 'No.' —
'Well, then, get married and buy me and my husband.'

"There was a girl among them whiter than I, who
roused my sympathies very much. I could not speak
to her, for the past and the future were too plainly told
in her face. I spoke to another, a bright-looking girl
of twelve. 'Where were you raised?' — 'In Kentucky.'
— 'And why are you to be sold?' — 'The trader came
to Kentucky, bought me, and brought me here.' I

thought what right had I to be homesick, when that poor girl had left all her kindred for life without her consent.

"I could hold my tongue and look around without much outward show of disgust, but to talk pleasantly to the trader I could not consent. He told me that he had been brought up in the business, but he thought it a pity.

"No buyers were present, so there was no examination that was painful to look upon.

"The slaves were intelligent-looking, and very healthy and neat in appearance. Those who belonged to one owner were dressed alike — some in striped pink and white dresses, others in plaid, all a little showy. The men were in thick trousers and coarse dark-blue jackets.

"April 5. We have been this morning to a negro church. We found it a miserable looking house, mostly unpainted and unplastered, but well filled with the swarthy faces. They were singing when we entered; we were pointed to a good seat.

"There may have been fifty persons present, all well dressed; the women in the fanciful checkered head-dresses so much favored by the negro race, the men in clean collars, nankin trousers, and dark coats. All showed that they were well kept and well fed.

"The audience was increased by new-comers frequently, and these, whatever the exercise might be, shook hands with those around them as they seated themselves, and joined immediately in the services. The singing was by the whole congregation, the minister

lining out the hymns as in the early times in New England.

"Several persons carried on the exercises from the
pulpit, and in the prayers and sermon the audience
took an active part, responding in groans, 'Oh, yes,' or
'Amen,' sometimes performing a kind of chant to
accompany the words. . . . A negro minister said
in his prayer, 'O God, we are not for much talking.'
I was delighted at the prospect of a short discourse, but
I found his 'not much talking' exactly corresponded
to 'a good deal' in my use of words. He talked for
a full hour.

"There was something pleasing in the earnestness of
the preacher and the sympathetic feeling of the audience, but their peculiar condition was not alluded to,
and probably was not felt.

"The discourse was almost ludicrous at times, and
at times was pathetic. I saved up a few specimens:

"'O God, you have said that where one or two are
gathered together in your name, there will you be; if anything stands between us that you can't come, put it aside.'

"'God wants a kingdom upon earth with which he
can coin—cide, and that kingdom are your heart.'

"'God is near you when you are at the wash-tub or
the ironing-table.'

"'Brethren, I thought last Sabbath I wouldn't live
to this; a man gets such a notion sometimes.'

"April 9, Alabama River. Some lessons we of the
North might learn from the South, and one is a greater
regard for human life. I asked the captain of our boat
if they had any accidents in these waters. He said,

'We don't kill people at the South, we gave that up some years ago; we leave it to the North, and the North seems to be capable of doing it.'

"The reason for this is, that they are in no hurry. The Southern character is opposed to haste. Safety is of more worth than speed, and there is no hurry.

"Every one at the South introduces its 'peculiar institution' into conversation.

"They talk as I expected Southern people of intelligence to talk; they lament the evil, and say, 'It is upon us, what can we do? To give them freedom would be cruel.'

"Southerners fall back upon the Bible at once; there is more of the old-fashioned religion at the South than at the North; that is, they are not intellectual religionists. They are shocked by the irreligion of Massachusetts, and by Theodore Parker. They read the Bible, and can quote it; they are ready with it as an argument at every turn. I am of course not used to the warfare, and so withdraw from the fight.

"One argument which three persons have brought up to me is the superior condition of the blacks now, to what it would have been had their parents remained in Africa, and they been children of the soil. I make no answer to this, for if this is an argument, it would be our duty to enslave the heathen, instead of attempting to enlighten them.

"We hear some anecdotes which are amusing. A Judge Smith, of South Carolina, moved to Alabama, and became a prominent man there. He was sent to the Senate. He was violently opposed by a young man

who said that but for his gray hair he would challenge
him. Judge Smith said, 'You are not the first coward
who has taken shelter beneath my gray hairs.'

"The same Judge Smith, when a proposition came
before the Senate to build a State penitentiary, said,
'Wall in the city of Mobile; you will have your penitentiary and its inmates.'

"So far I have found it easier to travel without an
escort South and West than at the North; that is, I
have more care taken of me. Every one is courteous,
too, in speech. I know that they cannot love Massachusetts, but they are careful not to wound my feelings.
They acknowledge it to be the great State in education;
they point to a pretty village and say, 'Almost as neat
as a New England village.'

"Savannah, April 15. . . . To-day we left town
at ten o'clock for a drive in any direction that we liked.
Mr. F. and I went in a buggy, and Miss S. cantered
behind us on her horse.

"The road that we took led to some rice plantations
ten miles out of the city. Our path was ornamented
by the live-oaks, cedar trees, the dogwood, and occasionally the mistletoe, and enlivened sometimes by the
whistle of the mocking-bird. Down low by the wheels
grew the wild azalea and the jessamine. Above our
heads the Spanish moss hung from the trees in beautiful drapery.

"By mistake we drove into the plantation grounds of
Mr. Gibbons, a man of wealth, who is seldom on his
lands, and where the avenues are therefore a little wild,
and the roads a little rough.

" We came afterwards upon a road leading under the most magnificent oaks that I ever saw. I felt as if I were under the arched roof of some ancient cathedral.

" The trees were irregularly grouped and of immense size, throwing their hundreds of arms far upon the background of heaven, and bearing the drapery of the Spanish moss fold upon fold, as if they sought to keep their raiment from touching the earth. I was perfectly delighted, and think it the finest picture I have yet seen.

" Retracing our steps, we sought the plantation of Mr. Potter — a very different one from that of Mr. Gibbons, as all was finish and neatness; a fine mansion well stored with books, and some fine oaks, some of which Mr. Potter had planted himself.

" Mr. Potter walked through the fields with us, and, stopping among the negro huts, he said to a little boy, ' Call the children and give us some singing.' The little boy ran off, shouting, ' Come and sing for massa; ' and in a few minutes the little darkies might be seen running through the fields and tumbling over the fences in their anxiety to get to us, to the number of eighteen.

" They sat upon the ground around us and began their song. The boy who led sang ' Early in the Morning,' and the other seventeen brought in a chorus of ' Let us think of Jesus.' Then the leader set up something about ' God Almicha,' to which the others brought in another chorus.

" They were a dirty and shabby looking set, but as usual fat, even to the little babies, whom the larger boys were tending. One little girl as she passed Mr. Potter carelessly put her hand in his and said, ' Good morning, massa.'

" Mrs. G. tells me an anecdote which shows the Southern sentiment on the one subject. The ladies of Charleston were much pleased with Miss Murray, and got up for her what they called a Murray testimonial, a collection of divers pretty things made by their own hands. The large box was ready to be sent to England, but alas for Miss Murray! While they were debating in what way it should be sent to ensure its reaching her without cost to herself, in an unwise moment she sent twenty-five dollars to ' Bleeding Kansas,' and the fit of good feeling towards her ebbed; the ' testimonial' remains unsent.

" April 23, Charleston. This place is somewhat like Boston in its narrow streets, but unlike Boston in being quiet; as is all the South. Quiet and moderation seem to be the attributes of Southern cities. You need not hurry to a boat for fear it will leave at the hour appointed; it never does.

" We took a carriage and drove along the Battery. The snuff of salt air did me good.

" Then we went on to a garden of roses, owned and cultivated by a colored woman. She has some twenty acres devoted to flowers and vegetables, and she owns twenty ' niggers.' The universal term for slaves is ' niggers.' ' Nigger, bring that horse,' ' Nigger, get out of the way,' will be said by the finest gentleman, and ' My niggers ' is said by every one.

" I do not believe that the slaves are badly treated;

there may be cases of it, but I have seen them only sleek, fat, and lazy.

"The old buildings of Charleston please me exceedingly. The houses are built of brick, standing end to the street, three stories in height, with piazza above piazza at the side; with flower gardens around, and magnolias at the gates; the winding steps to the mansions festooned with roses.

"I have just called on Miss Rutledge, who lives in the second oldest house in the city; herself a fine specimen of antiquity, in her double-ruffled cap and plaided black dress; she chatted away like a young person, using the good old English.

"April 26. To-day Mr. Capers called on me. I was pleased with the account he gave me of his college life, and of a meeting held by his class thirty years after they graduated. Some thirty of them assembled at the Revere House in Boston; they spread a table with viands from all sections of the country. Mr. Capers sent watermelons, and another gentleman from Kentucky sent the wines of his State.

"They sat late at table; they renewed the old friendships and talked over college scenes, and when it was near midnight some one proposed that each should give a sketch of his life, so they went through in alphabetical order.

"Adams was the first. He said, 'You all remember how I waited upon table in commons. You know that I afterwards went through college, but you do not know that to this man [and he pointed to a classmate] I was indebted for the money that paid for my college course.'

" Anderson was the second, and he told of his two wives: of the first, much; of the second, little. Bowditch came next, and he said he would tell of Anderson's second wife, who was a Miss Lockworth, of Lexington, Ky.

" Anderson, a widower, and his brother went to Lexington, carrying with them a letter of introduction to the father of the young lady.

" While the brother was making an elaborate toilet, Anderson strolled out, and came, in his walk, upon a beautiful residence, and saw, within the enclosure, some inviting grounds. He stopped and spoke to the porter, and found it was Mr. Lockworth's. He told the porter that he had letters to Mr. Lockworth, and was intending to call upon him. The porter was very communicative, and told him a good deal. Anderson asked if there were not a pretty daughter. The porter asked him to walk around. As he entered the gate he reached a dollar to the man, and, being much pleased, when he came out he reached the porter another dollar.

" Anderson went back to the hotel, told his brother about it, and they set out together to deliver the letter. The brother knew Mr. Lockworth, and as they met him in the parlor, he walked up, shook hands with him, and asked to present his brother, Lars Anderson. ' No introduction is necessary,' said Mr. Lockworth; and putting his hand into his pocket, drawing out the two dollars, he added, ' I am already in your debt just this sum!' The 'pretty daughter' was sitting upon the sofa.

" Mr. Capers told me that their autobiographies drew

smiles and tears alternately; they continued till one
o'clock; then one of the class said, ' Brothers, do you
know that not a wineglass has yet been turned up, not
a drop of wine drunk? And all were at once so impressed with the conviction that they had all been lifted
above the needs of the flesh that they refused to drink,
and one of the clergymen of the class kneeling in
prayer, they all knelt at once, even to some idle
spectators who were looking on.

" April 28. Nothing can exceed the hospitality shown
to us. We have several invitations for each day, and
calls without limit.

" I had heard Mrs. Holbrook described as a wonder,
and I found her a very pleasing woman, all ready to
talk, and talking with a richness of expression which
shows a full mind. Mrs. Holbrook was a Rutledge, and
it was amusing, after seeing her, to open Miss Bremer's
' Homes of the New World,' and read her extravagant
comments. Miss Bremer was certainly made happy at
Belmont.

" April 29. To-day I have been to see Miss Pinckney. She is the last representative of her name, is over
eighty, and still retains the animation of youth, though
somewhat shaken in her physical strength by age.
I found her sitting in an armchair, her feet resting
upon a cushion, surrounded by some half-dozen callers.

" She rose at once when I entered, and insisted upon
my occupying her seat, while she took a less comfortable one.

" The walls of the room were ornamented with portraits of Major-General Pinckney by Stuart, Stuart's

Washington, one by Morris of General Thomas Pinckney, and a portrait of Miss Pinckney's mother.

"Miss Pinckney is a very plain woman, but much
beloved for her benevolence.

"It is said that on looking over her diary which she
keeps, recording the reasons for her many gifts to her
friends and to her slaves, such entries as these will be
found :

"'$ to Mary, because she is married.'

"'$ to Julia, because she has no husband.'

"Miss Pinckney showed me among her centre-table
ornaments a miniature of Washington; one of her
grandmother, of exceeding beauty; one of each of the
Pinckneys whose portraits are on the walls.

"Charleston is full of ante-Revolution houses, and they
please me. They were built when there was no hurry;
they were built to last, and they have lasted, and will
yet last for the children of their present possessors.

"Nothing can be happier in expression than the faces
of the colored children. They have what must be the
ease of the lower classes in a despotic country. The
slaves have no care, no ambition; their place is a fixed
one — they know it, and take all the good they can get.
The children are fat, sleek, and, inheriting no nervous
longings from their parents, are on a constant grin — at
play with loud laughs and high leaps.

"May 1. 'It does not follow because the slaves are
sleek and fat and really happy — for happy I believe
they are — that slavery is not an evil; and the great evil
is, as I always supposed, in the effect upon the whites.
The few Southern gentlemen that I know interest me

from their courtesy, agreeable manners, and ready speech. They also strike me as childlike and fussy. I catch myself feeling that I am the man and they are women; and I see this even in the captain of a steamer. Then they all like to talk sentiment — their religion is a feeling.

" May 2. The negroes are remarkable for their courtesy of manner. Those who belong to good families seem to pride themselves upon their dress and style.

" A lady walking in Charleston is never jostled by black or white man. The white man steps out of her way, the black man does this and touches his hat. The black woman bows — she is distinguished by her neat dress, her clean plaid head-dress, and her upright carriage. It would be well for some of our young ladies to carry burdens on their heads, even to the risk of flattening the instep, if by that means they could get the straight back of a slave.

" Mrs. W., who takes us out to drive, comes with her black coachman and a little boy. The coachman wears white gloves, and looks like a gentleman. The little boy rings door-bells when we stop.

" When it rained the other day, Mrs. W. dropped the window of the carriage, and desired the two to put on their shawls, for fear they would take cold. They are plainly a great care to their owners, for they are like children and cannot take care of themselves; and yet in another way the masters are like children, from the constant waiting upon that they receive. One would think, where one class does all the thinking and the

other all the working, that masters would be active
thinkers and slaves ready workers; but neither result
seems to happen — both are listless and inactive.

"May 3.   I asked Miss Pinckney to-day if she remembered George Washington.   She and Mrs. Poinsett
spoke at once.   "'Oh, yes, we were children,' said Mrs.
Poinsett; 'but my father would have him come to see
us, and he took each of us in his arms and kissed us;
and at another time we went to Mt. Vernon and made
him a visit.'

"Never were more intelligent old ladies than Mrs.
Poinsett and Miss Pinckney.   The latter stepped around
like a young girl, and brought a heavy book to show
me the sketch of her sister, Marie Henrietta Pinckney,
who, in the nullification time of 1830, wrote a pamphlet
in defence of the State.

"Miss Pinckney's father was the originator of the
celebrated maxim, 'Millions for defence, but not one
cent for tribute.'   Their house was the headquarters
for the nullifiers, and they had serenades, she said, without number.

"It was pleasant to hear the old ladies chatter
away, and it was interesting to think of the distinguished men who had been under that roof, and of the
cultivated and beautiful women who had adorned the
mansion.

"Miss Pinckney, when I left, followed me to the door,
and put into my hands an elegant little volume of
poems, called 'Reliquiai.'

"They seem to be simple effusions of some person
who died early.

"May 9. We left Charleston, its old houses and its good people, on Monday, and reached Augusta the same day.

"Augusta is prettily laid out, but the place is of little interest; and for the hotel where we stayed, I can only give this advice to its inmates: ' Don't examine a black spot upon your pillow-case; go to sleep at once, and keep asleep if you can.'

"When we were on the road from Augusta to Atlanta, the conductor said, 'If you are going on to Nashville, you will be on the road in the night; people don't love to go on that road in the night. I don't know why.'

"When we came to the Nashville road, I thought that I knew 'why.' The road runs around the base of a mountain, while directly beneath it, at a great depth, runs a river. A dash off the track on one side would be against the mountain, on the other side would be into the river, while the sharp turns seem to invite such a catastrophe. When we were somewhat wrought up to a nervous excitement, the cars would plunge into the darkness of a tunnel — darkness such as I almost felt.

"It was a picturesque but weary ride, and we were tired and hungry when we reached Nashville.

"May 11. To-day we have been out for a two-hours' drive. It is warm, cloudy, and looks like a tempest; we are too tired for much effort.

"Mrs. Fogg, of Nashville, took us to call on the widow of President Polk. We found her at home though apparently just ready for a walk. She is still in mourning, and tells me that she has not travelled fifty miles from home in the last eight years.

" She spoke to me of Governor Briggs (of Massachusetts), an old friend; of Professor Hare; and said that among her cards, on her return from a journey some years ago, she found Charles Sumner's; and forgetting at the moment who he was, she asked the servant who he was. ' The Abolitionist Senator from Massachusetts — I asked him in,' was the reply.

" Mrs. Polk talks readily, is handsome, elegant in figure, and shows at once that she is well read. She told me that she reads all the newspaper reports of the progress of science. She lives simply, as any New England woman would, though her house is larger than most private residences.

" Mrs. Fogg told me many anecdotes of Dorothea Dix. That lady was, at one time, travelling alone, and was obliged to stop at some little village tavern. As she lay half asleep upon the sofa, the driver of the stage in which she was to take passage came into the room, approached her, and held a light to her closed eyes. She did not dare to move nor utter a sound, but when he turned away she opened her eyes and watched him. He went to the mail-bags, opened them, took out the letters, hastily broke the seals, took out money enclosed, put it into his pocket, closed the bags, and again approached her with his lamp. She shut her eyes and pretended to sleep again; then at the proper time entered the stage and pursued her journey. At the end of the journey she reported his conduct to the proper authorities.

" I was a little doubtful about the propriety of going to the Mammoth Cave without a gentleman escort, but

if two ladies travel alone they must have the courage of
men. So I called the landlord as soon as we arrived at
the Cave House, and asked if we could have Mat, who I
had been told was the best guide now that Stephen is
ill. The landlord promised Mat to me for two days.
After dinner we made our first attempt.

"The ground descends for some two hundred feet
towards the mouth of the cave; then you come to a low
hill, and you descend through a small aperture not at
all imposing, in front of which trickles a little stream.
For some little while we needed no light, but soon the
guide lighted and gave to each of us a little lamp.
Mat took the lead, I came next, Miss S. followed, and
an old slave brought up in the rear.

" I confess that I shuddered as I came into the darkness. Our lamps, of course, gave but feeble light; we
barely saw at first where our feet must step.

" I looked up, trying in vain to find the ceiling or the
walls. All was darkness. In about an hour we saw
more clearly. The chambers are, many of them, elliptical in shape; the ceiling is of mixed dark and white
color, and looks much like the sky on a cloudy moonlight evening.

"A friend of ours, who has been much in the cave,
says, 'If the top were lifted off, and the whole were
exposed to view, no woman would ever enter it again.'

"We clambered over heaps of rocks, we descended
ladders, wound through narrow passages, passed. along
chambers so low that we crouched for the whole
length, entered upon lofty halls, ascended ladders, and
crossed a bridge over a yawning abyss.

" Every nightmare scene that I had ever dreamed of seemed to be realized. I shuddered several times, and was obliged to reason with myself to assure me of safety. Occasionally we sat down and rested upon some flat rock.

" Miss S., who has a great taste for costuming, wound her plaid shawl about her shoulders, turbaned her head with a green veil, swung her lamp upon a stick which she rested upon her shoulder, and then threw herself upon a rock in a most picturesque attitude. The guide took a lower seat, and his dirty tin cup, swung across his breast, looked like an ornament as the light struck it; his swarthy face was bright, and I wondered what our friends at home would give for a picture.

" One of these elliptical halls has its ceiling immensely far off, and of the deepest black, until our feeble little lights strike upon innumerable points, when it shines forth like a dark starlight night. The stars are faint, but they look so exceedingly like the heavens that one easily forgets that it is not reality.

" The guide asked us to be seated, while he went behind down a descent with the lights, to show us the creeping over of the shadows of the rocks, as if a dark cloud passed over the starlit vault. The black cloud crept on and on as the guide descended, until a fear came over us, and we cried out together to him to come back, not to leave us in total darkness. He begged that he might go still lower and show us entire darkness, but we would not permit it.

" Guin's Dome. What the name means I can't say. The guide tells you to pause in your scrambling over loose stones and muddy soil, — which you are always willing to do, — and to put your head through a circular aperture, and to look up while he lights the Bengal light; you obey, and look up upon columns of fluted, snowy whiteness; he tells you to look down, and you follow the same pillars down — up to heights which the light cannot climb, down to depths on which it cannot fall.

"You shudder as you look up, and you shudder as you look down. Indeed, the march of the cave is a series of shudders. Geologists may enjoy it, a large party may be merry in it; but if the ' underground railroad ' of the slaves is of that kind, I should rather remain a slave than undertake a runaway trip!

" May 18. To-day we retraced our steps from Nashville to Chattanooga. It had been raining nearly all night, and we found, when not far from the latter place, that the streams were pouring down from the high lands upon the car-track, so that we came through rivers. When we dashed into the dark tunnel it was darker than ever from the darkness of the day, and it seemed to me that the darkness pressed upon me. I am sure I should keep my senses a very little while if I were confined in a dark place.

" As we came out of the tunnel, the water from the hill above dashed upon the cars; and although it did not break the panes of glass, it forced its way through and sprinkled us. .

" The route, with all its terrors, is beautiful, and the trees are now much finer than they were ten days ago.

" May 27. There is this great difference between

Niagara and other wonders of the world : that of it you get no idea from descriptions, or even from paintings. Of the ' Mammoth Cave ' you have a conception from what you are told ; of the Natural Bridge you get a really truthful impression from a picture. But cave and bridge are in still life. Niagara is all activity and change. No picture gives you the varying form of the water or the change of color; no description conveys to your mind the ceaseless roar. So, too, the ocean must be unrepresentable to those who have not looked upon it.

" The Natural Bridge stands out bold and high, just as you expect to see it. You are agreeably disappointed, however, on finding that you can go under the arch and be completely in the coolness of its shade while you look up for two hundred feet to the rocky black and white ceiling above.

" One of the prettiest peculiarities is the fringing above of the trees which hang over the edge, and looking out past the arch the wooded banks of the ravine are very pleasant. From above, one has the pain always attendant to me upon looking down into an abyss, but at the same time one obtains a better conception of the depth of the valley. It is well worth seeing, partly for itself, partly because it can be reached only by a ride among the hills of the Blue Ridge."

CHAPTER V

1857

FIRST EUROPEAN TOUR — LIVERPOOL — THE HAWTHORNES —
LONDON — GREENWICH OBSERVATORY — ADMIRAL SMYTH
— DR. LEE

SHORTLY after her return from the South, Miss Mitchell started again for a tour in Europe with the same young girl.

Miss Mitchell carried letters from eminent scientific people in this country to such persons as it would be desirable for her to know in Europe; especially to astronomers and mathematicians.

When Miss Mitchell went to Europe she took her Almanac work with her, and what time she was not sight-seeing she was continuing that work. Her wisdom in this respect was very soon apparent. She had not been in England many weeks when a great financial crisis took place in the United States, and the father of her young charge succumbed to the general failure. The young lady was called home, but after considering the matter seriously Miss Mitchell decided to remain herself, putting the young lady into careful hands for the return passage from Liverpool.

Miss Mitchell enjoyed the society of the scientific people whom she met in England to her heart's content. She was very cordially received, and the astronomers not only opened their observatories to her, but welcomed her into their family life.

On arriving at Liverpool, Miss Mitchell delivered the letters to the astronomers living in or near that city, and visited their observatories.

" Aug. 3, 1857. I brought a letter from Professor Silliman to Mr. John Taylor, cotton merchant and astronomer; and to-day I have taken tea with him. He is an old man, nearly eighty I should think, but full of life, and talks by the hour on heathen mythology. He was the principal agent in the establishment of the Liverpool Observatory, but disclaims the honor, because it was established on so small a scale, compared with his own gigantic plan. Mr. Taylor has invented a little machine, for showing the approximate position of a comet, having the elements.

" He has also made additions to the globes made by De Morgan, so that they can be used for any year and show the correct rising and setting of the stars.

" He struck me as being a man of taste, but of no great profundity. He has a painting which he believes to be by Guido; it seemed to me too fresh in its coloring for the sixteenth century.

" August 4, 3 P.M. I put down my pen, because old Mr. Taylor called, and while he was here Rev. James Martineau came. Mr. Martineau is one of the handsomest men I ever saw. He cannot be more than thirty, or if he is he has kept his dark hair remarkably. He has large, bluish-gray eyes, and is tall and elegant in manner. He says he is just packed to move to London. He gave me his London address and hoped he should see me there; but I doubt if he does, for I did not like to tell him my address unless he asked for it, for fear of seeming to be pushing.

"August, . . . I have been to visit Mr. Lassell. He called yesterday and asked me to dine with him to-day. He has a charming place, about four miles out of Liverpool; a pretty house and grounds.

"Mr. Lassell has constructed two telescopes, both on the Newtonian plan; one of ten, the other of twenty, feet in length. Each has its separate building, and in the smaller building is a transit instrument.

"Mr. Lassell must have been a most indefatigable worker as well as a most ingenious man; for, besides constructing his own instruments, he has found time to make discoveries. He is, besides, very genial and pleasant, and told me some good anecdotes connected with astronomical observations.

"One story pleased me very much. Our Massachusetts astronomer, Alvan Clark, has long been a correspondent of Mr. Dawes, but has never seen him. Wishing to have an idea of his person, and being a portrait painter, Mr. Clark sent to Mr. Dawes for his daguerreotype, and from that painted a likeness, which he has sent out to Liverpool, and which is said to be excellent.

"Mr. Lassell looks in at the side of his reflecting telescopes by means of a diagonal eye-piece; when the instrument is pointed at objects of high altitude he hangs a ladder upon the dome and mounts; the ladder moves around with the dome. Mr. Lassell works only for his own amusement, and has been to Malta, —

carrying his larger telescope with him, — for the sake of clearer skies. Neither Mr. Lassell nor Mr. Hartnup [1] makes regular observations.

"The Misses Lassell, four in number, seem to be very accomplished. They take photographs of each other which are beautiful, make their own picture-frames, and work in the same workshop with their father. One of them told me that she made observations on my comet, supposing it to belong to Mr. Dawes, who was a friend of hers.

"They keep an album of the autographs of their scientific visitors, and among them I saw those of Professor Young, of Dartmouth, and of Professor Loomis.

"August 4. I have just returned from a visit to the Liverpool Observatory, under the direction of Mr. Hartnup. It is situated on Waterloo dock, and the pier of the observatory rests upon the sandstone of that region. The telescope is an equatorial; like many good instruments in our country, it is almost unused.

"Mr. Hartnup's observatory is for nautical purposes. I found him a very gentlemanly person, and very willing to show me anything of interest about the observatory; but they make no regular series of astronomical observations, other than those required for the commerce of Liverpool.

"Mr. Hartnup has a clock which by the application of an electric current controls the action of other clocks, especially the town clock of Liverpool — distant some miles. The current of electricity is not the motive power, but a corrector.

---

[1] Of the Liverpool Observatory.

" Much attention is paid to meteorology. The pressure of the wind, the horizontal motion, and the course
are recorded upon sheets of paper running upon cylin-
ders and connected with the clock; the instrument
which obeys the voice of the wind being outside.

" Aug. 5, 1857. I did not send my letter to Mr.
Hawthorne until yesterday, supposing that he was not
in the city; but yesterday when Rev. James Martineau
called on me, he said that he had not yet left. Mr.
Martineau said that it would be a great loss to Liverpool when Mr. Hawthorne went away.

" I sent my letter at once; from all that I had heard
of Mr. Hawthorne's shyness, I thought it doubtful if he
would call, and I was therefore very much pleased when
his card was sent in this morning. Mr. Hawthorne was
more chatty than I had expected, but not any more
diffident. He remained about five minutes, during
which time he took his hat from the table and put it
back once a minute, brushing it each time. The engravings in the books are much like him. He is not
handsome, but looks as the author of his books should
look; a little strange and odd, as if not of this earth.
He has large, bluish-gray eyes; his hair stands out on
each side, so much so that one's thoughts naturally
turn to combs and hair-brushes and toilet ceremonies
as one looks at him."

Later, when Miss Mitchell was in Paris, alone, on
her way to Rome, she sent to the Hawthornes, who
were also in Paris, asking for the privilege of joining
them, as they too were journeying in the same
direction. She says in her diary:

" Mrs. Hawthorne was feeble, and she told me that she objected, but that Mr. Hawthorne assured her that I was a person who would give no trouble; therefore she consented. We were about ten days on the journey to Rome, and three months in Rome; living, however, some streets asunder. I saw them nearly every day. Like everybody else, I found Mr. Hawthorne very taciturn. His few words were, however, very telling. When I talked French, he told me it was capital: 'It came down like a sledge-hammer.' His little satirical remarks were such as these: It was March and I took a bunch of violets to Rosa; notched white paper was wound around them, and Mr. Hawthorne said, 'They have on a cambric ruffle.'"

" Generally he sat by an open fire, with his feet thrust into the coals, and an open volume of Thackeray upon his knees. He said that Thackeray was the greatest living novelist. I sometimes suspected that the volume of Thackeray was kept as a foil, that he might not be talked to. He shrank from society, but rode and walked."

EXTRACT FROM A LETTER.

ROME, Feb. 16, 1858.

. . . The Hawthornes are invaluable to me, because the little ones come to my room every day and I go there when I like. Mrs. Hawthorne sometimes walks with us, Mr. H. *never*. He has a horror of sight-seeing and of emotions in general, but I like him very much, and when I say I like *him* it only means that I like *her* a little more. Julian, the boy, is in love with me. When I was last there Mr. H. came home with me; as he put on his coat he turned to Julian and said, " Julian, I should think with your *tender interest* in Miss Mitchell you wouldn't let me escort her home."

"We arrived in Rome in the evening. Mrs. H. was somewhat of an invalid, and Mr. Hawthorne tried in vain to make the servant understand that she must have a fire in her room. He spoke no word of French, German, or Italian, but he said emphatically, ' Make a fire in Mrs. Hawthorne's room.' Worn out with his efforts, he turned to me and said, ' Do, Miss Mitchell, tell the servant what I want; your French is excellent! Englishmen and Frenchmen understand it equally well.' So I said in execrable French, ' Make a fire,' and pointed to the grate; of course the gesture was understood.

" Mr. Hawthorne was minutely and scrupulously honest; I should say that he was a rigid temperance man. Once I heard Mrs. Hawthorne say to the clerk, ' Send some brandy to Mr. Hawthorne at once.' We were six in the party. When I paid my bill I heard Mr. Hawthorne say to Miss S., the teacher, who took all the business cares, ' Don't let Miss Mitchell pay for one-sixth of my brandy.'

" So if we ordered tea for five, and six partook of it, he called the waiter and said, ' Six have partaken of the tea, although there was no tea added to the amount.'

" I told Mr. Hawthorne that a friend of mine, Miss W., desired very much to see him, as she admired him very much. He said, ' Don't let her see me, let her keep her little lamp burning.'

" He was a sad man; I could never tell why. I never could get at anything of his religious views.

" He was wonderfully blest in his family. Mrs.

Hawthorne almost worshipped him.   She was of a very
serious and religious turn of mind.

"I dined with them the day that Una was sixteen
years old. We drank her health in cold water. Mr.
Hawthorne said, 'May you live happily, and be ready
to go when you must.'

"He joined in the family talk very pleasantly.   One
evening we made up a story.   One said, 'A party was
in Rome;' another said, 'It was a pleasant day;' another
said, 'They took a walk.'   It came to Hawthorne's turn,
and he said, 'Do put in an incident;' so Rosa said,
'Then a bear jumped from the top of St. Peter's!'   The
story went no further.

"I was with the family when they first went to St.
Peter's. Hawthorne turned away saying, 'The St. Peter's
of my imagination was better.'

"I think he could not have been well, he was so very
inactive.   If he walked out he took Rosa, then a child
of six, with him.   He once came with her to my room,
but he seemed tired from the ascent of the stairs.   I was
on the fifth floor.

"I have been surprised to see that he made severe
personal remarks in his journal, for in the three months
that I knew him I never heard an unkind word; he was
always courteous, gentle, and retiring.   Mrs. Hawthorne
said she took a wifely pride in his having no small
vices.   Mr. Hawthorne said to Miss S., 'I have yet to
find the first fault in Mrs. Hawthorne.'

"One day Mrs. Hawthorne came to my room, held
up an inkstand, and said, 'The new book will be begun
to-night.'

" This was 'The Marble Faun.' She said, ' Mr. Hawthorne writes after every one has gone to bed. I never see the manuscript until it is what he calls *clothed*' . . . Mrs. H. says he never knows when he is writing a story how the characters will turn out; he waits for *them* to influence *him*.

" I asked her if Zenobia was intended for Margaret Fuller, and she said, ' No ; ' but Mr. Hawthorne admitted that Margaret Fuller seemed to be around him when he was writing it.

" London, August. We went out for our first walk as soon as breakfast was over, and we walked on Regent street for hours, looking in at the shop windows. The first view of the street was beautiful, for it was a misty morning, and we saw its length fade away as if it had no end. I like it that in our first walk we came upon a crowd standing around ' Punch.' It is a ridiculous affair, but as it is as much a ' peculiar institution ' as is Southern slavery, I stopped and listened, and after we came into the house Miss S. threw out some pence for them. We rested after the shop windows of Regent street, took dinner, and went out again, this time to Piccadilly.

" The servility of the shopkeepers is really a little offensive. ' What shall I have the honor of showing you? ' they say.

" Our chambermaid, at our lodgings, thanks us every time we speak to her.

" I feel ashamed to reach a four-penny piece to a stout coachman who touches his hat and begs me to remember him. Sometimes I am ready to say, ' How can I forget you, when you have hung around me so closely for half an hour?'

"Our waiter at the Adelphi Hotel, at Liverpool, was a very respectable middle-aged man, with a white neck-cloth; he looked like a Methodist parson. He waited upon us for five days with great gravity, and then another waiter told us that we could give our waiter what we pleased. We were charged £1 for 'attendance' in the bill, but I very innocently gave half as much more, as fee to the 'parson.'

"August 14. To-day we took a brougham and drove around for hours. Of course we didn't *see* London, and if we stay a month we shall still know nothing of it, it is so immense. I keep thinking, as I go through the streets, of 'The rats and the mice, they made such a strife, he had to go to London,' etc., and especially 'The streets were so wide, and the lanes were so narrow;' for I never saw such narrow streets, even in Boston.

"We have begun to send out letters, but as it is 'out of season' I am afraid everybody will be at the watering-places.

THE GREENWICH OBSERVATORY. "The observatory was founded by Charles II. The king that 'never said a foolish thing and never did a wise one' was yet sagacious enough to start an institution which has grown to be a thing of might, and this, too, of his own will, and not from the influence of courtiers. One of the hospital buildings of Greenwich, then called the 'House of Delights,' was the residence of Henrietta Maria, and the young prince probably played on the little hill now the site of the observatory.

" But Charles, though he started an observatory, did not know very well what was needed. The first building consisted of a large, octagonal room, with windows all around; it was considered sufficiently firm without any foundation, and sufficiently open to the heavens with no opening higher than windows. This room is now used as a place of deposit for instruments, and busts and portraits of eminent men, and also as the dancing-hall for the director's family.

" Under Mr. Airy's[1] direction, the walls of the observing-room have become pages of its history. The transit instruments used by Halley, Bradley, and Pond hang side by side; the zenith sector with which Bradley discovered the 'aberration of light,' now moving rustily on its arc, is the ornament of another room; while the shelves of the computing-room are filled with volumes of unpublished observations of Flamstead and others.

" The observatory stands in Greenwich Park, the prettiest park I have yet seen; being a group of small hills. They point out oaks said to belong to Elizabeth's time — noble oaks of any time. The observatory is one hundred and fifty feet above the sea level. The view from it is, of course, beautiful. On the north the river, the little Thames, big with its fleet, is winding around the Isle of Dogs; on the left London, always overhung with a cloud of smoke, through which St. Paul's and the Houses of Parliament peep.

" Mr. Airy was exceedingly kind to me, and seemed to take great interest in showing me around. He appeared to be much gratified by my interest in the

---

[1] The late Sir George Airy.

history of the observatory.   He is naturally a despot, and his position increases this tendency.   Sitting in his chair, the zero-point of longitude for the world, he commands not only the little knot of observers and computers around him, but when he says to London, ' It is one o'clock,' London adopts that time, and her ships start for their voyages around the globe, and continue to count their time from that moment, wherever the English flag is borne.

" It is singular what a quiet motive-power Science is, the breath of a nation's progress.

" Mr. Airy is not favorable to the multiplication of observatories.   He predicted the failure of that at Albany.   He says that he would gladly destroy one-half of the meridian instruments of the world, by way of reform.   I told him that my reform movement would be to bring together the astronomers who had no instruments and the instruments which had no astronomers.

" Mr. Airy is exceedingly systematic.   In leading me by narrow passages and up steep staircases, from one room to another of the irregular collection of rooms, he was continually cautioning me about my footsteps, and in one place he seemed to have a kind of formula: ' Three steps at this place, ten at this, eleven at this, and three again.'   So, in descending a ladder to the birthplace of the galvanic currents, he said, ' Turn your back to the stairs, step down with the right foot, take hold with the right hand; reverse the operation in ascending; do not, on coming out, turn around at once, but step backwards one step first.'

" Near the throne of the astronomical autocrat is

another proof of his system, in a case of portfolios. These contain the daily bills, letters, and papers, as they come in and are answered in order. When a portfolio is full, the papers are removed and are sewed together. Each year's accumulation is bound, and the bound volumes of Mr. Airy's time nearly cover one side of his private room.

"Mr. Airy replies to all kinds of letters, with two exceptions: those which ask for autographs, and those which request him to calculate nativities. Both of these are very frequent.

"In the drawing-room Mr. Airy is cheery; he loves to recite ballads and knows by heart a mass of verses, from 'A, Apple Pie,' to the 'Lady of the Lake.'

"A lover of Nature and a close observer of her ways, as well in the forest walk as in the vault of heaven, Mr. Airy has roamed among the beautiful scenery of the Lake region until he is as good a mountain guide as can be found. He has strolled beside Grassmere and ascended Helvellyn. He knows the height of the mountain peaks, the shingles that lie on their sides, the flowers that grow in the valleys, the mines beneath the surface.

"At one time the Government Survey planted what is called a 'Man' on the top of one of the hills of the Lake region. In a dry season they built up a stone monument, right upon the bed of a little pond. The country people missed the little pond, which had seemed to them an eye of Nature reflecting heaven's blue light. They begged for the removal of the surveyor's pile, and Mr. Airy at once changed the station.

" The established observatories of England do not step out of their beaten path to make discoveries — these come from the amateurs. In this respect they differ from America and Germany. The amateurs of England do a great deal of work, they learn to know of what they and their instruments are capable, and it is done.

" The library of Greenwich Observatory is large. The transactions of learned societies alone fill a small room; the whole impression of the thirty volumes of printed observations fills a wall of another room, and the unpublished papers of the early directors make of themselves a small manuscript library.

" October 22, 1857. We have just returned from our fourth visit to Greenwich, like the others twenty-four hours in length. We go again to-morrow to meet the Sabines.

" Herr Struve, the director of the Pulkova Observatory, is at Greenwich, with his son Karl. The old gentleman is a magnificent-looking fellow, very large and well proportioned; his great head is covered with white hair, his features are regular and handsome. When he is introduced to any one he thrusts both hands into the pockets of his pantaloons, and bows. I found that the son considered this position of the hands particularly *English*. However, the old gentleman did me the honor to shake hands with me, and when I told him that I brought a letter to him from a friend in America, he said, ' It is quite unnecessary, I know you without.' He speaks very good English.

" Herr Struve's mission in England is to see if he can

connect the trigonometrical surveys of the two countries. It is quite singular that he should visit England for this purpose, so soon after Russia and England were at war. One of his sons was an army surgeon at the Crimea.

"Five visitors remained all night at the observatory. I slept in a little round room and Miss S. in another, at the top of a little jutting-out, curved building. Mrs. Airy says, ' Mr. Airy got permission of the Board of Visitors to fit up some of the rooms as lodging-rooms.' Mr. Airy said, ' My dear love, I did as I always do: I fitted them up first, and then I reported to the Board that I had done it.'

" October 23. Another dinner-party at the observatory, consisting of the Struves, General and Mrs. Sabine, Professor and Mrs. Powell, Mr. Main, and ourselves; more guests coming to tea.

" Mrs. Airy told me that she should arrange the order of the guests at table to please herself; that properly all of the married ladies should precede me, but that I was really to go first, with Mr. Airy. To effect this, however, she must explain it to Mrs. Sabine, the lady of highest rank.

" So we went out, Professor Airy and myself, Professor Powell and Mrs. Sabine, General Sabine and Mrs. Powell, Mr. Charles Struve and Miss S., Mr. Main, Mrs. Airy, and Professor Struve.

" General Sabine is a small man, gray haired and sharp featured, about seventy years old. He smiles very readily, and is chatty and sociable at once. He speaks with more quickness and ease than most of the

Englishmen I have met.   Mrs. Sabine is very agreeable and not a bit of a blue-stocking.

"The chat at table was general and very interesting. Mr. Airy says, 'The best of a good dinner is the amount of talk.' He talked of the great 'Leviathan' which he and Struve had just visited, then anecdotes were told by others, then they went on to comic poetry. Mr. Airy repeated 'The Lost Heir,' by Hood. General Sabine told droll anecdotes, and the point was often lost upon me, because of the local allusions. One of his anecdotes was this: 'Archbishop Whately did not like a professor named Robert Daly; he said the Irish were a very contented people, they were satisfied with one *bob daily.*' I found that a 'bob' is a shilling.

"When the dinner was over, the ladies left the room, and the gentlemen remained over their wine ; but not for long, for Mr. Airy does not like it, and Struve hates it.

"Then, before tea, others dropped in from the neighborhood, and the tea was served in the drawing-room, handed round informally.

"August 15.   Westminster Abbey interested me more than I had expected.   We went into the chapels and admired the sculpture when the guide told us we ought, and stopped with interest sometimes over some tomb which he did not point out.

"I stepped aside reverently when I found I was standing on the stone which covers the remains of Dr. Johnson.   It is cracked across the middle.   Garrick lies by the side of Johnson, and I thought at first that Goldsmith lay near; but it is only a monument — the body is interred in Temple churchyard.

"You are continually misled in this way unless you refer at every minute to your guide-book, and to go through Europe reading a guide-book which you can read at home seems to be a waste of time. On the stone beneath which Addison lies is engraved the verse from Tickell's ode:

" ' Ne'er to these chambers where the mighty rest,' etc.

"The base of Newton's monument is of white marble, a solid mass large enough to support a coffin; upon that a sarcophagus rests. The remains are not enclosed within. As I stepped aside I found I had been standing upon a slab marked ' Isaac Newton,' beneath which the great man's remains lie.

"On the side of the sarcophagus is a white marble slab, with figures in bas-relief. One of these imaginary beings appears to be weighing the planets on a steelyard. They hang like peas! Another has a pair of bellows and is blowing a fire. A third is tending a plant.

"On this sarcophagus reclines a figure of Newton, of full size. He leans his right arm upon four thick volumes, probably ' The Principia,' and he points his left hand to a globe above his head on which the goddess Urania sits; she leans upon another large book.

"Newton's head is very fine, and is probably a portrait. The left hand, which is raised, has lost two fingers. I thought at first that this had been the work of some ' undevout astronomer,' but when I came to ' read up' I found that at one time soldiers were quartered in the abbey, and probably one of them

' wanted a finger with which to crowd the tobacco into his pipe, and so broke off one.

"August 17. To-day we have been to the far-famed British Museum. I carried an 'open sesame' in the form of a letter given to me by Professor Henry, asking for me special attention from all societies with which the 'Smithsonian' at Washington is connected.

"I gave the paper first to a police officer; a police officer is met at every turn in London. He handed it to another official, who said, 'You'd better go to the secretary.'

"I walked in the direction towards which he pointed, a long way, until I found the secretary. He called another man, and asked him to show me whatever I wanted to see.

"This man took me into another room, and consigned me to still another man — the fifth to whom I had been referred. No. 5 was an intelligent and polite person, and he began to talk about America at once.

"I asked to see anything which had belonged to Newton, and he told me they had one letter only, — from Newton to Leibnitz, — which he showed me. It was written in Latin, with diagrams and formulæ interspersed. The reply of Leibnitz, copied by Newton, was also in their collection, and an order from Newton written while he was director of the mint.

"No. 5 also showed me the illuminated manuscripts of the collection; they are kept locked in glass-topped cases, and a curtain protects them from the light. We saw also the oldest copy of the Bible in the world.

"The art of printing has brought incalculable blessings; but as I looked at a neat manuscript book by Queen Elizabeth, copied from another as a present to her father, I could not help thinking it was much better than worsted work!

"A much-worn prayer-book was shown me, said to be the one used by Lady Jane Grey when on the scaffold. Nothing makes me more conscious that I am on foreign soil than the constant recurrence of associations connected with the executioner's block. We hung the Quakers and we burned the witches, but we are careful not to remember the localities of our barbarisms; we show instead the Plymouth Rock or the Washington Elm.

"Among other things, we were shown the 'Magna Charta' — a few fragments of worn-out paper on which some words could be traced; now carefully preserved in a frame, beneath a glass.

"Thus far England has impressed me seriously; I cannot imagine how it has ever earned the name of 'Merrie England.'

"August 19. There are four great men whose haunts I mean to seek, and on whose footsteps I mean to stand: Newton, Shakspere, Milton, and Johnson.

"To-day I told the driver to take me to St. Martin's, where the guide-book says that Newton lived. He put me down at the Newton Hotel, but I looked in vain to its top to see anything like an observatory.

"I went into a wine-shop near, and asked a girl, who was pouring out a dram, in which house Newton lived. She pointed, not to the hotel, but to a house next to a church, and said, 'That's it — don't you see a place on the top? That's where he used to study nights.'

" It is a little, oblong-shaped observatory, built apparently of wood, and blackened by age. The house is a good-looking one — it seems to be of stone. The girl said the rooms were let for shops.

"Next I told the driver to take me to Fleet street, to Gough square, and to Bolt court, where Johnson lived and died.

" Bolt court lies on Fleet street, and it is but few steps along a narrow passage to the house, which is now a hotel, where Johnson died; but you must walk on farther through the narrow passage, a little fearful to a woman, to see the place where he wrote the dictionary. The house is so completely within a court, in which nothing but brick walls could be seen, that one wonders what the charm of London could be, to induce one to live in that place. But a great city always draws to itself the great minds, and there Johnson probably found his enjoyment.

"August 27. We took St. Paul's Church to-day. We took tickets for the vaults, the bell, the crypt, the whispering-gallery, the clock and all. We did not know what was before us. It was a little tiresome as far as the library and the room of Nelson's trophies, but to my surprise, when the guide said, 'Go that way for the clock,' he did not take the lead, but pointed up a staircase, and I found myself the pioneer in the narrowest and darkest staircase I ever ascended. It was really perfect darkness in some of the places, and we had to feel our way. We all took a long breath when a gleam of light came in at some narrow windows scattered along. At the top, in front of the clock works, stood a woman, who began at once to tell us the statistics of the pendulum, to which recital I did not choose to listen. She was not to go down with us, and, panting with fatigue and trembling with fright, we groped our way down again.

"There was another long, but easy, ascent to the 'whispering-gallery,' which is a fine place from which to look down upon the interior of the church. The man in attendance looked like a respectable elderly gentleman. He told us to go to the opposite side of the gallery, and he would whisper to us. We went around, and, worn out with fatigue, dropped upon a bench.

"The man began to whisper, putting his mouth to an opening in the wall; we heard noises, but could not tell what he said.

"To my amazement, this very respectable-looking elderly gentleman, as we passed him in going out, whispered again, and as this time he put his mouth close to my ear, I understood! He said, 'If you will give anything for the whisper, it will be gratefully received.' There are notices all over the church forbidding fees, and I felt that the man was a beggar at best — more properly a pickpocket.

"A figure of Dr. Johnson stands in one of the aisles of the church. It must be like him, for it is exceedingly ugly.

"September 3. We have been three weeks in London 'out of season,' but with plenty of letters. At present we have as many acquaintances as we desire. Last night we were at the opera, to-night we go out to dine, and to-morrow evening to a dance, the next day to Admiral Smyth's.

"The opera fatigued me, as it always does. I tired my eyes and ears in the vain effort to appreciate it. Mario was the great star of the evening, but I knew no difference.

"One little circumstance showed me how an American, with the best intentions, may offend against good manners. American-like we had secured very good seats, were in good season, and as comfortable as the very narrow seats would permit us to be, before most of the audience arrived. The house filled, and we sat at our ease, feeling our importance, and quite unconscious that we were guilty of any impropriety. While the curtain was down, I heard a voice behind me say to the gentleman who was with us, 'Is the lady on your left with you?' — 'Yes,' said Mr. R. — 'She wears a bonnet, which is not according to rule.' — 'Too late now,' said Mr. R. — 'It is my fault,' said the attendant; 'I ought not to have admitted her; I thought it was a hood.'

"I was really in hopes that I should be ordered out, for I was exceedingly fatigued and should have been glad of some fresh air. On looking around, I saw that only the 'pit' wore bonnets.

"September 6. We left London yesterday for Aylesbury. It is two hours by railroad. Like all railroads in England, it runs seemingly through a garden. In many cases flowers are cultivated by the roadside.

"From Aylesbury to Stone, the residence of Admiral Smyth, it is two miles of stage-coach riding.

Stage-coaches are now very rare in England, and I was delighted with the chance for a ride.

"We found the stage-coach crowded. The driver asked me if we were for St. John's Lodge, and on my replying in the affirmative gave me a note which Mrs. Smyth had written to him, to ask for inside seats. The note had reached him too late, and he said we must go on the outside. He brought a ladder and we got up. For a minute I thought, 'What a height to fall from!' but the afternoon was so lovely that I soon forgot the danger and enjoyed the drive. There were six passengers on top.

"Aylesbury is a small town, and Stone is a very small village. The driver stopped at what seemed to be a cultivated field, and told me that I was at my journey's end. On looking down I saw a wheelbarrow near the fence, and I remembered that Mrs. Smyth had said that one would be waiting for our luggage, and I soon saw Mrs. Smyth and her daughter coming towards us. It was a walk of about an eighth of a mile to the 'Lodge'— a pleasant cottage surrounded by a beautiful garden.

"Admiral Smyth's family go to a little church seven hundred years old, standing in the midst of tombstones and surrounded by thatched cottages. English scenery seems now (September) much like our Southern scenery in April — rich and lovely, but wanting mountains and water. An English village could never be mistaken for an American one : the outline against the sky differs ; a thatched cottage makes a very wavy line on the blue above.

"We find enough in St. John's Lodge, in the admiral's

library, and in the society of the cultivated members of his family to interest us for a long time.

"The admiral himself is upwards of sixty years of age, noble-looking, loving a good joke, an antiquarian, and a good astronomer. I picked up many an anecdote from him, and many curious bits of learning.

"He tells a good story, illustrative of his enthusiasm when looking at a crater in the moon. He says the night was remarkably fine, and he applied higher and higher powers to his glass until he seemed to look down into the abyss, and imagining himself standing on its verge he felt himself falling in, and drew back with a shudder which lasted even after the illusion was over.

"In speaking of Stratford-upon-Avon, the admiral told me that the Lucy family, one of whose ancestors drove Shakspere from his grounds, and who is caricatured in Justice Shallow, still resides on the same spot as in Shakspere's time. He says no family ever retained their characteristics more decidedly.

"Some years ago one of this family was invited to a Shakspere dinner. He resented the well-meant invitation, saying they must surely have forgotten how that *person* treated his ancestor!

"The amateur astronomers of England are numerous, but they are not like those of America.

"In America a poor schoolmaster, who has some bright boys who ask questions, buys a glass and becomes a star-gazer, without time and almost without instruments; or a watchmaker must know the time, and therefore watches the stars as time-keepers. In almost all cases they are hard-working men.

" In England it is quite otherwise. A wealthy gentleman buys a telescope as he would buy a library, as an ornament to his house.

" Admiral Smyth says that no family is quite civilized unless it possesses a copy of some encyclopædia and a telescope. The English gentleman uses both for amusement. If he is a man of philosophical mind he soon becomes an astronomer, or if a benevolent man he perceives that some friend in more limited circumstances might use it well, and he offers the telescope to him, or if an ostentatious man he hires some young astronomer of talent, who comes to his observatory and makes a name for him. Then the queen confers the honor of knighthood, not upon the young man, but upon the owner of the telescope. Sir James South was knighted for this reason.

" We have been visiting Hartwell House, an old baronial residence, now the property of Dr. Lee, a whimsical old man.

" This house was for years the residence of Louis XVIII., and his queen died here. The drawing-room is still kept as in those days; the blue damask on the walls has been changed by time to a brown. The rooms are spacious and lofty, the chimney-pieces of richly carved marble. The ceiling of one room has fine bas-relief allegorical figures.

" Books of antiquarian value are all around — one whole floor is covered with them. They are almost never opened. In some of the rooms paintings are on the walls above the doors.

" Dr. Lee's modern additions are mostly paintings of

himself and a former wife, and are in very bad taste.
He has, however, two busts of Mrs. Somerville, from
which I received the impression that she is handsome,
but Mrs. Smyth tells me she is not so; certainly she is
sculpturesque.

"The royal family, on their retreat from Hartwell
House, left their prayer-book, and it still remains on its
stand. The room of the ladies of the bedchamber is
papered, and the figure of a pheasant is the prevailing
characteristic of the paper. The room is called 'The
Pheasant Room.' One of the birds has been carefully
cut out, and, it is said, was carried away as a memento
by one of the damsels.

" Dr. Lee is second cousin to Sir George Lee, who
died childless. He inherits the estate, but not the title.
The estate has belonged to the Lees for four hundred
years. As the doctor was a Lee only through his
mother, he was obliged to take her name on his acces-
sion to the property. He applied to Parliament to be
permitted to assume the title, and, being refused, from a
strong Tory he became a Liberal, and delights in curry-
ing favor with the lowest classes; he has twice married
below his rank. Being remotely connected with the
Hampdens, he claims John Hampden as one of his
family, and keeps a portrait of him in a conspicuous
place.

" A summer-house on the grounds was erected by
Lady Elizabeth Lee, and some verses inscribed on its
walls, written by her, show that the Lees have not
always been fools.

" But Dr. Lee has his way of doing good. Being

fond of astronomy, he has bought an eight and a half feet equatorial telescope, and with a wisdom which one could scarcely expect, he employed Admiral Smyth to construct an observatory. He has also a fine transit instrument, and the admiral, being his near neighbor, has the privilege of using the observatory as his own In the absence of the Lees he has a private key, with which he admits himself and Mrs. Smyth. They make the observations (Mrs. Smyth is a very clever astronomer), sleep in a room called 'The Admiral's Room,' find breakfast prepared for them in the morning, and return to their own house when they choose.

"I saw in the observatory a timepiece with a double second-hand; one of these could be stopped by a touch, and would, in that way, show an observer the instant when he thought a phenomenon, as an occultation for instance, had occurred, and yet permit him to go on with his count of the seconds, and, if necessary, correct his first impression.

"Admiral Smyth is a hard worker, but I suspect that many of the amateur astronomers of England are Dr. Lees — rich men who, as a hobby, ride astronomy and employ a good astronomer. Dr. Lee gives the use of a good instrument to the curate; another to Mr. Payson, of Cambridge, who has lately found a little planet.

"I saw at Admiral Smyth's some excellent photographs of the moon, but in England they have not yet photographed the stars."

CHAPTER VI

1857

FIRST EUROPEAN TOUR CONTINUED   CAMBRIDGE UNIVERSITY —
AMBLESIDE — MISS SOUTHEY — THE HERSCHELS — A LONDON
ROUT — EDINBORO' AND GLASGOW OBSERVATORIES   " REFLEC-
TIONS AND MUTTERINGS "

" IF any one wishes to know the customs of centuries
ago in England, let him go to Cambridge.

" Sitting at the window of the hotel, he will see the
scholars, the fellows, the masters of arts, and the
masters of colleges passing along the streets in their
different gowns. Very unbecoming gowns they are, in
all cases; and much as the wearers must be accustomed
to them, they seem to step awkwardly, and to have an
ungraceful feminine touch in their motions.

" Everything that you see speaks of the olden time.
Even the images above the arched entrance to the courts
around which the buildings stand are crumbling slowly,
and the faces have an unearthly expression.

" If the visitor is fortunate enough to have an introduction to one of the college professors, he will be taken
around the buildings, to the libraries, the 'Combination' room to which the fellows retire to chat over their
wine, and perhaps even to the kitchen.

" Our first knowledge of Cambridge was the entrance
to Trinity College and the Master's Lodge.

"We arrived in Cambridge just about at lunch time — one o'clock.

"Mrs. Airy said to me, 'Although we are invited to be guests of Dr. Whewell, he is quite too mighty a man to come to meet us.' Her sons, however, met us, and we walked with them to Dr. Whewell's.

"The Master's Lodge, where Dr. Whewell lives, is one of the buildings composing the great pile of Trinity College. One of the rooms in the lodge still remains nearly as in the time of Henry VIII. It is immense in size, and has two oriel windows hung with red velvet. In this room the queen holds her court when she is in Cambridge; for the lodge then becomes a palace, and the 'master' retires to some other apartments, and comes to dinner only when asked.

"It is said that the present master does not much like to submit to this position.

"In this great room hang full-length portraits of Henry and Elizabeth. On another wall is a portrait of Newton, and on a third the sweet face of a young girl, Dr. Whewell's niece, of whom I heard him speak as 'Kate.'

"Dr. Whewell received us in this room, standing on a rug before an open fireplace; a wood fire was burning cheerily. Mrs. Airy's daughter, a young girl, was with us.

"Dr. Whewell shook hands with us, and we stood. I was very tired, but we continued to stand. In an American gentleman's house I should have asked if I might sit, and should have dropped upon a chair; here, of course, I continued to stand. After, perhaps,

fifteen minutes, Dr. Whewell said, ' Will you sit? ' and
the four of us dropped upon chairs as if shot!

" The master is a man to be noted, even physically.
He is much above ordinary size, and, though now gray-
haired, would be extraordinarily handsome if it were
not for an expression of ill-temper about the mouth.

" An Englishmen is proud ; a Cambridge man is the
proudest of Englishmen ; and Dr. Whewell, the proudest of Cambridge men.

" In the opinion of a Cambridge man, to be master
of Trinity is to be master of the world!

" At lunch, to which we stayed, Dr. Whewell talked
about American writers, and was very severe upon
them ; some of them were friends of mine, and it was
not pleasant. But I was especially hurt by a remark
which he made afterwards. Americans are noted in
England for their use of slang. The English suppose
that the language of Sam Slick or of Nasby is the
language used in cultivated society. They do not seem
to understand it, and I have no doubt to-day that
Lowell's comic poems are taken seriously. So at this
table, Dr. Whewell, wishing to say that we would do
something in the way of sight-seeing very thoroughly,
turning to me, said, ' We'll go the whole hog, Miss
Mitchell, as you say in America.'

" I turned to the young American girl who sat next
to me, and said, ' Miss S., did you ever hear that expression except on the street? ' ' Never,' she replied.

" Afterwards he said to me, ' You in America think
you know something about the English language,
and you get out your Webster's dictionary, and your

Worcester's dictionary, but we here in Cambridge think we know rather more about English than you do.'

" After lunch we went to the observatory. The Cambridge Observatory has the usual number of meridian instruments, but it has besides a good equatorial telescope of twenty feet in length, mounted in the English style; for Mr. Airy was in Cambridge at the time of its establishment. In this pretty observatory, overlooking the peaceful plains, with some small hills in the distance, Mr. and Mrs. Airy passed the first year of their married life.

" Professor Challis, the director, is exceedingly short, thick-headed (in appearance), and, like many of the English, thick-tongued. While I was looking at the instruments, Mrs. Airy came into the equatorial house, bringing Mr. Adams, the rival of Leverrier,[1] — another short man, but bright-looking, with dark hair and eyes, and again the thick voice, this time with a nasal twang. He is a fellow of Pembroke College, and master of arts. If Mr. Adams had become a fellow of his own college, St. John, he must have gone into holy orders, as it is called; this he was not willing to do; he accepted a fellowship from Pembroke.

" Mr. Adams is a merry little man, loves games with children, and is a favorite with young ladies.

" At 6.30 we went again to the lodge to dine. We were a little late, and the servant was in a great hurry to announce us; but I made him wait until my gloves were on, though not buttoned. He announced us with a loud voice, and Dr. Whewell came forward to receive

---

[1] See Chapter VII.

us. Being announced in this way, the other guests do
not wait for an introduction. There was a group of
guests in the drawing-room, and those nearest me spoke
to me at once.

" Dinner was announced immediately, and Dr. Whewell escorted me downstairs, across an immense hall,
to the dining-room, outside of which stood the waiters,
six in number, arranged in a straight line, in livery, of
course. One of them had a scarlet vest, short clothes,
and drab coat.

" As I sat next to the master, I had a good deal of talk
with him. He was very severe upon Americans; he said
that Emerson did not write good English, and copied
Carlyle! I thought his severity reached really to
discourtesy, and I think he perceived it when he asked
me if I knew Emerson personally, and I replied that
I did, and that I valued my acquaintance with him
highly.

" I got a little chance to retort, by telling him that we
had outgrown Mrs. Hemans in America, and that we
now read Mrs. Browning more. He laughed at it, and
said that Mrs. Browning's poetry was so coarse that he
could not tolerate it, and he was amused to hear that
any people had got above Mrs. Hemans; and he asked
me if we had outgrown Homer! To which I replied
that they were not similar cases.

" Altogether, there was a tone of satire in Dr. Whewell's remarks which I did not think amiable.

" There were, as there are very commonly in English
society, some dresses too low for my taste; and the wine-
drinking was universal, so that I had to make a special

point of getting a glass of water, and was afraid I might drink all there was on the table !

" Before the dessert came on, saucers were placed before each guest, and a little rose-water dipped into them from a silver basin ; then each guest washed his face thoroughly, dipping his napkin into the saucer. Professor Willis, who sat next to me, told me that this was a custom peculiar to Cambridge, and dating from its earliest times.

" The nnger bowls came on afterwards, as usual.

" It is customary for the lady of the house or the ' first lady ' to turn to her nearest neighbor at the close of dinner and say, ' Shall we retire to the drawing-room ? ' Now, there was no lady of the house, and I was in the position of first lady. They might have sat there for a thousand years before I should have thought of it. I drew on my gloves when the other ladies drew on theirs, and then we waited. Mrs. Airy saw the dilemma, made the little speech, and the gentlemen escorted us to the door, and then returned to their wine.

" We went back to the drawing-room and had coffee ; after coffee new guests began to come, and we went into the magnificent room with the oriel windows.

" Professor Sedgwick came early — an old man of seventy-four, already a little shattered and subject to giddiness. He is said to be very fond of young ladies even now, and when younger made some heartaches ; for he could not give up his fellowship and leave Cambridge for a wife ; which, to me, is very unmanly. He is considered the greatest geologist in England, and of course they would say 'in the world,' and is much loved by all who know him. He came to Cambridge a young man, and the elms which he saw planted are now sturdy trees. It is pleasant to hear him talk of Cambridge and its growth; he points to the stately trees and says, 'Those trees don't look as old as I, and they are not.'

"I did not see Professor Adams at that time, but I spent the whole of Monday morning walking about the college with him. I asked him to show me the place where he made his computations for Neptune, and he was evidently well pleased to do so.

"We laughed over a roll, which we saw in the College library, containing a list of the ancestors of Henry VIII.; among them was Jupiter.

"Professor Adams tells me that in Wales genealogical charts go so far back that about half-way between the beginning and the present day you find this record: 'About this time the world was created'!

"November 2. At lunch to-day Dr. Whewell was more interesting than I had seen him before. He asked me about Laura Bridgman, and said that he knew a similar case. He contended, in opposition to Mrs. Airy and myself, that loss of vision was preferable to loss of hearing, because it shut one out less from human companionship.

"Dr. Whewell's self-respect and immense self-esteem led him to imperiousness of manner which touches the border of discourtesy. He loves a good joke, but his jests are serious. He writes verses that are touchingly beautiful, but it is difficult to believe, in his presence, that he writes them. Mrs. Airy said that Dr. Whewell and I *riled* each other!

"I was at an evening party, and the Airy boys, young men of eighteen and twenty, were present. They stood the whole time, occasionally leaning against a table or the piano, in their blue silk gowns. I urged them to sit. 'Of course not,' they said; 'no undergraduate sits in the master's presence!'

"I went to three services on 'Scarlet Sunday,' for the sake of seeing all the sights.

"The costumes of Cambridge and Oxford are very amusing, and show, more than anything I have seen, the old-fogyism of English ways. Dr. Whewell wore, on this occasion, a long gown reaching nearly to his feet, of rich scarlet, and adorned with flowing ribands. The ribands did not match the robe, but were more of a crimson.

"I wondered that a strong-minded man like Dr. Whewell could tolerate such trappings for a moment; but it is said that he is rather proud of them, and loves all the etiquette of the olden time, as also, it is said, does the queen.

"In these robes Dr. Whewell escorted me to church — and of course we were a great sight!

"Before dinner, on this Scarlet Sunday, there was an interval when the master was evidently tried to know what to do with me. At length he hit upon an expedient. 'Boys,' he said to the young Airys, 'take Miss Mitchell on a walk!'

"I was a little surprised to find myself on a walk, 'nolens volens;' so as soon as we were out of sight of the master of Trinity, I said, ' Now, young gentlemen, as I do not want to go to walk, we won't go ! '

" It was hard for me to become accustomed to English ideas of caste.   I heard Professor Sedgwick say that Miss Herschel, the daughter of Sir John and niece to Caroline, married a Gordon.   ' Such a great match for her ! ' he added ; and when I asked what match could be great for a daughter of the Herschels, I was told that she had married one of the queen's household, and was asked to *sit* in the presence of the queen !

" When I hear a missionary tell that the pariah caste sit on the ground, the peasant caste lift themselves by the thickness of a leaf, and the next rank by the thickness of a stalk, it seems to me that the heathen has reached a high state of civilization — precisely that which Victoria has reached when she permits a Her-schel to sit in her presence !

" The University of Cambridge consists of sixteen colleges.   I was told that, of these, Trinity leads and St. John comes next.

" Trinity has always led in mathematics ; it boasts of Newton and Byron among its graduates.   Milton belonged to Christ Church College ; the mulberry tree which he planted still flourishes.

" Even to-day, a young scholar of Trinity expressed his regret to me that Milton did not belong to the college in which he himself studied.   He pointed out the rooms occupied by Newton, and showed us ' Newton's Bridge,' ' which will surely fall when a greater man than he walks over it ' !

" Milton first planned the great poem, ' Paradise Lost,'

as a drama, and this manuscript, kept within a glass case, is opened to the page on which the *dramatis personæ* are planned and replanned. On the opposite page is a part of ' Lycidas,' neatly written and with few corrections.

" The most beautiful of the college buildings is King's Chapel. A Cambridge man is sure to take you to one of the bridges spanning the wretched little stream called the ' Silver Cam,' that you may see the architectural beauties of this building.

" It is well to attend service in one or the other of the chapels, to see assembled the young men, who are almost all the sons of the nobility or gentry. The propriety of their conduct struck me. •

" The fellows of the colleges are chosen from the ' scholars ' who are most distinguished, as the ' scholars ' are chosen from the undergraduates. They receive an income so long as they remain connected with the college and unmarried.

" They have also the use of rooms in the college ; they dine in the same hall with the undergraduates, but their tables are placed upon a raised dais ; they have also little garden-places given them.

" ' What are their duties ? ' I asked Mr. Airy. ' None at all ; *they* are the college. It would not be a seat of learning without them.'

" They say in Cambridge that Dr. Whewell's book, ' Plurality of Worlds,' reasons to this end : The planets were created for this world ; this world for man ; man for England ; England for Cambridge ; and Cambridge for Dr. Whewell !

"Ambleside, September 13. We have spent the Sunday in ascending a mountain. I have a minute route marked out for me by Professor Airy, who has rambled among the lakes and mountains of Cumberland and Westmoreland for months, and says that no man lives who knows them better than he.

"In accordance with these directions, I took a one-horse carriage this morning for Coniston Waters, in order to ascend the 'Old Man.' The waiter at the 'Salutation' at Ambleside, which we made head-quarters, told me that I could not make the ascent, as the day would not be fine; but I have not travelled six months for nothing, and I knew he was saying, 'You are fine American geese; you are not to leave my house until you have been well plucked!'—which threat he will of course keep, but I shall see all the 'Old Men' that I choose. So I borrowed the waiter's umbrella, when he said it would rain, and off we went in an open carriage, a drive of seven miles, up hill and down dale, among mountains and around ponds (lakes *they* called them), in the midst of rich lands and pretty mansions, with occasionally a castle, and once a ruin, to diversify the scenery.

"Arrived at Coniston Hotel, the waiter said the same thing: 'It's too cloudy to ascend the "Old Man;"' but as soon as it was found that if it was too cloudy we did not intend to stay, it cleared off amazingly fast, and the ponies were ordered. I thought at first of walking up, but, having a value for my feet and not liking to misuse them, I mounted a pony and walked him.

"He was beautifully stupid, but I could not help

thinking of Henry Colman, the agriculturist, who, when in England, went on a fox-hunt. He said, ' Think of my poor wife's old husband leaping a fence ! '

"But I soon forgot any fear, for the pony needed nothing from me or the guide, but scrambled about any way he chose; and the scenery was charming, for although the mountains are not very high, they are thrown together very beautifully and remind me of those of the Hudson Highlands. Then the little lakes were lovely, and occasionally we came to a tarn or pond, and exceedingly small waterfalls were rushing about everywhere, without any apparent object in view, but evidently looking for something. And spite of the weatherwise head-waiter of the ' Salutation ' and of him of Coniston Inn, the day was beautiful. We had to give up the ponies when we were half a mile from the top, and clamber up ourselves. The guide was very intelligent, and pointed out the lakes, Windermere, Coniston; and the mountains, Helvellyn, Skiddaw, and Saddleback; but at one time he spoke a name that I couldn't understand, and forgetting that I was in England and not in America, I asked him to *spell* it. He replied, ' Theys call it so always.' He did not fail, however, to ask questions like a Yankee, if he couldn't spell like one. ' Which way be ye coming? ' — ' From America.' — ' Ye'll be going to Scotland like? ' — ' Yes.' — ' Ye'll be spending much money before ye are home again.'

"When we were quite on top of the mountain I asked what the white glimmering was in the distance, and he said it was, what I supposed, an arm of the sea.

" The shadows of the flying clouds were very pretty falling on the hills around us, and the villages in the valleys beneath looked like white dots on the green.

" Sunday, Sept. 20, 1857. We have been to see Miss Southey to-day. I sent the letter which Mrs. Airy gave me yesterday, and with it a note saying that I would call to-day if convenient.

" Miss Southey replied at once, saying that she should be happy to see me. She lives in a straggling, irregular cottage, like most of the cottages around Keswick, but beautifully situated, though far from the lake.

" Southey himself lived at Greta Hall, a much finer place, for many years, but he never owned it, and the gentleman who bought it will permit no one to see it.

" Miss Southey's house is overgrown with climbing plants, has windows opening to the ground, and is really a summer residence, not a good winter home.

" When Southey, in his decline, married a second wife, the family scattered, and this daughter, the only unmarried one, left him.

" We were shown into a pleasant parlor comfortably furnished, especially with books and engravings, portraits of Southey, Wordsworth, and others.   .

" Miss Southey soon came down ; she is really pretty, having the fresh English complexion and fair hair. She seems to be a very simple, pleasant person ; chatty, but not too much so. She is much engrossed by the care of three of her brother's children, an old aunt, and a servant, who, having been long in the family, has become a dependant. Miss Southey spoke at once of the Americans whom she had known, Ticknor being one.

The old aunt asked after a New York lady who had visited Southey at Greta Hall, but her niece reminded her that it must have been before I was born!

"Miss Southey said that her father felt that he knew as many Americans as Englishmen, and that she wanted very much to go to America. I told her that she would be in danger of being ' lionized; ' she said, ' Oh, I should like that, for of course it is gratifying to know how much my father was valued there.'

" I asked after the children, and Miss Southey said that the little boy had called out to her, ' Oh! Aunt Katy, the Ameriky ladies have come!

" The three children were called in; the boy, about six years old, of course wouldn't speak to me.

" The best portrait of Southey in his daughter's collection is a profile in wax — a style that I have seen several times in England, and which I think very pretty.

" We went down to Lodore, the scene of the poem, 'How does the Water come Down,' etc., and found it about as large as the other waterfalls around here — a little dripping of water among the stones.

COLLINGWOOD, Nov. 14, 1857.

MY DEAR FATHER: This is Sir John Herschel's place. I came last night just at dusk.

According to English ways, I ought to have written a note, naming the hour at which I should reach Etchingham, which is four miles from Collingwood; but when I left Liverpool I went directly on, and a letter would have arrived at the same time that I did. I stopped in London one night only, changed my lodging-house, that I might pay a pound a week only for letting my trunk live in a room, instead of two pounds, and started off again.

I reached Etchingham at ten minutes past four, took a cab, and set off for Sir John's. It is a large brick house, no way handsome, but surrounded by fine grounds, with beautiful trees and a very large pond.

The family were at dinner, and I was shown into the drawing-room.

There was just the light of a coal fire, and as I stood before it Sir John bustled in, an old man, much bent, with perfectly white hair standing out every way. He reached both hands to me, and said, " We had no letter and so did not expect you, but you are always welcome in this house." Lady Herschel followed — very noble looking ; she does not look as old as I, but of course must be ; but English women, especially of her station, do not wear out as we do, who are " Jacks at all trades."

I found a fire in my room, and a cup of tea and crackers were immediately sent up.

The Herschels have several children ; I have not seen Caroline, Louise, William, and Alexander, but Belle, and Amelie, and Marie, and Julie, and Rosa, and Francesca, and Constance, and John are at home !

The children are not handsome, but are good-looking, and well brought up of course, and highly educated. The children all come to table, which is not common in England. Think what a table they must set when the whole twelve are at home !

The first object that struck me in the house was Borden's map of Massachusetts, hanging in the hall opposite the entrance. Over the mantelpiece in the dining-room is a portrait of Sir William Herschel. In the parlor is a portrait of Caroline Herschel, and busts of Sir William, Sir John, and the eldest daughter.

I spent the evening in looking at engravings, sipping tea, and talking. Sir John is like the elder Mr. Bond, except that he talks more readily ; but he is womanly in his nature, not a tyrant like Whewell. Sir John is a better listener than any man I have met in England. He joins in all the chit-chat, is one of the domestic circle, and tells funny little anecdotes. (So do Whewell and Airy.)

The Herschels know Abbot Lawrence and Edward Everett —

and everywhere these two have left a good impression. But I am certainly mortified by anecdotes that I hear of " pushing " Americans. Mrs. —— sought an introduction to Sir John Herschel to tell him about an abridgment of his Astronomy which she had made, and she intimated to him that in consequence of her abridgment his work was, or would be, much more widely known in America. Lady Herschel told me of it, and she remarked, " I believe Sir John was not much pleased, for he does not like abridgments." I told her that I had never heard of the abridgment.

There are other guests in the house : a lady whose sister was among those killed in India ; and her husband, who is an officer in the army. We have all been playing at " Spelling " this evening, with the letters, as we did at home last winter.

Sunday, 15th. I thought of going to London to-day, but was easily persuaded to stay and go with Lady Herschel to-morrow. All this afternoon I have spent listening to Sir John, who has shown me his father's manuscript, his aunt's, beautifully neat, and he told me about his Cape observations.

The telescope used at the Cape of Good Hope lies in the barn (the glass, of course, taken care of) unused ; and Sir John now occupies himself with writing only. He made many drawings at the Cape, which he showed me, and very good ones they are. Lady Herschel offers me a letter to Mrs. Somerville, who is god-mother to one of her children. I am afraid I shall have no letter to Leverrier, for every one seems to dislike him. Lady Herschel says he is one of the few persons whom she ever asked for an autograph ; he was her guest, and he refused !

Just as I was coming away, Sir John bustled up to me with a sheet of paper, saying that he thought I would like some of his aunt's handwriting and he would give it to me. He had before given me one of his own calculations ; he says if there were no " war, pestilence, or famine," and one pair of human beings had been put upon the globe at the time of Cheops, they would not only now fill the earth, but if they stood upon each other's heads, they would reach a hundred times the distance to Neptune !

I turned over their scrap-books, and Sir John's poetry is much better than many of the specimens they had carefully kept, by Sir William Hamilton. Sir William Hamilton's sister had some specimens in the book, and also Lady Herschel and her brother.

Lady Herschel is the head of the house — so is Mrs. Airy — so, I suspect, is the wife in all well-ordered households! I perceived that Sir John did not take a cup of tea until his wife said, "You can have some, my dear."

Mr. Airy waits and waits, and then says, "My dear, I shall lose all my flesh if I don't have something to eat and drink."

I am hoping to get to Paris next week, about the 23d. I have had just what I wanted in England, as to society.

"November 26. A few days ago I received a card, 'Mrs. Baden Powell, at home November 25.' Of course I did not know if it was a tea party or a wedding reception. So I appealed to Mrs. Airy. She said, 'It is a London rout. I never went to one, but you'll find a crowd and a good many interesting people.'

"I took a cab, and went at nine o'clock. The servant who opened the door passed me to another who showed me the cloak-room. The girl who took my shawl numbered it and gave me a ticket, as they would at a public exhibition. Then she pointed to the other end of the room, and there I saw a table with tea and coffee. I took a cup of coffee, and then the servant asked my name, *yelled* it up the stairs to another, and he announced it at the drawing-room door just as I entered.

"Mrs. Powell and the professor were of course standing near, and Mrs. Admiral Smyth just behind. To my delight, I met four English persons whom I knew, and also Prof. Henry B. Rogers, who is a great society man.

"People kept coming until the room was quite full. I was very glad to be introduced to Professor Stokes, who is called the best mathematician in England, and is a friend of Adams. He is very handsome — almost all Englishmen are handsome, because they look healthy; but Professor Stokes has fine black eyes and dark hair and good features. He looks very young and innocent. Stokes is connected with Cambridge, but lives in London, just as Professor Powell is connected with Oxford, but also lives in London. Several gentlemen spoke to me without a special introduction — one told me his name was Dr. Townby [Qy., Toynbie], and he was a great admirer of Emerson — the first case of the sort I have met.

"Dr. Townby is a young man not over thirty, full of enthusiasm and progress, like an American. He really seemed to me all alive, and is either a genius or crazy — the shade between is so delicate that I can't always tell to which a person belongs! I asked him if Babbage was in the room, and he said, 'Not yet,' so I hoped he would come.

"He told me that a fine-looking, white-headed, good-featured old man was Roget, of the 'Thesaurus;' and another old man in the corner was Dr. Arnott, of the 'Elements of Physics.' I had supposed he was dead long ago. Afterwards I was introduced to him. He is an old man, but not much over sixty; his hair is white, but he is full of vigor, short and stout, like almost all Englishmen and Englishwomen. I have met only two women taller than myself, and most of them are very much shorter. Dr. Arnott told me he was

only now finishing the 'Elements,' which he first published in 1827. He intends now to publish the more
mathematical portions with the other volumes. He was
very sociable, and I told him he had twenty years ago a
great many readers in America. He said he supposed
he had more there than in England, and that he believed
he had made young men study science in many instances.

"I asked him if Babbage was in the room, and he too
said, 'Not yet.' Dr. Arnott asked me if I wore as many
stockings when I was observing as the Herschels — he
said Sir William put on twelve pairs and Caroline fourteen!

"I stayed until eleven o'clock, then I said 'Good-
by,' and just as I stepped upon the threshold of the
drawing-room to go out, a broad old man stepped
upon it, and the servant announced 'Mr. Babbage,' and
of course that glimpse was all I shall ever have!

"Edinboro', September 30. The people of Edinboro',
having a passion for Grecian architecture, and being
very proud of the Athenian character of their city,
seek to increase the resemblance by imitations of
ancient buildings.

"Grecian pillars are seen on Calton Hill in great
numbers, and the observatory would delight an old
Greek; its four fronts are adorned by Grecian pillars,
and it is indeed beautiful as a structure; but the Greeks
did not build their temples for astronomical observations; they probably adapted their architecture to their
needs.

"This beautiful building was erected by an association of gentlemen, who raised a good deal of money,

but, of course, not enough. They built the Grecian temple, but they could not supply it with priests.

"About a hundred years ago Colin Maclaurin had laid the foundation of an observatory, and the curious Gothic building, which still stands, is the first germ. We laugh now at the narrow ideas of those days, which seemed to consider an observatory a lookout only ; but the first step in a work is a great step — the others are easily taken. There was added to the building of Maclaurin a very small transit room, and then the present edifice followed.

"When the builders of the observatory found that they could not support it, they presented it to the British government ; so that it is now a government child, but it is not petted, like the first-born of Greenwich.

"There are three instruments ; an excellent transit instrument of six and a half inches' aperture, resting on its y's of solid granite. The corrections of the errors of the instrument by means of little screws are given up, and the errors which are known to exist are corrected in the computations.

"Professor Smyth finds that although the two pillars upon which the instrument rests were cut from the same quarry, they are unequally affected by changes of temperature ; so that the variation of the azimuth error, though slight, is irregular.

"The collimation plate they correct with the micrometer, so that they consider some position-reading of the micrometer-head the zero point, and correct that for the error, which they determine by reflection in a trough of mercury. With this instrument they observe

on certain stars of the British Catalogue, whose places
are not very well determined, and with a mural circle of
smaller power they determine declinations.

"The observatory possesses an equatorial telescope,
but it is of mixed composition. The object glass was
given by Dr. Lee, the eye-pieces by some one else,
and the two are put together in a case, and used by
Professor Smyth for looking at the craters in the moon;
of these he has made fine drawings, and has published
them in color prints.

"The whole staff of the observatory consists of Professor Smyth, Mr. Wallace, an old man, and Mr. Will-
iamson, a young man.

"The city of Edinboro' has no amateur astronomers, and there are two only, of note, in Scotland: Sir
William Bisbane and Sir William Keith Murray.

"From the observatory, the view of Edinboro' is
lovely. 'Auld Reekie,' as the Scotch call it, always
looks her best through a mist, and a Scotch mist is not
a rare event — so we saw the city under its most becoming veil.

"October, 1857. I stopped in Glasgow a few hours,
and went to the observatory, which is also the private
residence of Professor Nichol. Miss Nichol received
me, and was a very pleasant, blue-eyed young lady.

"I found that the observatory boasts of two good instruments: a meridian circle, which must be good, from
its appearance, and a Newtonian telescope, differently
mounted from any I had seen; cased in a composition
tube which is painted bright blue — rather a striking
object. The iron mounting seemed to me good. It

was of the German kind, but modified. It seemed to me that it could be used for observations far from the meridian. The iron part was hollow, so that the clock was inside, as was the azimuth circle, and thus space was saved.

" They have a wind and rain self-register, and a self-registering barometer, marking on a cylinder turned by a clock, the paper revolving once an hour.

" When I was at Dungeon Ghyll, a little ravine among the English lakes, down which trickles an exceedingly small stream of water, but which is, nevertheless, very picturesque, — as I followed the old man who shows it for a sixpence, he asked if we had come a long way. 'From America,' I replied. 'We have many Americans here,' said he; 'it is much easier to understand their language than that of other foreigners; they speak very good English, better than the French or Germans.'

" I felt myself a little annoyed and a good deal amused. I supposed that I spoke the language that Addison wrote, and here was a Westmoreland guide, speaking a dialect which I translated into English before I could understand it, complimenting me upon my ability to speak my own tongue.

" I learned afterwards, as I journeyed on, to expect no appreciation of my country or its people. The English are strangely deficient in curiosity. I can scarcely imagine an Englishwoman a gossip.

" I found among all classes a knowledge of the extent of America; by the better classes its geography was understood, and its physical peculiarities. One astronomer had bound the scientific papers from America in green morocco, as typical of a country covered by forests. Among the most intelligent men whom I met I found an appreciation of the different characters of the States. Everywhere Massachusetts was honored; everywhere I met the horror of the honest Englishman at the slave system; but anything like a discriminating knowledge of our public men I could not meet. Webster had been heard of everywhere. They assured me that our *really great* men were known, our really great deeds appreciated; but this is not true. They make mistakes in their measure of our men; second-rate men who have travelled are of course known to the men whom they have met; these travellers have not perhaps thought it necessary to mention that they represent a secondary class of people, and they are considered our 'first men.' The English forget that all Americans travel.

" I was vexed when I saw some of our most miserable novels, bound in showy yellow and red, exposed for sale. A friend told me that they had copied from the cheap publications of America. It may be so, but they have outdone us in the cheapness of the material and the showy covers. I never saw yellow and red together on any American book.

"The English are far beyond us in their highest scholarship, but why should they be ignorant of our scholars? The Englishman is proud, and not without reason; but he may well be proud of the American offshoot. It is not strange that England produces fine scholars, when we consider that her colleges confer fellowships on the best undergraduates.

" England differs from America in the fact that it has a past. Well may the great men of the present be proud of those who have gone before them; it is scarcely to be hoped that the like can come after them; and yet I suppose we must admit that even now the strong minds are born across the water.

" At the same time England has a class to which we have happily no parallel in our country — a class to which even English gentlemen liken the Sepoys, and who would, they admit, under like circumstances be guilty of like enormities. But the true Englishman shuts his eyes for a great part of the time to the steps in the social scale down which his race descends, and looks only at the upper walks. He has therefore a glance of patronizing kindness for the people of the United States, and regards us of New England as we regard our rich brethren of the West.

" I wondered what was to become of the English people! Their island is already crowded with people, the large towns are numerous and are very large. Suppose for an instant that her commerce is cut off, will they starve? It is an illustration of moral power that, little island as that of Great Britain is, its power is the great power of the world.

" Crowded as the people are, they are healthy. I never saw, I thought, so. many ruddy faces as met me at once in Liverpool. Dirty children in the street have red cheeks and good teeth. Nowhere did I see little children whose minds had outgrown their bodies. They do not live in the school-room, but in the streets. One continually meets little children carrying smaller

ones in their arms; little girls hand in hand walk the
streets of London all day. There are no free schools,
and they have nothing to do. Beggars are everywhere,
and as importunate as in Italy. For a well-behaved
common people I should go to Paris; for clean work-
ing-women I should look in Paris.

"I saw a little boy in England tormenting a smaller
one. He spat upon his cap, and then declared that
the little one did it. The little one sobbed and said he
didn't. I gave the little one a penny; he evidently did
not know the value of the coin, and appealed to the
bigger boy. 'Is it a penny?' he asked, with a look of
amazement. 'Yes,' said the bigger. Off ran the
smaller one triumphant, and the bigger began to cry,
which I permitted him to do."

CHAPTER VII

1857-1858

FIRST EUROPEAN TOUR CONTINUED — LEVERRIER AND THE PARIS OBSERVATORY — ROME — HARRIET HOSMER — OBSERVATORY OF THE COLLEGIO ROMANO — SECCHI

AT this time, the feeling between astronomers of Great Britain and those of the United States was not very cordial. It was the time when Adams and Leverrier were contending to which of them belonged the honor of the discovery of the planet Neptune, and each side had its strong partisans.

Among Miss Mitchell's papers we find the following with reference to this subject:

". . . Adams, a graduate of Cambridge, made the calculations which showed how an unseen body must exist whose influences were felt by Uranus. It was a problem of great difficulty, for he had some half-dozen quantities touching Uranus which were not accurately known, and as many wholly unknown concerning the unseen planet. We think it a difficult question which involves three or four unknown quantities with too few circumstances, but this problem involved twelve or thirteen, so that x, y, z reached pretty high up into the alphabet. But Adams, having worked the problem, carried his work to Airy, the Astronomer Royal of England, and awaited his comments. A little later

Leverrier, the French astronomer, completed the same problem, and waiting for no authority beyond his own, flung his discovery out to the world with the self-confidence of a Frenchman. . . .

" . . . When the news of the discovery of Neptune reached this country, I happened to be visiting at the observatory in Cambridge, Mass. Professor Bond (the elder) had looked for the planet the night before I arrived at his house, and he looked again the evening that I came.

" His observatory was then a small, round building, and in it was a small telescope; he had drawn a map of a group of stars, one of which he supposed was not a star, but the planet. He set the telescope to this group, and asking his son to count the seconds, he allowed the stars to pass by the motion of the earth across the field. If they kept the relative distance of the night before, they were all stars; if any one had approached or receded from the others, it was a planet; and when the father looked at his son's record he said, ' One of those has moved, and it is the one which I thought last night was the planet.' He looked again at the group, and the son said, ' Father, do give me a look at the new planet — you are the only man in America that can do it ! ' And then we both looked; it looked precisely like a small star, and George and I both asked, ' What made you think last night that it was the new planet ? ' Mr. Bond could only say, ' I don't know, it looked different from the others.'

" It is always so — you cannot get a man of genius to explain steps, he leaps.

" After the discovery of this planet, Professor Peirce, in our own country, declared that it was not the planet of the theory, and therefore its discovery was a happy accident. But it seemed to me that it was the planet of the theory, just as much if it varied a good deal from its prescribed place as if it varied a little. So you might have said that Uranus was not the Uranus of the theory.

" Sir John Herschel said, ' Its movements have been felt trembling along the far-reaching line of our analysis, with a certainty hardly inferior to ocular demonstration.' I consider it was superior to ocular demonstration, as the action of the mind is above that of the senses. Adams, in his study at Cambridge, England, and Leverrier in his closet at Paris, poring over their logarithms, knew better the locus of that outside planet than all the practical astronomers of the world put together. . . .

" Of course in Paris I went to the Imperial Observatory, to visit Leverrier. I carried letters from Professor Airy, who also sent a letter in advance by post. Leverrier called at my hotel, and left cards ; then came a note, and I went to tea.

" Leverrier had succeeded Arago. Arago had been a member of the Provisional Government, and had died. Leverrier took exactly opposite ground, politically, to that of Arago ; he stood high with the emperor.

"He took me all over the observatory. He had a large room for a ballroom, because in the ballroom science and politics were discussed ; for where a press is not free, salons must give the tone to public opinion.

" Both Leverrier and Madame Leverrier said hard

things about the English, and the English said hard
things about Leverrier.

"The Astronomical Observatory of Paris was founded
on the establishment of the Academy of Sciences, in
the reign of Louis XIV. The building was begun in
1667 and finished in 1672; like other observatories of
that time, it was quite unfit for use.

"John Dominie Cassini came to it before it was
finished, saw its defects, and made alterations; but the
whole building was afterwards abandoned. M. Leverrier showed me the transit instrument and the mural
circle. He has, like Mr. Airy, made the transit instrument incapable of mechanical change for its corrections
of error, so that it depends for accuracy upon its faults
being known and corrected in the computations.

"All the early observatories of Europe seem to have
been built as temples to Urania, and not as working-
chambers of science. The Royal Observatory at
Greenwich, the Imperial Observatory of Paris, and the
beautiful structure on Calton Hill, Edinboro', were at
first wholly useless as observatories. That of Greenwich had no steadiness, while every pillar in the astronomical temple of Edinboro', though it may tell of the
enlightenment of Greece, hides the light of the stars
from the Scottish observer. Well might Struve say that
' An observatory should be simply a box to hold instruments.'

"The Leverriers speak English about as well as I do
French, and we had a very awkward time of it. M. Leverrier talked with me a little, and then talked wholly to one
of the gentlemen present. Madame was very chatty.

" Leverrier is very fine-looking; he is fair-haired full-faced, altogether very healthy-looking. His wife is really handsome, the children beautiful. I was glad that I could understand when Leverrier said to the children, ' If you make any more noise you go to bed.'

"While I was there, a woman as old as I rushed in, in bonnet and shawl, and flew around the room, kissed madame, jumped the children about, and shook hands with monsieur; and there was a great amount of screaming and laughing, and all talked at once. As I could not understand a word, it seemed to me like a theatre.

" I asked monsieur when I could see the observatory, and he answered, ' Whenever it suits your convenience.'

" December 15. I went to Leverrier's again last evening by special invitation. Four gentlemen and three ladies received me, all standing and bowing without speaking. Monsieur was, however, more sociable than before, and shrieked out to me in French as though I were deaf.

" The ladies were in blue dresses; a good deal of crinoline, deep flounces, high necks, very short, flowing sleeves, and short undersleeves; the dresses were brocade and the flounces much trimmed, madame's with white plush.

" The room was cold, of course, having no carpet, and a wood fire in a very small fireplace.

" The gentlemen continued standing or promenading, and taking snuff.

" Except Leverrier, no one of them spoke to me. The

ladies all did, and all spoke French. The two children were present again — the little girl five years old played on the piano, and the boy of nine played and sang like a public performer. He promenaded about the room with his hands in his pockets, like a man. I think his manners were about equal to ——'s, as occasionally he yelled and was told to be quiet.

" About ten o'clock M. Leverrier asked me to go into the observatory, which connects with the dwelling. They are building immense additional rooms, and are having a great telescope, twenty-seven feet in focal length, constructed.

" With Leverrier's bad English and my bad French we talked but little, but he showed me the transit instrument, the mural circle, the computing-room, and the private office. He put on his cloak and cap, and said, ' Voila le directeur ! '

" One room, he told me, had been Arago's, and Arago had his bed on one side. M. Leverrier said, ' I do not wish to have it for my room.' He is said to be much opposed to Arago, and to be merciless towards his family.

" He showed me another room, intended for a reception-room, and explained to me that in France one had to make science come into social life, for the government must be reached in order to get money.

" There were huge globes in one room that belonged to Cassini. If what he showed me is not surpassed in the other rooms, I don't think much of their instruments.

" M. Leverrier said he had asked M. Chacornac to meet me, but he was not there. I felt that we got on a little better, but not much, and it was evident that he did not expect me to understand an observatory. We did not ascend to the domes.

"Leverrier has telegraphic communication with all Europe except Great Britain.

"It was quite singular that they made such different remarks to me. Leverrier said that they had to make science popular.

"Airy said, 'In England there is no astronomical public, and we do not need to make science popular.'

"Jan. 24, 1858. I am in Rome! I have been here four days, and already I feel that I would rather have that four days in Rome than all the other days of my travels! I have been uncomfortable, cold, tired, and subjected to all the evils of travelling; but for all that, I would not have missed the sort of realization that I have of the existence of the past of great glory, if I must have a thousand times the discomfort. I went alone yesterday to St. Peter's and the Vatican, and to-day, taking Murray, I went alone to the Roman Forum, and stood beside the ruined porticos and the broken columns of the Temple. Then I pushed on to the Coliseum, and walked around its whole circumference. I could scarcely believe that I really stood among the ruins, and was not dreaming! I really think I had more enjoyment for going alone and finding out for myself. Afterwards the Hawthornes called, and I took Mrs. H. to the same spot. . . .

"I really feel the impressiveness of Rome. All Europe has been serious to me; Rome is even sad in its seriousness. You cannot help feeling, in the

Coliseum, some little of the influence of the scenes that have been enacted there, even if you know little about them; you must remember that the vast numbers of people who have been within its walls for ages have not been common minds, whether they were Christian martyrs or travelling artists. . . .

"I think if I had never heard before of the reputation of the pictures and statues of the Vatican, I should have perceived their superiority. There is more idea of *action* conveyed by the statuary than I ever received before — they do not seem to be *dead*.

"January 25. I have finer rooms than I had in Paris, but the letting of apartments is better managed in Paris. There you always find a *concierge*, who tells you all you want to know, and who speaks several languages. In Rome you enter a narrow, dark passage, and look in vain for a door. Then you go up a flight of stairs, and see a door with a string; you pull the string, and a woman puts her mouth to a square hole, covered with tin punctured with holes, and asks what you want. You tell her, and she tells you to go up higher; you repeat the process, and at last reach the rooms. The higher up the better, because you get some sun, and one learns the value of sunlight. I saw no sun in Paris in my room, and here I have it half of the day, and it seems very pleasant.

"All the customs of the people differ from those of Paris. . . .

"A little of Italian art enters into the ornaments of rooms and furniture, but anything like mechanical skill seems to be unheard of; and I dare say the pretty stamp used on the butter I have, which represents some antique picture, was cut by some northern hand. I could make a better cart than those that I see on the streets, and I could *almost* make as good horses as those that draw them ! . . ..

"It is Holy Week. I have spent seven hours at a time at St. Peter's, in terrible crowds, for ten days, and now I go no more. The ladies are seated, but as the ceremonies are in different parts of the immense building, they rush wildly from one to the other; with their black veils they look like furies let loose! I stayed five hours to-day to see the Pope wash feet, which was very silly; for I saw mother wash them much more effectually twenty years ago!

" The crowd is better worth seeing than the ceremony, if one could only see it without being in it. I shall not try to hear the ' Miserere ' — I have given up the study of music! Since I failed to appreciate Mario, I sha'n't try any more!

"I go to the Storys' on Sunday evening to look at St. Peter's lighting up.

" March 21. I have been to vespers at St. Peter's. They begin an hour before sunset. When my work is done for the day, I walk to St. Peter's. This is Sunday, and the floor was full of kneeling worshippers, but that makes no difference. I walk about among them.

" I was there an hour to-day before I saw a person that I knew; then I met the Nicholses and went with them into a side chapel to hear vespers. Then I saw next the Waterstons, then Miss Lander; but I was unusually short of friends, I generally meet so many more.

"There were kneeling women to-day with babies in their arms. The babies of the lower classes have their legs so wrapped up that they cannot move them; they look like small pillows even when they are six months old. I think it must dwarf them. We Americans are a tall people. I am a very tall woman here. I think that P.'s height would cause a sensation in the streets. My servant admires my height very much.

"March 22. I called on Miss Bremer to-day, having heard that she desired to see me. She is a 'little woman in black,' but not so plain; her face is a little red, but her complexion is fair and the expression very pleasing. She chatted away a good deal; asked me about astronomy, and how I came to study it. I told her that my father put me to it, and she said she was just writing a story on the affection of father and daughter. She told me I had good eyes. It is a long time now since any one has told me that! . . .

"Miss Bremer and Mrs. W. met in my room and remained an hour. Miss Bremer is quiet and unpretending. Mrs. W. is flashy and brilliant, and, as I usually say when I don't understand a person, a little insane; she had the floor all the time after she came in. She gave a sketch of her life from her birth up, mentioning incidentally that she had been a belle, surrounded with beaux, the pride of her parents, with a reputation for intellect, etc.

"I had been urging Miss Bremer into an interesting talk before Mrs. W. appeared, and I felt what a pity it was that she hadn't the same propensity to talk that the latter had. She talked very pleasantly, however, and I thought what a pity it was that I shall not see her again; for I leave Rome in three days for Florence.

"I was in Rome for a winter, an idler by necessity for six weeks. It is the very place of all the world for an idler.

"On the pleasant days there are the ruins to visit, the Campagna to stroll over, the villas and their grounds to gather flowers in, the Forum to muse in, the Pincian Hill or the Capitoline for a gossiping walk with some friend.

"On rainy days it is all art. There are the cathedrals, the galleries, and the studios of the thousand artists; for every winter there are a thousand artists in Rome.

"A rainy day found me in the studio of Paul Akers. As I was looking at some of his models, the studio door opened and a pretty little girl, wearing a jaunty hat and a short jacket, into the pockets of which her hands were thrust, rushed into the room, seemingly unconscious of the presence of a stranger, began a rattling, all-alive talk with Mr. Akers, of which I caught enough to know that a ride over the Campagna was planned, as I heard Mr. Akers say, 'Oh, I won't ride with you — I'm afraid to!' after which he turned to me and introduced Harriet Hosmer.

"I was just from old conservative England, and I had been among its most conservative people. I had caught something of its old musty-parchment ideas, and the cricket-like manners of Harriet Hosmer rather troubled me. It took some weeks for me to get over the impression of her madcap ways; they seemed childish.

"I went to her studio and saw 'Puck,' a statue all fun and frolic, and I imagined all was fun to the core of her heart.

"As a general rule, people disappoint you as you know them.   To know them better and better is to know more and more weaknesses.   Harriet Hosmer parades her weaknesses with the conscious power of one who knows her strength, and who knows you will find her out if you are worthy of her acquaintance.   She makes poor jokes — she's a little rude — a good deal eccentric; but she is always *true*.   .

"In the town where she used to live in Massachusetts they will tell you a thousand anecdotes of her vagaries — but they are proud of her.

"She does not start on a false scent; she knows the royal character of the game before she hunts.

"A lady who is a great rider said to me a few days since: 'Of course I do not ride like Harriet Hosmer, but, if you will notice, there is method in Harriet Hosmer's madness.   She does not mount a horse until she has examined him carefully.'

"At the time when I saw her, she was thinking of her statue of Zenobia.   She was studying the history of Palmyra, reading up on the manners and customs of its people, and examining Eastern relics and costumes.

"If she heard that in the sacristy of a certain cathedral, hundreds of miles away, were lying robes of Eastern queens, she mounted her horse and rode to the spot, for the sake of learning the lesson they could teach.

"Day after day alone in her studio, she studied the

subject. Think what knowledge of the country, of the history of the people, must be gathered, must be moulded, to bring into the face and bearing of its queen the expression of the race! Think what familiar acquaintance with the human form, to represent a lifelike figure at all!

" For years after I came home I read the newspapers to see if I could find any notice of the statue of Zenobia; and I did at length see this announcement: ' The statue of Zenobia, by Miss Hosmer, is on exhibition at Childs & Jenks'.'

" It was after five years. All through those five years, Miss Hosmer had kept her projects steadily turned in this direction.

" Whatever may be the criticism of art upon her work, no one can deny that she is above the average artist.

" But she is herself, as a woman, very much above herself in art. If there came to any struggling artist in Rome the need of a friend, — and of the thousand artists in Rome very few are successful, — Harriet Hosmer was that friend.

" I knew her to stretch out a helping hand to an unfortunate artist, a poor, uneducated, unattractive American, against whom the other Americans in Rome shut their houses and their hearts. When the other Americans turned from the unsuccessful artist, Harriet Hosmer reached forth the helping hand.

" When Harriet Hosmer knew herself to be a sculptor, she knew also that in all America was no school for her. She must leave home, she must live where art could live. She might model her busts in

the clay of her own soil, but who should follow out in
marble the delicate thought which the clay expressed?
The workmen of Massachusetts tended the looms, built
the railroads, and read the newspapers. The hard-handed
men of Italy worked in marble from the designs put
before them; one copied the leaves which the sculptor
threw into the wreaths around the brows of his heroes;
another turned with his tool the folds of the drapery;
another wrought up the delicate tissues of the flesh;
none of them dreamed of ideas: they were copyists, —
the very hand-work that her head needed.

"And to Italy she went. For her school she sought
the studio of Gibson — the greatest sculptor of the time.

"She resolved 'To scorn delights and live laborious
days;' and there she has lived and worked for years.

"She fashions the clay to her ideal — every little
touch of her nngers in the clay is a thought; she thinks
in clay.

"The model finished and cast in the dull, hard, inex-
pressive plaster, she stands by the workmen while they
put it into the marble. She must watch them, for a
touch of the tool in the wrong place might alter the
whole expression of the face, as a wrong accent in
the reader will spoil a line of poetry.

"COLLEGIO ROMANO; SECCHI. There was another
observatory which had a reputation and was known
in America. It was the observatory of the Collegio
Romano, and was in the monastery behind the Church
of St. Ignasio. Its director was the Father Secchi who
had visited the United States, and was well known to
the scientists of this country.

"I said to myself, 'This is the land of Galileo, and this is the city in which he was tried. I knew of no sadder picture in the history of science than that of the old man, Galileo, worn by a long life of scientific research, weak and feeble, trembling before that tribunal whose frown was torture, and declaring that to be false which he knew to be true. And I know of no picture in the history of religion more weakly pitiable than that of the Holy Church trembling before Galileo, and denouncing him because he found in the Book of Nature truths not stated in their own Book of God — forgetting that the Book of Nature is also a Book of God.

"It seems to be difficult for any one to take in the idea that two truths cannot conflict.

"Galileo was the first to see the four moons of Jupiter; and when he announced the fact that four such moons existed, of course he was met by various objections from established authority. One writer declared that as astrologers had got along very well without these planets, there could be no reason for their starting into existence.

"But his greatest heresy was this: He was tried, condemned, and punished for declaring that the sun was the centre of the system, and that the earth moved around it; also, that the earth turned on its axis.

"For teaching this, Galileo was called before the assembled cardinals of Rome, and, clad in black cloth, was compelled to kneel, and to promise never again to teach that the earth moved. It is said that when he arose he whispered, 'It does move!'

"He was tried at the Hall of Sopre Minerva. In

fewer than two hundred years from that time the Church of St. Ignasio was built, and the monastery on whose walls the instruments of the modern observatory stand.

"It is a very singular fact, but one which seems to show that even in science 'the blood of the martyrs is the seed of the church,' that the spot where Galileo was tried is very near the site of the present observatory, to which the pope was very liberal.

"From the Hall of Sopre Minerva you make but two turns through short streets to the Fontenelle de Borghese, in the rear of which stands the present observatory.

"Indeed, if a cardinal should, at the Hall of Sopre Minerva, call out to Secchi, 'Watchman, what of the night?' Secchi could hear the question; and no bolder views emanate from any observatory than those which Secchi sends out.

"I sent a card to Secchi, and awaited a call, well satisfied to have a little more time for listless strolling among ruins and into the studios. And so we spent many an hour: picking up land shells from the top of the Coliseum, gathering violets in the upper chambers of the Palace of the Cæsars, — for the overgrown walls made climbing very easy, — or, resting upon some broken statue on the Forum, we admired the arches of the Temple of Peace, thrown upon the rich blue of the sunny skies.

"Returning one day from a drive, I met two priests descending one of the upper flights of stairs in the house where I lived. As my rooms had been blessed once.

and holy water sprinkled upon them, I thought perhaps
another process of that kind had just been gone through,
and was about to pass them, when one of them, accost-
ing me, asked if I were the Signorine Mitchell, — changing his Italian to good English as he saw that I was,
and introducing himself as Father Secchi. He told me
that the younger man was a young *religieux*, and the
two turned and went back with me.

"I recalled, as I saw Father Secchi, an anecdote I had
heard, no way to his credit, — except for ingenious
trickery. It was said that coming to America he
brought with him the object-glass of a telescope, at a
time when scientific apparatus paid a high duty. Being
asked by some official what the article was, he replied,
' My looking-glass,' and in that way passed it off as personal wardrobe, so escaped the duty. (It may have
been De Vico.)

" Father Secchi had brought with him, to show me,
negatives of the planet Saturn, — the rings showing
beautifully, although the image was not more than half
an inch in size.

" I was ignorant enough of the ways of papal institutions, and, indeed, of all Italy, to ask if I might visit the
Roman Observatory. I remembered that the days of
Galileo were days of two centuries since. I did not
know that my heretic feet must not enter the sanctuary,
— that my woman's robe must not brush the seats of
learning.

" The Father's refusal was seen in his face at once,
and I felt that I had done something highly improper.
The Father said that he would have been most happy to

have me visit him, but he had not the power — it was a religious institution — he had already applied to his superior, who was not willing to grant permission — the power lay with the Holy Father or one of his cardinals. I was told that Mrs. Somerville, the most learned woman in all Europe, had been denied admission; that the daughter of Sir John Herschel, in spite of English rank, and the higher stamp of Nature's nobility, was at that time in Rome, and could not enter an observatory which was at the same time a monastery.

"If I had before been mildly desirous of visiting the observatory, I was now intensely anxious to do so. Father Secchi suggested that I should see Cardinal Antonelli in person, with a written application in my hand. This was not to be thought of — to ask an interview with the wily cardinal!

FROM A LETTER TO HER FATHER.

. . . I am working to get admitted to see the observatory, but it cannot be done without special permission from the pope, and I don't like to be "presented." If I can get permission without the humbug of putting on a black veil and receiving a blessing from Pius, I shall; but I shrink from the formality of presentation. I know thou'd say "Be presented."

"Our minister at that time had the reputation of being very careless of the needs and wishes of his countrymen, and I was not surprised to find a long delay.

"In the course of my waiting, I had told my story to a young Italian gentleman, the nephew of a monseigneur; a monseigneur being next in rank to a cardinal. He assured me that permission would never be obtained by our minister.

"After a fortnight's waiting I received a permit, written on parchment, and signed by Cardinal Antonelli.

"When the young Italian next called, I held the parchment up in triumph, and boasted that Minister had at length moved in the matter. The young man coolly replied, 'Yes, I spoke to my uncle last evening, and asked him to urge the matter with Cardinal Antonelli; but for that it would never have come!' There had been 'red tape,' and I had not seen it.

"At the same time that the formal missive was sent to me, a similar one was sent to Father Secchi, authorizing him to receive me. The Father called at once to make the arrangements for my visit. I made the most natural mistake! I supposed that the doors which opened to one woman, opened to all, and I asked to take with me my Italian servant, a quick-witted and bright-eyed woman, who had escorted me to and from social parties in the evening, and who had learned in these walks the names of the stars, receiving them from me in English, and giving back to me the sweet Italian words; and who had come to think herself quite an astronomer. Father Secchi refused at once. He said I was to meet him at the Church of St. Ignasio at one and a half hours before Ave Marie, and he would conduct me through the church into the observatory. My servant might come into the church with me. The Ave Marie bell rings half an hour after sunset.

"At the appointed time, the next fine day, — and all days seem to be fine, — we set out on our mission.

"When we entered the church we saw, far in the distance, Father Secchi, standing just behind a pillar. He slipped out a little way, as much as to say, 'I await you,' but did not come forward to meet us; so the woman and I passed along through the rows of kneeling worshippers, by the strolling students, and past the lounging tourists — who, guide-book in hand, are seen in every foreign church — until we came to the standpoint from which the Father had been watching us.

"Then the Italian woman put up a petition, not one word of which I could understand, but the gestures and the pointing showed that she begged to go on and enter the monastery and see the observatory. Father Secchi said, 'No, the Holy Father gave permission to one only,' and alone I entered the monastery walls.

" Through long halls, up winding staircases, occasionally stopped by some priest who touched his broad hat and asked ' Parlate Italiano? ' occasionally passed by students, often stopped by pictures on the walls, — once to be introduced to a professor; then through the library of the monastery, full of manuscripts on which monks had worked away their lives; then through the astronomical library, where young astronomers were working away theirs, we reached at length the dome and the telescope.

" One observatory is so much like another that it does not seem worth while to describe Father Secchi's. This observatory has a telescope about the size of that at Washington (about twelve inches). Secchi had no staff, and no prescribed duties. The base of the observatory was the solid foundation of the old Roman building. The church was built in 1650, and the monastery in part at that time, certainly the dome of the room in which was the meridian instrument.

"The staircase is cut out of the old Roman walls, which no roll of carriage, except that of the earthquake chariot, can shake.

"Having no prescribed duties, Secchi could follow his fancies — he could pick up comets as he picked up bits of Mosaic upon the Roman forum. He learns what himself and his instruments can do, and he keeps to that narrow path.

"He was at that time much interested in celestial photography.

"Italy must be the very paradise of astronomers; certainly I never saw objects so well before; the purity of the air must be very superior to ours. We looked at Venus with a power of 150, but it was not good. Jupiter was beautiful, and in broad daylight the belts were plainly seen. With low powers the moon was charming, but the air would not bear high ones.

"Father Secchi said he had used a power of 2,000, but that 600 was more common. I have rarely used 400. Saturn was exquisite; the rings were separated all around; the dusky ring could be seen, and, of course, the shadow of the ball upon the ring.

"The spectroscopic method of observing starlight was used by Secchi as early as by any astronomer. By this method the starlight is analyzed, and the sunlight is analyzed, and the two compared. If it does not disclose absolutely what are the peculiarities of

starlight and sunlight, relatively, it traces the relation-
ship.

"In order to be successful in this kind of observation,
the telescope must keep very accurately the motion of
the earth in its axis; and so the papal government fur-
nishes nice machinery to keep up with this motion, —
the same motion for declaring whose existence Galileo
suffered! The two hundred years had done their
work.

"I should have been glad to stay until dark to look
at nebulæ, but the Father kindly informed me that
my permission did not extend beyond the daylight,
which was fast leaving us, and conducting me to the
door he informed me that I must make my way home
alone, adding, 'But we live in a civilized country.'

"I did not express to him the doubt that rose to my
thoughts! The Ave Marie bell rings half an hour
after sunset, and before that time I must be out of
the observatory and at my own house."

CHAPTER VIII

1858-1865

FIRST EUROPEAN TOUR CONCLUDED — MRS. SOMERVILLE — HUM-
BOLDT — MRS. MITCHELL'S DEATH — REMOVAL TO LYNN,
MASS. — PRESENT OF AN EQUATORIAL TELESCOPE — EXTRACTS
FROM LETTERS

" I HAD no hope, when I went to Europe, of knowing
Mrs. Somerville. American men of science did not
know her, and there had been unpleasant passages between the savants of Europe and those of the United
States which made my friends a little reluctant about
giving me letters.

" Professor Henry offered to send me letters, and
said that among them should be one to Mrs. Somerville; but when his package came, no such letter
appeared, and I did not like to press the matter, —
indeed, after I had been in England I was not surprised
at any amount of reluctance. They rarely asked to
know my friends, and yet, if they were made known
to them, they did their utmost.

" So I went to Europe with no letter to Mrs. Somerville, and no letter to the Herschels.

" I was very soon domesticated with the Airys, and
really felt my importance when I came to sleep in one
of the round rooms of the Royal Observatory. I dared
give no hint to the Airys that I wanted to know the

Herschels, although they were intimate friends. ' What
was I that I should love them, save for feeling of the
pain?' But one fine day a letter came to Mrs. Airy
from Lady Herschel, and she asked, ' Would not Miss
Mitchell like to visit us?' Of course Miss Mitchell
jumped at the chance! Mrs. Airy replied, and probably hinted that Miss Mitchell 'could be induced,'
etc.   .

" If the Airys were old friends of Mrs. Somerville, the
Herschels were older. The Airys were just and kind
to me; the Herschels were lavish, and they offered me
a letter to Mrs. Somerville.

" So, provided with this open sesame to Mrs. Somerville's heart, I called at her residence in Florence, in the
spring of 1858.

" I sent in the letter and a card, and waited in the
large Florentine parlor. In the open fireplace blazed
a wood fire very suggestive of American comfort —
very deceitful in the suggestion, for there is little of
home comfort in Italy.

" After some little delay I heard a footstep come
shuffling along the outer room, and an exceedingly tall
and very old man entered the room, in the singular
head-dress of a red bandanna turban, approached me,
and introduced himself as Dr. Somerville, the husband.

" He was very proud of his wife, and very desirous of
talking about her, a weakness quite pardonable in the
judgment of one who is desirous to know. He began
at once on the subject. Mrs. Somerville, he said, took
great interest in the Americans, for she claimed connection with the family of George Washington.

"Washington's half-brother, Lawrence, married Anne Fairfax, who was one of the Scotch family. When Lieutenant Fairfax was ordered to America, Washington wrote to him as a family relative, and asked him to make him a visit. Lieutenant Fairfax applied to his commanding officer for permission to accept, and it was refused. They never met, and much to the regret of the Fairfax family the letter of Washington was lost. The Fairfaxes of Virginia are of the same family, and occasionally some member of the American branch returns to see his Scotch cousins.

"While Dr. Somerville was eagerly talking of these things, Mrs. Somerville came tripping into the room, speaking at once with the vivacity of a young person. She was seventy-seven years old, but appeared twenty years younger. She was not handsome, but her face was pleasing; the forehead low and broad; the eyes blue; the features so regular, that in the marble bust by Chantrey, which I had seen, I had considered her handsome.

"Neither bust nor picture, however, gives a correct idea of her, except in the outline of the head and shoulders.

"She spoke with a strong Scotch accent, and was slightly affected with deafness, an infirmity so common in England and Scotland.

"While Mrs. Somerville talked, the old gentleman, seated by the fire, busied himself in toasting a slice of bread on a fork, which he kept at a slow-toasting distance from the coals. An English lady was present, learned in art, who, with a volubility worthy of an

American, rushed into every little opening of Mrs. Somerville's more measured sentences with her remarks upon recent discoveries in *her* specialty. Whenever this occurred, the old man grew fidgety, moved the slice of bread backwards and forwards as if the fire were at fault, and when, at length, the English lady had fairly conquered the ground, and was started on a long sentence, he could bear the eclipse of his idol no longer, but, coming to the sofa where we sat, he testily said, ' Mrs. Somerville would rather talk on science than on art.'

" Mrs. Somerville's conversation was marked by great simplicity; it was rather of the familiar and chatty order, with no tendency to the essay style. She touched upon the recent discoveries in chemistry or the discovery of gold in California, of the nebulæ, more and more of which she thought might be resolved, and yet that there might exist nebulous matters, such as compose the tails of comets, of the satellites, of the planets, the last of which she thought had other uses than as subordinates. She spoke with disapprobation of Dr. Whewell's attempt to prove that our planet was the only one inhabited by reasoning beings; she believed that a higher order of beings than ourselves might people them.

" On subsequent visits there were many questions from Mrs. Somerville in regard to the progress of science in America. She regretted, she said, that she knew so little of what was done in our country.

" From Lieutenant Maury, alone, she received scientific papers. She spoke of the late Dr. (Nathaniel)

Bowditch with great interest, and said she had corresponded with one of his sons. She asked after Professor Peirce, whom she considered a great mathematician, and of the Bonds, of Cambridge. She was much interested in their photography of the stars, and said it had never been done in Europe. At that time photography was but just applied to the stars. I had carried to the Royal Astronomical Society the first successful photograph of a star. It was that of Mizar and Alcor, in the Great Bear. (Since that time all these things have improved.)

"The last time I saw Mrs. Somerville, she took me into her garden to show me her rose-bushes, in which she took great pride. Mrs. Somerville was not a mathematician only, she spoke Italian fluently, and was in early life a good musician.

"I could but admire Mrs. Somerville as a woman. The ascent of the steep and rugged path of science had not unfitted her for the drawing-room circle; the hours of devotion to close study have not been incompatible with the duties of wife and mother; the mind that has turned to rigid demonstration has not thereby lost its faith in those truths which figures will not prove. 'I have no doubt,' said she, in speaking of the heavenly bodies, 'that in another state of existence we shall know more about these things.'

"Mrs. Somerville, at the age of seventy-seven, was interested in every new improvement, hopeful, cheery, and happy. Her society was sought by the most cultivated people in the world. [She died at ninety-two.]

" Berlin, May 7, 1858. Humboldt had replied to my letter of introduction by a note, saying that he should be happy to see me at 2 P.M., May 7. Of course I was punctual. Humboldt is one of several residents in a very ordinary-looking house on Oranienberge strasse.

" All along up the flight of stairs to his room were printed notices telling persons where to leave packages and letters for Alexander Humboldt.

" The servant showed me at first into a sort of ante-room, hung with deers' horns and carpeted with tigers' skins, then into the study, and asked me to take a seat on the sofa. The room was very warm; comfort was evidently carefully considered, for cushions were all around; the sofa was handsomely covered with worsted embroidery. A long study-table was full of books and papers.

" I had waited but a few moments when Humboldt came in; he was a smaller man than I had expected to see. He was neater, more ' trig,' than the pictures represent him; in looking at the pictures you feel that his head is too large, — out of proportion to the body, — but you do not perceive this when you see him.

" He bowed in a most courtly manner, and told me he was much obliged to me for coming to see him, then shook hands, and asked me to sit, and took a chair near me.

" There was a clock in sight, and I stayed but half an hour. He talked every minute, and on all kinds of subjects: of Dr. Bache, who was then at the head of the U.S. Coast Survey; of Dr. Gould, who had recently returned from long years in South America; of the Washington Observatory and its director, Lieutenant Maury; of the Dudley Observatory, at Albany; of Sir George Airy, of the Greenwich Observatory; of Professor Enke's comet reputation; of Argelander, who was there observing variable stars; of Mrs. Somerville and Goldschmidt, and of his brother.

"It was the period when the subject of admitting Kansas as a slave State was discussed — he touched upon that; it was during the administration of President Buchanan, and he talked about that.

"Having been nearly a year in Europe, I had not kept up my reading of American newspapers, but Humboldt could tell me the latest news, scientifically and politically. To my ludicrous mortification, he told me of the change of position of some scientific professor in New York State, and when I showed that I didn't know the location of the town, which was Clinton, he told me if I would look at the map, which lay upon the table, I should find the town somewhere between Albany and Buffalo.

"Humboldt was always considered a good-tempered, kindly-natured man, but his talk was a little fault-finding.

"He said: 'Lieutenant Maury has been useful, but for the director of an observatory he has put forth some strange statements in the 'Geography of the Sea.'

"He asked me if Mrs. Somerville was now occupied with pure mathematics. He said: 'There she is strong. I never saw her but once. She must be over sixty years old.' In reality she was seventy-seven. He spoke with admiration of Mrs. Somerville's ' Physical Geography,' — said it was excellent because so concise. ' A German woman would have used more words.'

"Humboldt asked me if they could apply photography to the small stars — to the eighth or ninth magnitude. I had asked the same question of Professor Bond, of Cambridge, and he had replied, ' Give me $500,000, and we can do it; but it is very expensive.'

"Humboldt spoke of the fifty-three small planets, and gave his opinion that they could not be grouped together; that there was no apparent connection.

"Having lost all his teeth, Humboldt's articulation was indistinct — he talked very rapidly. His hair was thin and very white, his eyes very blue, his nose too broad and too flat; yet he was a handsome man. He wore a white necktie, a black dress-coat, buttoned up, but not so much so that it hid a figured dark-blue and white waistcoat. He was a little deaf. He told me that he was eighty-nine years old, and that he and Bonpland, alone, were living of those who in early life were on expeditions together; that Bonpland was eighty-five, and much the more vigorous of the two.

"He said that we had gone backwards, morally, in America since he was there, — that then there were strong men there: Jefferson, and Hamilton, and Madison; that the three months he spent in America were spent almost wholly with Jefferson.

"In the course of conversation he told me that the fifth volume of ' Cosmos ' was in preparation. He urged me to go to see Argelander on my way to London; he followed me out, still urging me to do this, and at the same time assured me that Kansas would go all right.

" It was singular that Humboldt should advise me to use the sextant ; it was the first instrument that I ever used, and it is a very difficult one. No young aspirant in science ever left Humboldt's presence uncheered, and no petty animosities come out in his record. You never heard of Humboldt's complaining that any one had stolen his thunder, — he knew that no one could lift his bolts.

"When I came away, he thanked me again for the visit, followed me into the anteroom, and made a low bow."

In 1855 Mrs. Mitchell was taken suddenly ill, and although partial recovery followed, her illness lasted for six years, during which time Maria was her constant nurse. For most of the six years her mother's condition was such that merely a general care was needed, but it used to be said that Maria's eyes were always upon her. When the opportunity to go to Europe came, an older sister came with her family to take Maria's place in the home ; and when Miss Mitchell returned she found her mother so nearly in the state in which she had left her, that she felt justified in having taken the journey.

Mrs. Mitchell died in 1861, and a few months after her death Mr. Mitchell and his daughter removed to Lynn, Mass. — Miss Mitchell having purchased a small house in that city, in the rear of which she erected the little observatory brought from Nantucket. She was very much depressed by her mother's death, and absorbed herself as much as possible in her observations and in her work for the Nautical Almanac.

Soon after her return from Europe she had been presented with an equatorial telescope, the gift of American women, through Miss Elizabeth Peabody. The following letter refers to this instrument:

LETTER FROM ADMIRAL SMYTH.

St. John's Lodge, ⟩
near Aylesbury, ⟩ 25-7-'59.

My dear Miss Mitchell: . . . We are much pleased to hear of your acquisition of an equatorial instrument under a revolving roof, for it is a true scientific luxury as well as an efficient implement. The aperture of your object-glass is sufficient for doing much useful work, but, if I may hazard an opinion to you, do not attempt too much, for it is quality rather than quantity which is now desirable. I would therefore leave the multiplication of objects to the larger order of telescopes, and to those who are given to sweep and ransack the heavens, of whom there is a goodly corps. Now, for your purpose, I would recommend a batch of neat, but not overclose, binary systems, selected so as to have always one or the other on hand.

I, however, have been bestirring myself to put amateurs upon a more convenient and, I think, a better mode of examining double stars than by the wire micrometer, with its faults of illumination, fiddling, jumps, and dirty lamps. This is by the beautiful method of rock-crystal prisms, not the Rochon method of double-image, but by thin wedges cut to given angles. I have told Mr. Alvan Clark my " experiences." and I hope he will apply his excellent mind to the scheme. I am insisting upon this point in some astronomical twaddle which I am now printing, and of which I shall soon have to request your acceptance of a copy.

There is a very important department which calls for a zealous amateur or two, namely, the colors of double stars, for these have usually been noted after the eye has been fatigued with observing in illuminated fields. The volume I hope to forward— *en hommage* — will contain all the pros and cons of this branch.

There is, for ultimate utility, nothing like forming a plan and then steadily following it. Those who profess they will attend to everything often fall short of the mark. The division of labor leads to beneficial conclusions as well in astronomy as in mechanics and arts.

Mrs. Smyth and my daughter unite with me in wishing you all happiness and success; and believe me

My dear Miss Mitchell,

Yours very faithfully,

W. H. SMYTH.

In regard to the colors of stars, Miss Mitchell had already begun their study, as these extracts from her diary show:

"Feb. 19, 1853. I am just learning to notice the different colors of the stars, and already begin to have a new enjoyment. Betelgeuse is strikingly red, while Rigel is yellow. There is something of the same pleasure in noticing the hues that there is in looking at a collection of precious stones, or at a flower-garden in autumn. Blue stars I do not yet see, and but little lilac except through the telescope.

"Feb. 12, 1855. . . . I swept around for comets about an hour, and then I amused myself with noticing the varieties of color. I wonder that I have so long been insensible to this charm in the skies, the tints of the different stars are so delicate in their variety. . . . What a pity that some of our manufacturers shouldn't be able to steal the secret of dyestuffs from the stars, and astonish the feminine taste by new brilliancy in fashion." [1]

[NANTUCKET], April [1860].

MY DEAR: Your father just gave me a great fright by " tapping at my window " (I believe Poe's was a door, wasn't it?) and holding up your note. I was busy examining some star notices just received from Russia or Germany, — I never knew where Dorpat is, — and just thinking that my work was as good as theirs. I always noticed that when school-teachers took a holiday in order to visit other institutions they came home and quietly said, " No school is better or as good as mine." And then I read your note, and perceive your reading is as good as Mrs. Kemble's. Now, being *modest*, I always felt afraid the reason I thought you such a good reader was because I didn't know any better, but if all the world is equally ignorant, it makes it all right. .   .   .

I've been intensely busy. I have been looking for the little inferior planet to cross the sun, which it hasn't done, and I got an article ready for the paper and then hadn't the courage to publish — not for fear of the readers, but for fear that I should change my own ideas by the time 'twas in print.

I am hoping, however, to have something by the meeting of the Scientific Association in August, — some paper, — not to get reputation for myself, — my reputation is so much beyond me that as policy I should keep quiet, — but in order that my telescope may show that it is at work. I am embarrassed by the amount of work it might do — as you do not know which of Mrs. Browning's poems to read, there are so many beauties.

The little republic of San Marino presented Miss Mitchell, in 1859, with a bronze medal of merit, together with the *Ribbon* and *Letters Patent* signed by the two captains regent. This medal she prized as highly as the gold one from Denmark.

---

[1] See Chapter XI.

" Nantucket, May 12, 18[60]. . . . I send you a notice of an occultation; the last sentence and the last figures are mine. You and I can never occult, for have we not always helped one another to shine? Do you have Worcester's Dictionary? I read it continually. Did you feast on ' The Marble Faun ' ? I have a charming letter from Una Hawthorne, herself a poet by nature, all about ' papa's book.' Ought not Mr. Hawthorne to be the happiest man alive? He isn't, though! Do save all the anecdotes you possibly can, piquant or not; starved people are not over-nice.

Lynn, Jan. 5 [1864].

. . . I very rarely see the B——s; they go to a different church, and you know with that class of people '' not to be with us is to be against us." Indeed, I know very little of Lynn people. If I can get at Mr. J., when you come to see me I'll ask him to tea. He has called several times, but he's in such demand that he must be engaged some weeks in advance! Would you, if you lived in Lynn, want to fall into such a mass of idolaters?

I was wretchedly busy up to December 31, but have got into quiet seas again. I have had a great deal of company — not a person that I did not want to see, but I can't make the days more than twenty-four hours long, with all my economy of time. This week Professor Crosby, of Salem, comes up with his graduating class and his corps of teachers for an evening.

They remained in Lynn until Miss Mitchell was called to Vassar College, in 1865, as professor of astronomy and director of the observatory.

CHAPTER IX

1865-1885

LIFE AT VASSAR COLLEGE

IN her life at Vassar College there was a great deal
for Miss Mitchell to get accustomed to ; if her duties had
been merely as director of the observatory, it would
have been simply a continuation of her previous work.
But she was expected, of course, to teach astronomy ;
she was by no means sure that she could succeed as a
teacher, and with this new work on hand she could not
confine herself to original investigation — that which
had been her great aim in life.

But she was so much interested in the movement
for the higher education of women, an interest which
deepened as her work went on, that she gave up, in a
great measure, her scientific life, and threw herself heart
and soul into this work.

For some years after she went to Vassar, sne still
continued the work for the Nautical Almanac ; but after
a while she relinquished that, and confined herself
wholly to the work in the college.

" 1866. Vassar College brought together a mass of
heterogeneous material, out of which it was expected
that a harmonious whole would evolve — pupils from all
parts of the country, of different habits, different training, different views ; teachers, mostly from New England,

differing also; professors, largely from Massachusetts, yet differing much. And yet, after a year, we can say that there has been no very noisy jarring of the discordant elements; small jostling has been felt, but the president has oiled the rough places, and we have slid over them.

" . . . Miss —— is a bigot, but a very sincere one. She is the most conservative person I ever met. I think her a very good woman, a woman of great energy. . . . She is very kind to me, but had we lived in the colonial days of Massachusetts, and had she been a power, she would have burned me at the stake for heresy!

"Yesterday the rush began. Miss Lyman [the lady principal] had set the twenty teachers all around in different places, and I was put into the parlor to talk to 'anxious mothers.'

"Miss Lyman had a hoarse cold, but she received about two hundred students, and had all their rooms assigned to them.

"While she had one anxious mamma, I took two or three, and kept them waiting until she could attend to them. Several teachers were with me. I made a rush at the visitors as they entered, and sometimes I was asked if I were lady principal, and sometimes if I were the matron. This morning Miss Lyman's voice was gone. She must have seen five hundred people yesterday.

"Among others there was one Miss Mitchell, and, of course, that anxious mother put that girl under my special care, and she is very bright. Then there were two who were sent with letters to me, and several others whose mothers took to me because they were frightened by Miss Lyman's *style*.

"One lady, who seemed to be a bright woman, got me by the button and held me a long time — she wanted this, that, and the other impracticable thing for the girl, and told me how honest her daughter was; then with a flood of tears she said, 'But she is not a Christian. I know I put her into good hands when I put her here.' (Then I was strongly tempted to avow my Unitarianism.) Miss W., who was standing by, said, 'Miss Lyman will be an excellent spiritual adviser,' and we both looked very serious; when the mother wiped her weeping eyes and said, 'And, Miss Mitchell, will you ask Miss Lyman to insist that my daughter shall curl her hair? She looks very graceful when her hair is curled, and I want it insisted upon,' I made a note of it with my pencil, and as I happened to glance at Miss W. the corners of her mouth were twitching, upon which I broke down and laughed. The mother bore it very good-naturedly, but went on. She wanted to know who would work some buttonholes in her daughter's dress that was not quite finished, etc., and it all ended in her inviting me to make her a visit.

"Oct. 31, 1866. Our faculty meetings always try me in this respect: we do things that other colleges have done before. We wait and ask for precedent. If the earth had waited for a precedent, it never would have turned on its axis!

"Sept. 22, 1868. I have written to-day to give up the Nautical Almanac work. I do not feel sure that it will be for the best, but I am sure that I could not

THE FATHER AND DAUGHTER

hold the almanac and the college, and father is happy
here.

" I tell Miss Lyman that my father is so much pleased
with everything here that I am afraid he will be im-
mersed ! " [1]

Only those who knew Vassar College in its earlier
days can tell of the life that the father and daughter
led there for four years.

Mr. Mitchell died in 1869.

" Jan. 3, 1868. Meeting Dr. Hill at a private party,
I asked him if Harvard College would admit girls in
fifty years. He said one of the most conservative
members of the faculty had said, within sixteen days,
that it would come about in twenty years. I asked him
if I could go into one of Professor Peirce's recitations.
He said there was nothing to keep me out, and that
he would let me know when they came.

" At eleven A.M., the next Friday, I stood at Professor
Peirce's door. As the professor came in I went towards
him, and asked him if I might attend his lecture. He
said ' Yes.' I said ' Can you not say " I shall be happy
to have you " ? ' and he said ' I shall be happy to have
you,' but he didn't look happy !

" It was with some little embarrassment that Mrs.
K. and I seated ourselves. Sixteen young men came
into the room ; after the first glance at us there was not
another look, and the lecture went on. Professor Peirce
had filled the blackboard with formulæ, and went on
developing them. He walked backwards and forwards

---

[1] Vassar College, though professedly unsectarian, was mainly under Baptist
control.

all the time, thinking it out as he went. The students at first all took notes, but gradually they dropped off until perhaps only half continued. When he made simple mistakes they received it in silence; only one, that one his son (a tutor in college), remarked that he was wrong. The steps of his lesson were all easy, but of course it was impossible to tell whence he came or whither he was going. . . .

"The recitation-room was very common-looking — we could not tolerate such at Vassar. The forms and benches of the recitation-room were better for taking notes than ours are.)

"The professor was polite enough to ask us into the senior class, but I had an engagement. I asked him if a young lady presented herself at the door he *could* keep her out, and he said ' No, and I shouldn't.' I told him I would send some of my girls.

"Oct. 15, 1868. Resolved, in case of my outliving father and being in good health, to give my efforts to the intellectual culture of women, without regard to salary; if possible, connect myself with liberal Christian institutions, believing, as I do, that happiness and growth in this life are best promoted by them, and that what is good in this life is good in any life."

In August, 1869, Miss Mitchell, with several of her Vassar students, went to Burlington, Ia., to observe the total eclipse of the sun. She wrote a popular account of her observations, which was printed in "Hours at Home" for September, 1869. Her records were published in Professor Coffin's report, as she was a member of his party.

" Sept. 26, 1871. My classes came in to-day for the first time; twenty-five students — more than ever before; fine, splendid-looking girls. I felt almost frightened at the responsibility which came into my hands — of the possible *twist* which I might give them.

" 1871. I never look upon the mass of girls going into our dining-room or chapel without feeling their nobility, the sovereignty of their pure spirit."

The following letter from Miss Mitchell, though written at a later date, gives an idea of the practical observing done by her classes:

MY DEAR MISS——: I reply to your questions concerning the observatory which you propose to establish. And, first, let me congratulate you that you begin *small*. A large telescope is a great luxury, but it is an enormous expense, and not at all necessary for teaching. . . . My beginning class uses only a small portable equatorial. It stands out-doors from 7 A.M. to 9 P.M. The girls are encouraged to use it: they are expected to determine the rotation of the sun on its axis by watching the spots — the same for the planet Jupiter; they determine the revolution of Titan by watching its motions, the retrograde and direct motion of the planets among the stars, the position of the sun with reference to its setting in winter and summer, the phases of Venus. All their book learning in astronomy should be mathematical. The astronomy which is not mathematical is what is so ludicrously called " Geography of the Heavens " — is not astronomy at all.

My senior class, generally small, say six, is received as a class, but in practical astronomy each girl is taught separately. I believe in *small* classes. I instruct them separately, first in the use of the meridian instrument, and next in that of the ·equatorial. They obtain the time for the college by meridian passage of stars; they use the equatorial just as far as they can do with very insufficient mechanism. We work wholly on planets, and they are taught to

find a planet at any hour of the day, to make drawings of what
they see, and to determine positions of planets and satellites.
With the clock and chronograph they determine difference of right
ascension of objects by the electric mode of recording. They
make, sometimes, very accurate drawings, and they learn to know
the satellites of Saturn (Titan, Rhea, etc.) by their different physi-
ognomy, as they would persons. They have sometimes measured
diameters.

If you add to your observatory a meridian instrument, I should
advise a small one. *Size* is not so important as people generally
suppose. Nicety and accuracy are what is needed in all scientific
work; startling effects by large telescopes and high powers are too
suggestive of sensational advertisement.

The relation between herself and her pupils was
quite remarkable — it was very cordial and intimate; she
spoke of them always as her "girls," but at the same
time she required their very best work, and was intoler-
ant of shirking, or of an ambition to do what nature
never intended the girl in question to do.

One of her pupils writes thus: "If it were only
possible to tell you of what Professor Mitchell did for
one of her girls! 'Her girls!' It meant so much to
come into daily contact with such a woman! There is
no need of speaking of her ability; the world knows
what that was. But as her class-room was unique, having something of home in its belongings, so its atmosphere differed from that of all others. Anxiety and
nervous strain were left outside of the door. Perhaps
one clue to her influence may be found in her remark
to the senior class in astronomy when '76 entered upon
its last year: 'We are women studying together.'

" Occasionally it happened that work requiring two

hours or more to prepare called for little time in the class. Then would come one of those treats which she bestowed so freely upon her girls, and which seemed to put them in touch with the great outside world. Letters from astronomers in Europe or America, or from members of their families, giving delightful glimpses of home life; stories of her travels and of visits to famous people; accounts of scientific conventions and of large gatherings of women, — not so common then as now, — gave her listeners a wider outlook and new interests.

"Professor Mitchell was chairman of a standing committee of the American Association for the Advancement of Women, — that on women's work in science, — and some of her students did their first work for women's organizations in gathering statistics and filling out blanks which she distributed among them.

"The benefits derived from my college course were manifold, but time and money would have been well spent had there been no return but that of two years' intercourse with Maria Mitchell."

Another pupil, and later her successor at Vassar College, Miss Mary W. Whitney, has said of her method of teaching : "As a teacher, Miss Mitchell's gift was that of stimulus, not that of drill. She could not drill ; she would not drive. But no honest student could escape the pressure of her strong will and earnest intent. The marking system she held in contempt, and wished to have nothing to do with it. 'You cannot mark a human mind,' she said, 'because there is no intellectual unit ; ' and upon taking up her duties as professor she stipulated that she should not be held responsible for a strict application of the system."

"July, 1887. My students used to say that my way of teaching was like that of the man who said to his son, 'There are the letters of the English alphabet — go into that corner and learn them.'

"It is not exactly my way, but I do think, as a general rule, that teachers talk too much! A book is a very good institution! To read a book, to think it over, and to write out notes is a useful exercise; a book which will not repay some hard thought is not worth publishing. The fashion of lecturing is becoming a rage; the teacher shows herself off, and she does not try enough to develop her pupils.

"The greatest object in educating is to give a right habit of study. . . .

. . . .

" . . . Not too much mechanical apparatus — let the imagination have some play; a cube may be shown by a model, but let the drawing upon the blackboard represent the cube; and if possible let Nature be the blackboard; spread your triangles upon land and sky.

"One of my pupils always threw her triangles on the celestial vault above her head. . . .

"A small apparatus well used will do wonders. A celebrated chemist ordered his servant to bring in the laboratory — on a tray! Newton rolled up the cover of a book; he put a small glass at one end, and a large brain at the other — it was enough.

. . . .

"When a student asks me, 'What specialty shall I

follow?' I answer, 'Adopt some one, if none draws you, and wait.' I am confident that she will find the specialty engrossing.

"Feb. 10, 1887. When I came to Vassar, I regretted that Mr. Vassar did not give full scholarships. By degrees, I learned to think his plan of giving half scholarships better; and to-day I am ready to say, 'Give no scholarships at all.'

"I find a helping-hand lifts the girl as crutches do; she learns to like the help which is not self-help.

"If a girl has the public school, and wants enough to learn, she will learn. It is hard, but she was born to hardness — she cannot dodge it. Labor is her inheritance.

"I was born, for instance, incapable of appreciating music. I mourn it. Should I go to a music-school, therefore? No, avoid the music-school; it is a very expensive branch of study. When the public school has taught reading, writing, and arithmetic, the boy or girl has his or her tools; let them use these tools, and get a few hours for study every day.

". . . Do not give educational aid to sickly young people. The old idea that the feeble young man must be fitted for the ministry, because the more sickly the more saintly, has gone out. Health of body is not only an accompaniment of health of mind, but is the cause; the converse may be true, — that health of mind causes health of body; but we all know that intellectual cheer and vivacity act upon the mind. If the gymnastic exercise helps the mind, the concert or the theatre improves the health of the body.

"Let the unfortunate young woman whose health is delicate take to the culture of the woods and fields, or raise strawberries, and avoid teaching.

" Better give a young girl who is poor a common-school education, a little lift, and tell her to work out her own career. If she have a distaste to the homely routine of life, leave her the opportunity to try any other career, but let her understand that she stands or falls by herself.

" .   .   . Not every girl should go to college. The over-burdened mother of a large family has a right to be aided by her daughter's hands. I would aid the mother and not the daughter.

" I would not put the exceptionally smart girl from a *very* poor family into college, unless she is a genius; and a genius should wait some years to *prove* her genius.

" Endow the already established institution with money. Endow the woman who shows genius with *time*.

" A case at Johns Hopkins University is an excellent one. A young woman goes into the institution who is already a scholar; she shows what she can do, and she takes a scholarship; she is not placed in a happy valley of do nothing, — she is put into a workshop, where she can work.   .   .   .

" .   .   . We are all apt to say, ' Could we have had the opportunity in life that our neighbor had,' — and we leave the unfinished sentence to imply that we should have been geniuses.

" No one ever says, ' If I had not had such golden

opportunities thrust upon me, I might have developed by a struggle'! But why look back at all? Why turn your eyes to your shadow, when, by looking upward, you see your rainbow in the same direction?

"But our want of opportunity was our opportunity — our privations were our privileges — our needs were stimulants; we are what we are because we had little and wanted much; and it is hard to tell which was the more powerful factor. . . .

.   .   .   .

"Small aids to individuals, large aid to masses.

.   .   .   .

"The Russian Czar determined to found an observatory, and the first thing he did was to take a million dollars from the government treasury. He sends to America to order a thirty-five inch telescope from Alvan Clark, — not to promote science, but to surpass other nations in the size of his glass. 'To him that hath shall be given.' Read it, 'To him that hath *should* be given.'

.   .   .   .

"To give wisely is hard. I do not wonder that the millionaire founds a new college — why should he not? Millionaires are few, and he is a man by himself — he must have views, or he could not have earned a million. But let the man or woman of ordinary wealth seek out the best institution already started, — the best girl already in college, — and give the endowment.

"I knew a rich woman who wished to give aid to some girls' school, and she travelled in order to find that institution which gave the most solid learning with

the least show.   She found it where few would expect
it, — in Tennessee.   It was worth while to travel.

"The aid that comes need not be money; let it be a
careful consideration of the object, and an evident
interest in the cause.

"When you aid a teacher, you improve the education of your children.   It is a wonder that teachers
work as well as they do.   I never look at a group of
them without using, mentally, the expression, 'The
noble army of martyrs'!

"The chemist should have had a laboratory, and the
observatory should have had an astronomer; but we
are too apt to bestow money where there is no man,
and to find a man where there is no money.

.   .   .   .

"If every girl who is aided were a very high order of
scholar, scholarship would undoubtedly conquer poverty; but a large part of the aided students are ordinary.   They lack, at least, executive power, as their
ancestors probably did.   Poverty is a misfortune; mis-
fortunes are often the result of blamable indiscretion,
extravagance, etc.

"It is one of the many blessings of poverty that
one is not obliged to 'give wisely.' "

1866.   *To her students :* "I cannot expect to make
astronomers, but I do expect that you will invigorate
your minds by the effort at healthy modes of thinking.
. . . When we are chafed and fretted by small cares,
a look at the stars will show us the littleness of our
own interests.

" .   .   . But star-gazing is not science.   The

entrance to astronomy is through mathematics. You must make up your mind to steady and earnest work. You must be content to get on slowly if you only get on thoroughly.   . . .

"The phrase 'popular science' has in itself a touch of absurdity.   That knowledge which is popular is not scientific.

"The laws which govern the motions of the sun, the earth, planets, and other bodies in the universe, cannot be understood and demonstrated without a solid basis of mathematical learning.

.   .   .   .

"Every formula which expresses a law of nature is a hymn of praise to God.

.   .   .   .

"You cannot study anything persistently for years without becoming learned, and although I would not hold reputation up to you as a very high object of ambition, it is a wayside flower which you are sure to have catch at your skirts.

"Whatever apology other women may have for loose, ill-finished work, or work not finished at all, you will have none.

"When you leave Vassar College, you leave it the *best educated women in the world*.   Living a little outside of the college, beyond the reach of the little currents that go up and down the corridors, I think I am a fairer judge of your advantages than you can be yourselves ; and when I say you will be the best educated women in the world, I do not mean the education of text-books, and class-rooms, and apparatus, only, but that broader education which you receive unconsciously, that higher teaching which comes to you, all unknown to the givers, from daily association with the noble-souled women who are around you."

" 1871. When astronomers compare observations made by different persons, they cannot neglect the constitutional peculiarities of the individuals, and there enters into these computations a quantity called ' personal equation.' In common terms, it is that difference between two individuals from which results a difference in the *time* which they require to receive and note an occurrence. If one sees a star at one instant, and records it, the record of another, of the same thing, is not the same.

" It is true, also, that the same individual is not the same at all times ; so that between two individuals there is a mean or middle individual, and each individual has a mean or middle self, which is not the man of to-day, nor the man of yesterday, nor the man of to-morrow ; but a middle man among these different selves. . . .

.   .   .   .

" We especially need imagination in science. It is not all mathematics, nor all logic, but it is somewhat beauty and poetry.

" There will come with the greater love of science greater love to one another. Living more nearly to Nature is living farther from the world and from its follies, but nearer to the world's people ; it is to be of them, with them, and for them, and especially for their improvement. We cannot see how impartially Nature gives of her riches to all, without loving all, and helping all; and if we cannot learn through Nature's laws the certainty of spiritual truths, we can at least learn to promote spiritual growth while we are together, and live in a trusting hope of a greater growth in the future.

". . . The great gain would be freedom of thought. Women, more than men, are bound by tradition and authority. What the father, the brother, the doctor, and the minister have said has been received undoubtingly. Until women throw off this reverence for authority they will not develop. When they do this, when they come to truth through their investigations, when doubt leads them to discovery, the truth which they get will be theirs, and their minds will work on and on unfettered.

[1874.] "I am but a woman!

"For women there are, undoubtedly, great difficulties in the path, but so much the more to overcome. First, no woman should say, 'I am but a woman!' But a woman! What more can you ask to be?

"Born a woman — born with the average brain of humanity — born with more than the average heart — if you are mortal, what higher destiny could you have? No matter where you are nor what you are, you are a power — your influence is incalculable; personal influence is always underrated by the person. We are all centres of spheres — we see the portions of the sphere above us, and we see how little we affect it. We forget the part of the sphere around and before us — it extends just as far every way.

"Another common saying, 'It isn't the way,' etc. Who settles the way? Is there any one so forgetful of the sovereignty bestowed on her by God that she accepts a leader — one who shall capture her mind?

" There is this great danger in student life. Now, we rest all upon what Socrates said, or what Copernicus taught; how can we dispute authority which has come down to us, all established, for ages?

" We must at least question it; we cannot accept anything as granted, beyond the first mathematical formulæ. Question everything else.

> " ' The world is round, and like a ball
> Seems swinging in the air.' [1]

" No such thing! the world is not round, it does not swing, and it doesn't *seem* to swing!

" I know I shall be called heterodox, and that unseen lightning flashes and unheard thunderbolts will be playing around my head, when I say that women will never be profound students in any other department except music while they give four hours a day to the *practice* of music. I should by all means encourage every woman who is born with musical gifts to study music; but study it as a science and an art, and not as an accomplishment; and to every woman who is not musical, I should say, ' Don't study it at all; ' you cannot afford four hours a day, out of some years of your life, just to be agreeable in company upon *possible* occasions.

" If for four hours a day you studied, year after year, the science of language, for instance, do you suppose

---

[1] From Peter Parley's Primary Geography.

you would not be a linguist? Do you put the mere pleasing of some social party, and the reception of a few compliments, against the mental development of four hours a day of study of something for which you were born?

"When I see that girls who are required by their parents to go through with the irksome practising really become respectable performers, I wonder what four hours a day at something which they loved, and for which God designed them, would do for them.

"I should think that to a real scientist in music there would be something mortifying in this rush of all women into music; as there would be to me if I saw every girl learning the constellations, and then thinking she was an astronomer!

"Jan. 8, 1876. At the meeting of graduates at the Deacon House, the speeches that were made were mainly those of Dr. R. and Professor B. I am sorry now that I did not at least say that the college is what it is mainly because the early students pushed up the course to a collegiate standard.

"Jan. 25, 1876. It has become a serious question with me whether it is not my duty to beg money for the observatory, while what I really long for is a quiet life of scientific speculation. I want to sit down and study on the observations made by myself and others."

During her later years at Vassar, Miss Mitchell interested herself personally in raising a fund to endow the chair of astronomy. In March, 1886, she wrote: "I have been in New York quite lately, and am quite hopeful that Miss —— will do something for Vassar.

Mrs. C., of Newburyport, is to ask Whittier, who is said to be rich, and —— told me to get anything I could out of her father. But after all I am a poor beggar; my ideas are small!'"

Since Miss Mitchell's death, the fund has been completed by the alumnæ, and is known as the Maria Mitchell Endowment Fund. With $10,000 appropriated by the trustees it amounts to $50,000.

"June 18, 1876. I had imagined the Emperor of Brazil to be a dark, swarthy, tall man, of forty-five years; that he would not really have a crown upon his head, but that I should feel it was somewhere around, handy-like, and that I should know I was in royal presence. But he turns out to be a large, old man, — say, sixty-five, — broad-headed and broad-shouldered, with a big white beard, and a very pleasant, even chatty, manner.

"Once inside of the dome, he seemed to feel at home; to my astonishment he asked if Alvan Clark made the glass of the equatorial. As he stepped into the meridian-room, and saw the instruments, he said, 'Collimators?' I said, 'You have been in observatories before.' 'Oh, yes, Cambridge and Washington,' he replied. He seemed much more interested in the observatory than I could possibly expect. I asked him to go on top of the roof, and he said he had not time; yet he stayed long enough to go up several times. I am told that he follows out, remarkably, his own ideas as to his movements."

In 1878, Miss Mitchell went to Denver, Colorado, to observe the total eclipse of the sun. She was accompanied by several of her former pupils. She prepared an account of this eclipse, which will be found in Chapter XI.

"Aug. 20, 1878. Dr. Raymond [President of Vassar College] is dead. I cannot quite take it in. I have never known the college without him, and it will make all things different.

"Personally, I have always been fond of him; he was very enjoyable socially and intellectually. Officially he was, in his relations to the students, perfect. He was cautious to a fault, and has probably been very wise in his administration of college affairs. He was broad in his religious views. He was not broad in his ideas of women, and was made to broaden the education of women by the women around him.

"June 18, 1881. The dome party to-day was sixty-two in number. It was breakfast, and we opened the dome; we seated forty in the dome and twenty in the meridian-room."

This "dome party" requires a few words of explanation, because it was unique among all the Vassar festivities. The week before commencement, Miss Mitchell's pupils would be informed of the approaching gathering by a notice like the following:

CIRCULAR.

The annual dome party will be held at the observatory on Saturday, the 19th, at 6 P.M. You are cordially invited to be present.

M. M.

[As this gathering is highly intellectual, you are invited to bring poems.]

It was, at first, held in the evening, but during the last years was a breakfast party, its character in other respects remaining the same. Little tables were spread under the dome, around the big telescope; the flowers were roses from Miss Mitchell's own garden. The "poems" were nonsense rhymes, in the writing of which Miss Mitchell was an adept. Each student would have a few verses of a more or less personal character, written by Miss Mitchell, and there were others written by the girls themselves; some were impromptu; others were set to music, and sung by a selected glee-club.

"June 5, 1881. We have written what we call our dome poetry. Some nice poems have come in to us. I think the Vassar girls, in the main, are magnificent, they are so all-alive. . . .

"May 20, 1882. Vassar is getting pretty. I gathered lilies of the valley this morning. The young robins are out in a tree close by us, and the phœbe has built, as usual, under the front steps.

"I am rushing dome poetry, but so far show no alarming symptoms of brilliancy."

A former student writes as follows about the dome poetry:

"At the time it was read, though it seemed mere merry nonsense, it really served a more serious purpose in the work of one who did nothing aimlessly. This apparent nonsense served as the vehicle to convey an expression of approbation, affection, criticism, or disapproval in such a merry mode that even the bitterest draught seemed sweet."

"1881, July 5. We left Vassar, June 24, on the

steamer 'Galatea,' from New York to Providence. I
looked out of my state-room window, and saw a strange-
looking body in the northern sky. My heart sank; I
knew instantly that it was a comet, and that I must
return to the observatory. Calling the young people
around me, and pointing it out to them, I had their
assurance that it was a comet, and nothing but a comet.

" We went to bed at nine, and I arose at six in the
morning. As soon as I could get my nieces started
for Providence, I started for Stonington, — the most
easy of the ways of getting to New York, as I should
avoid Point Judith.

" I went to the boat at the Stonington wharf about
noon, and remained on board until morning — there
were few passengers, it was very quiet, and I slept well.

" Arriving in New York, I took cars at 9 A.M. for
Poughkeepsie, and reached the college at dinner-time.
I went to work the same evening.

" As I could not tell at what time the comet would
pass the meridian, I stationed myself at the telescope in
the meridian-room by 10 P.M., and watched for the
comet to cross. As it approached the meridian, I saw
that it would go behind a scraggy apple-tree. I sent
for the watchman, Mr. Crumb, to come with a saw, and
cut off the upper limbs. He came back with an axe,
and chopped away vigorously; but as one limb after
another fell, and I said, 'I need more, cut away,' he
said, 'I think I must cut down the whole tree.' I said,
'Cut it down.' I felt the barbarism of it, but I felt
more that a bird might have a nest in it.

" I found, when I went to breakfast the next morning,

that the story had preceded me, and I was called
' George Washington.'

"But for all this, I got almost no observation; the
fog came up, and I had scarcely anything better than
an estimation. I saw the comet blaze out, just on the
edge of the field, and I could read its declination only.

"On the 28th, 29th, and July 1st, I obtained good
meridian passages, and the R.A. must be very good.

"Jan. 12, 1882. There is a strange sentence in the
last paragraph of Dr. Jacobi's article on the study of
medicine by women, to the effect that it would be
better for the husband always to be superior to the
wife. Why? And if so, does not it condemn the ablest
women to a single life?

"March 13, 1882, 3 P.M. I start for faculty, and
we probably shall elect what are called the ' honor
girls.' I dread the struggle that is pretty certain to
come. Each of us has some favorite whom she wishes
to put into the highest class, and whom she honestly
believes to be of the highest order of merit. I never
have the whole ten to suit me, but I can truly say
that at this minute I do not care. I should be sorry
not to see S., and W., and P., and E., and G., and K.
on the list of the ten, but probably that is more than I
ought to expect. The whole system is demoralizing
and foolish. Girls study for prizes and not for learning, when ' honors ' are at the end. The unscholarly
motive is wearing. If they studied for sound learning,
the cheer which would come with every day's gain
would be health-preserving.

". . . I have seven advanced students, and to-day, when I looked around to see who should be called to help look out for meteors, I could consider only *one* of them not already overworked, and she was the postgraduate, who took no honors, and never hurried, and has always been an excellent student.

". . . We are sending home some girls already [November 14], and —— is among them. I am somewhat alarmed at the dropping down, but —— does an enormous amount of work, belongs to every club, and writes for every club and for the 'Vassar Miscellany,' etc.; of course she has the headache most of the time.

" Sometimes I am distressed for fear Dr. Clarke[1] is not so far wrong; but I do not think it is the study — it is the morbid conscientiousness of the girls, who think they must work every minute.

" April 26, 1882. Miss Herschel came to the college on the 11th, and stayed three days. She is one of the little girls whom I saw, twenty-three years since, playing on the lawn at Sir John Herschel's place, Collingwood.

". . . Miss Herschel was just perfect as a guest; she fitted in beautifully. The teachers gave a reception for her, —— gave her his poem, and Henry, the gardener, found out that the man in whose employ he lost a finger was her brother-in-law, in Leeds!

" Jan. 9, 1884. Mr. [Matthew] Arnold has been to the college, and has given his lecture on Emerson. The audience was made up of three hundred students, and three hundred guests from town. Never was a man listened to with so much attention. Whether he is right

---

[1] Author of " Sex in Education."

in his judgment or not, he held his audience by his manly way, his kindly dissection, and his graceful English. Socially, he charmed us all. He chatted with every one, he smiled on all. He said he was sorry to leave the college, and that he felt he must come to America again. We have not had such an awakening for years. It was like a new volume of old English poetry.

"March 16, 1885. In February, 1831, I counted seconds for father, who observed the annular eclipse at Nantucket. I was twelve and a half years old. In 1885, fifty-four years later, I counted seconds for a class of students at Vassar; it was the same eclipse, but the sun was only about half-covered. Both days were perfectly clear and cold."

CHAPTER X

1873

SECOND EUROPEAN TOUR — RUSSIA — FRANCES POWER COBBE —
" THE GLASGOW COLLEGE FOR GIRLS "

IN 1873, Miss Mitchell spent the summer in Europe,
and availed herself of this opportunity to visit the
government observatory at Pulkova, in Russia.

"Eydkuhnen, Wednesday, July 30, 1873. Certainly,
I never in my life expected to spend twenty-
four hours in this small town, the frontier town
of Prussia. Here I remembered that our little bags
would be examined, and I asked the guard about it,
but he said we need not trouble ourselves; we should
not be examined until we reached the first Russian
town of Wiersbelow. So, after a mile more of travel,
we came to Wiersbelow. Knowing that we should
keep our little compartment until we got to St. Petersburg, we had scattered our luggage about; gloves
were in one place, veil in another, shawl in another,
parasol in another, and books all around.

"The train stopped. Imagine our consternation!
Two officials entered the carriage, tall Russians in full
uniform, and seized everything — shawls, books, gloves,
bags; and then, looking around very carefully, espied
W's poor little ragged handkerchief, and seized that, too,
as a contraband article! We looked at one another,

and said nothing. The tall Russian said something to us; we looked at each other and sat still. The tall Russians looked at one another, and there was almost an official smile between them.

"Then one turned to me, and said, very distinctly, 'Passy-port.' 'Oh,' I said, 'the passports are all right; where are they?' and we produced from our pockets the passports prepared at Washington, with the official seal, and we delivered them with a sort of air as if we had said, 'You'll find that they do things all right at Washington.'

"The tall Russians got out, and I was about to breathe freely, when they returned, and said something else — not a word did I understand; they exchanged a look of amusement, and W. and I, one of amazement; then one of them made signs to us to get out. The sign was unmistakable, and we got out, and followed them into an immense room, where were tables all around covered with luggage, and about a hundred travellers standing by; and our books, shawls, gloves, etc., were thrown in a heap upon one of these tables, and we awoke to the disagreeable consciousness that we were in a custom-house, and only two out of a hundred travellers, and that we did not understand one word of Russian.

"But, of course, it could be only a few minutes of delay, and if German and French failed, there is always left the language of signs, and all would be right.

"After, perhaps, half an hour, two or three officials approached us, and, holding the passports, began to talk to us. How did they know that those two passports belonged to us? Out of two hundred persons, how could they at once see that the woman whose age was given at more than half a century, and the lad whose age was given at less than a score of years, were the two fatigued and weary travellers who stood guarding a small heap of gloves, books, handkerchiefs, and shawls? Two of the officials held up the passports to us, pointed to the blank page, shook their heads ominously; the third took the passports, put them into his vest pocket, buttoned up his coat, and motioned to us to follow him.

"We followed; he opened the door of an ordinary carriage, waved his hand for us to get in, jumped in himself, and we found we were started back. We could not cross the line between Germany and Russia.

"We meekly asked where we were to go, and were relieved when we found that we went back only to the nearest town, but that the passports must be sent to Konigsberg, sixty miles away, to be endorsed by the Russian ambassador — it might take some days. W. was very much inclined to refuse to go back and to attempt a war of words, but it did not seem wise to me to undertake a war against the Russian government; I know our country does not lightly go into an 'unpleasantness' of that kind. . . .

"So we went back to Eydkuhnen, — a little miserable German village. We took rooms at the only hotel, and there we stayed twenty-four hours. Before the end of that time, we had visited every shop in the village, and aired our German to most of our fellow-travellers whom we met at the hotel.

"The landlord took our part, and declared it was hard enough on simple travellers like ourselves to be stopped in such a way, and that Russia was the only country in Europe which was rigid in that respect. Happily, our passports were back in twenty-four hours, and we started again; our trunks had been registered for St. Petersburg, and to St. Petersburg they had gone, ahead of us; and of the small heap of things thrown down promiscuously at the custom-house, the whole had not come back to us — it was not very important. I learned how to wear one glove instead of two, or to go without.

"We had the ordeal of the custom-house to pass again; but once passed, and told that we were free to go on, it was like going into a clear atmosphere from a fog. We crossed the custom-house threshold into another room, and we found ourselves in Russia, and in an excellent, well-furnished, and cheery restaurant. We lost the German smoke and the German beer; we found hot coffee and clean table-cloths.

"We did not return to our dusty, red-velvet palace, but we entered a clean, comfortable compartment, with easy sofas, for the night. We started again for St. Petersburg; we were now four days from London. I will omit the details of a break-down that night, and another change of cars. We had some sleep, and awoke in the morning to enjoy Russia.

"And, first, of Russian railroads. When the railroads of Russia were planned, the Emperor Nicholas allowed a large sum of money for the building. The engineer showed him his plan. The road wound by slight curves from one town to another. This did not suit the emperor at all. He took his ruler, put it down upon the table, and said: 'I choose to have my roads run so.' Of course the engineer assented — he had his large fund granted; a straight road was much cheaper to build than a curved one. As a consequence, he built and furnished an excellent road.

"At every 'verst,' which is not quite a mile, a small house is placed at the roadside, on which, in very large figures, the number of versts from St. Petersburg is told. The train runs very smoothly and very slowly; twenty miles an hour is about the rate. Of course the journey seemed long. For a large part of the way it was an uninhabited, level plain; so green, however, that it seemed like travelling on prairies. Occasionally we passed a dreary little village of small huts, and as we neared St. Petersburg we passed larger and better built towns, which the dome of some cathedral lighted up for miles.

"The road was enlivened, too, by another peculiarity. The restaurants were all adorned by flags of all colors, and festooned by vines. At one place the green arches ran across the road, and we passed under a bower of evergreens. I accepted this, at first, as a Russian peculiarity, and was surprised that so much attention was paid to travellers; but I learned that it was not for us at all. The Duke of Edinboro' had passed over the road a few days before, on his way to St. Petersburg, for his betrothal to the only daughter of the czar, and the decorations were for him; and so we felt that we were of the party, although we had not been asked.

"We approached St. Petersburg just at night, and caught the play of the sunlight on the domes. It is a city of domes — blue domes, green domes, white domes, and, above all, the golden dome of the Cathedral of St. Isaac's.

"It is almost never a single dome. St. Isaac's central, gilded dome looms up above its fellow domes, but four smaller ones surround it.

"It was summer; the temperature was delightful, about like our October. The showers were frequent, there was no dust and no sultry air.

"There must be a great deal of nice mechanical work required in St. Petersburg, for on the Nevsky Perspective, the principal street, there were a great many shops in which graduating and measuring instruments of very nice workmanship were for sale. Especially I noticed the excellence of the thermometers, and I naturally stopped to read them. Figures are a common language, but it was clear that I was in another planet; I could not read the thermometers! I judged that the weather was warm enough for the thermometer to be at 68. I read, say, 16. And then I remembered that the Russians do not put their freezing point at 32, as we do, and I was obliged to go through a troublesome calculation before I could tell how warm it was.

"But I came to a still stranger experience. I dated my letters August 3, and went to my banker's, before I sealed them, to see if there were letters for me. The banker's little calendar was hanging by his desk, and the day of the month was on exhibition, in large figures. I read, July 22! This was distressing! Was I like Alice in Wonderland? Did time go backward? Surely, I had dated August 3. Could I be in error twelve days? And then I perceived that twelve days was just the difference of old and new calendars.

"How many times I had taught students that the Russians still counted their time by the 'old style,' but had never learned it myself! And so I was obliged to teach myself new lessons in science. The earth turns on its axis just the same in Russia as in Boston, but you don't get out of the sunlight at the Boston sunset hour.

"When the thermometer stands at 32 in St. Petersburg, it does not freeze as it does in Boston. On the contrary, it is very warm in St. Petersburg, for it means what 104 does in Boston. And if you leave London on the 22d of July, and are five days on the way to St. Petersburg, a week after you get there it is still the 22d of July! And we complain that the day is too short!

"Another peculiarity. We strolled over the city all day; we came back to our hotel tired; we took our tea; we talked over the day; we wrote to our friends; we planned for the next day; we were ready to retire. We walked to the window — the sun was striking on all the chimney tops. It doesn't seem to be right even for the lark to go to sleep while the sun shines. We looked at our watches; but the watches said nine o'clock, and we went off to our beds in daytime; and we awoke after the first nap to perceive that the sun still shone into the room.

"Like all careful aunts, I was unwilling that my nephew should be out alone at night. He was desirous of doing the right thing, but urged that at home, as a little boy, he was always allowed to be out until dark, and he asked if he could stay out until dark! Alas for the poor lad! There was no dark at all! I could not consent for him to be out all night, and the twilight was not over. You may read and read that the summer day at St. Petersburg is twenty hours long, but until you see that the sun scarcely sets, you cannot take it in.

"I wondered whether the laboring man worked eight or ten hours under my window; it seemed to me that he was sawing wood the whole twenty-four!

"W. came in one night after a stroll, and described a beautiful square which he had come upon accidentally. I listened with great interest, and said, 'I must go there in the morning; what is the name of it?' — 'I don't know,' he replied. — 'Why didn't you read the sign?' I asked. — 'I can't read,' was the reply. — 'Oh, no; but why didn't you ask some one?' — 'I can't speak,' he answered. Neither reading nor speaking, we had to learn St. Petersburg by our observation, and it is the best way. Most travellers read too much.

"There are learned institutions in St. Petersburg: universities, libraries, picture-galleries, and museums; but the first institution with which I became acquainted was the drosky. The drosky is a very, very small phaeton. It has the driver's seat in front, and a very narrow seat behind him. One person can have room enough on this second seat, but it usually carries two.

Invariably the drosky is lined with dark-blue cloth, and the drosky-driver wears a dark-blue wrapper, coming to the feet, girded around the waist by a crimson sash. He also wears a bell-shaped hat, turned up at the side. You are a little in doubt, if you see him at first separated from his drosky, whether he is a market-woman or a serving-man, the dress being very much like a morning wrapper. But he is rarely six feet away from his carriage, and usually he is upon it, sound asleep!

"The trunks having gone to St. Petersburg in advance of ourselves, our first duty was to get possession of them. They were at the custom-house, across the city. My nephew and I jumped upon a drosky — we could not say that we were really *in* the drosky, for the seat was too short. The drosky-driver started off his horse over the cobble-stones at a terrible rate. I could not keep my seat, and I clung to W. He shouted, ' Don't hold by me ; I shall be out the next minute ! ' What could be done? I was sure I shouldn't stay on half a minute. Blessings on the red sash of the drosky-man — I caught at that! He drove faster and faster, and I clung tighter and tighter, but alarmed at two immense dangers : first, that I should stop his breath by dragging the girdle so tightly ; and, next, that when it became unendurable to him, he would loosen it in front.

" I could not perceive that he was aware of my existence at all ! He had only one object in life, — to carry us across the city to our place of destination, and to get his copecks in return.

"In a few days I learned to like the jolly vehicles very much. They are so numerous that you may pick one up on any street, whenever you are tired of walking.

"My principal object in visiting St. Petersburg was the astronomical observatory at Pulkova, some twelve miles distant.

"I had letters to the director, Otto von Struve, but our consul declared that I must also have one from him, for Struve was a very great man. I, of course, accepted it.

"We made the journey by rail and coach, but it would be better to drive the whole way.

"Most observatories are temples of silence, and quiet reigns. As we drove into the grounds at Pulkova, a small crowd of children of all ages, and servants of all degrees, came out to meet us. They did not come out to do us honor, but to gaze at us. I could not understand it until I learned that the director of the observatory has a large number of aids, and they, with all their families, live in large houses, connected with the central building by covered ways.

"All about the grounds, too, were small observatories, — little temples, — in which young men were practising for observations on the transit of Venus. These little buildings, I afterwards learned, were to be taken down and transported, instruments and all, to the coast of Asia.

"The director of the observatory is Otto Struve — his father, Wilhelm Struve, preceded him in this office. Properly, the director is Herr Von Struve; but the old

Russian custom is still in use, and the servants call him Wilhelm-vitch; that is, ' the son of William.'

" When I bought a photograph of the present emperor, Alexander, I saw that he was called Nicholas-vitch.

" Herr Struve received us courteously, and an assistant was called to show us the instruments. All observatories are much alike; therefore I will not describe this, except in its peculiarities. One of these was the presence of small, light, portable rooms, *i.e.*, baseless boxes, which rolled over the instruments to protect them; two sides were of wood, and two sides of green silk curtains, which could, of course, be turned aside when the boxes, or little rooms, were rolled over the apparatus. Being covered in this way, the heavy shutters can be left open for weeks at a time.

" Everything was on a large scale — the rooms were immense.

" The director has three assistants who are called ' elder astronomers,' and two who are called ' adjunct astronomers.' Each of these has a servant devoted to him. I asked one of the elder astronomers if he had rooms in the observatory, and he answered, ' Yes, my rooms are 94 ft. by 50.'

" They seem to be amused at the size of their lodgings, for Mr. Struve, when he told me of his apartments, gave me at once the dimensions, — 200 ft. by 100 ft.

" The room in which we dined with the family of Herr Struve was immense. I spoke of it, and he said, ' We cannot open our windows in the winter, — the winters are so severe, — and so we must have good air without it.' Their drawing room was also very large; the chairs (innumerable, it seemed to me) stood stiffly around the walls of the room. The floor was painted and highly varnished, and flower-pots were at the numerous windows on little stands. It was scrupulously neat everywhere.

"There was very little ceremony at dinner; we had the delicious wild strawberries of the country in great profusion; and the talk, the best part of the dinner, was in German, Russian, and English.

"Madame Struve spoke German, Russian, and French, and complained that she could not speak English. She said that she had spent three weeks with an English lady, and that she must be very stupid not to speak English.

"I noticed that in one of the rooms, which was not so very immense, there was a circular table, a small centre-carpet, and chairs around the table; I have been told that 'in society' in Russia, the ladies sit in a circle, and the gentlemen walk around and talk consecutively with the ladies, — kindly giving to each a share of their attention.

"They assured me that the winters were charming, the sleighing constant, and the social gatherings cheery; but think of four hours, only, of daylight in the depth of the winter. Their dread was the spring and the autumn, when the mud is deep.

"Everything in the observatory which could be was built of wood. They have the fir, which is very indestructible; it is supposed to show no mark of change in two hundred years.

"Wood is so susceptible of ornamentation that the pretty villages of Russia — and there are some that look like New England villages — struck us very pleasantly, after the stone and brick villages of England.

"I try, when I am abroad, to see in what they are superior to us, — not in what they are inferior.

"Our great idea is, of course, freedom and self-government; probably in that we are ahead of the rest of the world, although we are certainly not so much in advance as we suppose; but we are sufficiently inflated with our own greatness to let that subject take care of itself when we travel. We travel to learn; and I have never been in any country where they did not do something better than we do it, think some thoughts better than we think, catch some inspiration from heights above our own — as in the art of Italy, the learning of England, and the philosophy of Germany.

"Let us take the scientific position of Russia. When, half a century ago, John Quincy Adams proposed the establishment of an astronomical observatory, at a cost of $100,000, it was ridiculed by the newspapers, considered Utopian, and dismissed from the public mind. When our government, a few years since, voted an appropriation of $50,000 for a telescope for the National Observatory, it was considered magnificent. Yet, a quarter of a century since (1838), Russia founded an astronomical observatory. The government spent $200,000 on instruments, $1,500,000 on buildings, and annually appropriated $38,000 for salaries of observers. I naturally thought that a million and a half dollars, and Oriental ideas, combined, would make the observatory a showy place; I expected that the observatory would be surmounted by a gilded dome, and that 'pearly gates' would open as I approached. There is not even a dome!

"The central observation-room is a cylinder, and its doors swing back on hinges. Wherever it is possible, wood is used, instead of stone or brick. I could not detect, in the whole structure, anything like carving, gilding, or painting, for mere show. It was all for science; and its ornamentations were adapted to its uses, and came at their demand.

"In our country, the man of science leads an isolated life. If he has capabilities of administration, our government does not yet believe in them.

"The director of the observatory at Pulkova has the military rank of general, and he is privy councillor to the czar. Every subordinate has also his military position — he is a soldier.

"What would you think of it, if the director of any observatory were one of the President's cabinet at Washington, in virtue of his position? Struve's position is that of a member of the President's cabinet.

"Here is another difference: Ours is a democratic country. We recognize no caste; we are born 'free and equal.' We honor labor; work is ennobling. These expressions we are all accustomed to use. Do we live up to them? Many a rich man, many a man in fine social position, has married a school-teacher; but I never heard it spoken of as a source of pride in the alliance until I went to despotic Russia. Struve told me, as he would have told of any other honor which had been his, that his wife, as a girl, had taught school in St. Petersburg. And then Madame Struve joined in the conversation, and told me how much the subject of woman's education still held her interest.

" St. Petersburg is about the size of Philadelphia. Struve said, ' There are thousands of women studying science in St. Petersburg.' How many thousand women do you suppose are studying science in the whole State of New York? I doubt if there are five hundred.

" Then again, as to language. It is rare, even among the common people, to meet one who speaks one language only. If you can speak no Russian, try your poor French, your poor German, or your good English. You may be sure that the shopkeeper will answer in one or another, and even the drosky-driver picks up a little of some one of them.

" Of late, the Russian government has founded a medical school for women, giving them advantages which are given to men, and the same rank when they graduate; the czar himself contributed largely to the fund.

" One wonders, in a country so rich as ours, that so few men and women gratify their tastes by founding scholarships and aids for the tuition of girls — it must be such a pleasant way of spending money.

" Then as regards religion. I am never in a country where the Catholic or Greek church is dominant, but I see with admiration the zeal of its followers. I may pity their delusions, but I must admire their devotion. If you look around in one of our churches upon the congregation, five-sixths are women, and in some towns nineteen-twentieths; and if you form a judgment from that fact, you would suppose that religion was entirely a 'woman's right.' In a Catholic church or Greek church, the men are not only as numerous as the women, but they are as intense in their worship. Well-dressed men, with good heads, will prostrate themselves before the image of the Holy Virgin as many times, and as devoutly, as the beggar-woman.

"I think I saw a Russian gentleman at St. Isaac's touch his forehead to the floor, rise and stand erect, touch the floor again, and rise again, ten times in as many minutes; and we were one day forbidden entrance to a church because the czar was about to say his prayers; we found he was making the pilgrimage of some seventy churches, and praying in each one.

"Christians who believe in public prayer, and who claim that we should be instant in prayer, would consider it a severe tax upon their energies to pray seventy times a day — they don't care to do it!

"Then there is the *democracy* of the church. There are no pews to be sold to the highest bidder — no 're-served seats;' the oneness and equality before God are always recognized. A Russian gentleman, as he prays, does not look around, and move away from the poor beggar next to him. At St. Peter's the crowd stands or kneels — at St. Isaac's they stand; and they stand literally on the same plane.

"I noticed in the crowd at St. Isaac's, one festival day, young girls who were having a friendly chat; but their religion was ever in their thoughts, and they crossed themselves certainly once a minute. Their religion is not an affair of Sunday, but of every day in the week.

"The drosky-driver, certainly the most stupid class of my acquaintance in Russia, never forgets his prayers; if his passenger is never so much in a hurry, and the bribe never so high, the drosky-driver will check his horse, and make the sign of the cross as he passes the little image of the Virgin, — so small, perhaps, that you have not noticed it until you wonder why he slackens his pace.

"Then as to government. We boast of our national freedom, and we talk about universal suffrage, the 'Home of the Free,' etc. Yet the serfs in Russia were freed in March, 1861, just before our Civil war began. They freed their serfs without any war, and each serf received some acres of land. They freed twenty-three millions, and we freed four or five millions of blacks; and all of us, who are old enough, remember that one of the fears in freeing the slaves was the number of lawless and ignorant blacks who, it was supposed, would come to the North.

"We talk about *universal* suffrage; a larger part of the antiquated Russians vote than of Americans. Just as I came away from St. Petersburg I met a Moscow family, travelling. We occupied the same compartment car. It was a family consisting of a lady and her three daughters. When they found where I had been, they asked me, in excellent English, what had carried me to St. Petersburg, and then, why I was interested in Pulkova; and so I must tell them about American girls, and so, of course, of Vassar College.

"They plied me with questions: 'Do you have women in your faculty? Do men and women hold the same rank?' I returned the questions: 'Is there a girl's college in Moscow?' 'No,' said the youngest sister, with a sigh, 'we are always *going* to have one.' The eldest sister asked: 'Do women vote in America?' 'No,' I said. 'Do women vote in Russia?' She said 'No;' but her mother interrupted her, and there was a spicy conversation between them, in Russian, and then the mother, who had rarely spoken, turned to me, and said: 'I vote, but I do not go to the polls myself. I send somebody to represent me; my vote rests upon my property.'

"Have you not read a story, of late, in the newspapers, about some excellent women in a little town in Connecticut whose pet heifers were taken by force and sold because they refused to pay the large taxes levied upon them by their townsmen, they being the largest holders of property in the town? That circumstance could not have happened in barbarous Russia; there, the owner of property has a right to say how it shall be used.

"'Why do you ask me about our government?' I said to the Russian girls. 'Are you interested in questions of government?' They replied, 'All Russian women are interested in questions of that sort.' How many American women are interested in questions concerning government?

"These young girls knew exactly what questions to ask about Vassar College, — the course of study, the diploma, the number of graduates, etc. The eldest said: 'We are at once excited when we hear of women studying; we have longed for opportunities to study all our lives. Our father was the engineer of the first Russian railroad, and he spent two years in America.'

"I confess to a feeling of mortification when one of these girls asked me, 'Did you ever read the translation of a Russian book?' and I was obliged to answer 'No.' This girl had read American books in the original. They were talking Russian, French, German, and English, and yet mourning over their need of education; and in general education, especially in that of women, I think we must be in advance of them.

"One of these sisters, forgetting my ignorance, said something to me in Russian. The other laughed. 'What did she say?' I asked. The eldest replied, 'She asked you to take her back with you, and educate her.' 'But,' I said, 'you read and speak your languages — the learning of the world is open to you — found your own college!' And the young girl leaned back on the cushions, drew her mantle around her, and said, 'We have not the energy of the American girl!'

"The energy of the American girl! The rich inheritance which has come down to her from men and women who sought, in the New World, a better and higher life.

"When the American girl carries her energy into the great questions of humanity, into the practical problems of life; when she takes home to her heart the interests of education, of government, and of religion, what may we not hope for our country!

London, 1873. "It was the 26th of August, and I had

no hope that Miss Cobbe could be at her town residence,
but I felt bound to deliver Mrs. Howe's letter, and I wished
to give her a Vassar pamphlet; so I took a cab and drove;
it was at an enormous distance from my lodging — she
told me it was six miles.   I was as much surprised as
delighted when the girl said she was at home, for the
house had painters in it, the carpets were up, and everything looked uninhabitable.   The girl came back, after
taking my card, and asked me if I would go into the
studio, and so took me through a pretty garden into a
small building of two rooms, the outer one filled with
pictures and books.   I had never heard that Miss Cobbe
was an artist, and so I looked around, and was afraid
that I had got the wrong Miss Cobbe.   But as I glanced
at the table I saw the 'Contemporary Review,' and I
took up the first article and read it — by Herbert
Spencer.   I had become somewhat interested in a
pretty severe criticism of the modes of reasoning of
mathematical men, and had perceived that he said the
problems of concrete sciences were harder than any of
the physical sciences (which I admitted was all true),
when a very white dog came bounding in upon me, and
I dropped the book, knowing that the dog's mistress
must be coming, — and Miss Cobbe entered. She looked
just as I expected, but even larger; but then her head
is magnificent because so large.   She was very cordial
at once, and told me that Miss Davies had told her I was
in London.   She said the studio was that of her friend.
I could not refrain from thanking her for her books, and
telling her how much we valued them in America, and
how much good I believed they had done. She colored

a very little, and said, 'Nothing could be more gratifying to me.'

"I had heard that she was not a women's rights
woman, and she said, 'Who could have told you that?
I am remarkably so. I write suffrage articles continually — I sign petitions.'

"I was delighted to find that she had been an intimate friend of Mrs. Somerville; had corresponded with
her for years, and had a letter from her after she was
ninety-two years of age, when she was reading Qua-
ternions for amusement. She said that Mrs. Somerville
would probably have called herself a Unitarian, but
that really she was a Theist, and that it came out more
in her later life. She said she was correcting proof of
the Life by the daughters; that the Life was intensely
interesting; that Mrs. Somerville mourned all her life
that she had not had the advantages of education.

"I asked her how I could get a photograph of Mrs.
Somerville, and she said they could not be bought.
She told me, without any hint from me, that she would
give Vassar College a plaster cast of the bust of Mrs.
Somerville.[1] She said, as women grew older, if they
lived independent lives, they were pretty sure to be
'women's rights women.' She said the clergy — the
broadest, who were in harmony with her — were very
courteous, and that since she had grown old (she's
about forty-five) all men were more tolerant of her and
forgot the difference of sex.

"I felt drawn to her when she was most serious. I
told her I had suffered much from doubt, and asked her

---

[1] This bust always stood in Miss Mitchell's parlor at the observatory.

if she had; and she said yes, when she was young; but that she had had, in her life, rare intervals when she believed she held communion with God, and on those rare periods she had rested in the long intermissions. She laughed, and the tears came to her eyes, all together; she was *quick*, and all-alive, and so courteous. When she gave me a book she said, ' May I write your whole name? and may I say " from your friend "? '

" Then she hurried on her bonnet, and walked to the station with me ; and her round face, with the blond hair and the light-blue eyes, seemed to me to become beautiful as she talked.

" In Edinburgh I asked for a photograph of Mary Somerville, and the young man behind the counter replied, ' I don't know who it is.'

" In London I asked at a bookstore, which the Murrays recommended, for a photograph of Mrs. Somerville and of Sir George Airy, and the man said if they could be had in London he would get them; and then he asked, ' Are they English?' and I informed him that Sir George Airy was the astronomer royal !

. . ..

" ' The Glasgow College for Girls.' Seeing a sign of this sort, I rang the door-bell of the house to which it was attached, entered, and was told the lady was at home. As I waited for her, I took up the ' Prospectus,' and it was enough, — ' music, dancing, drawing, needlework, and English' were the prominent features, and the pupils were children. All well enough, — but why call it a college?

"When the lady superintendent came in, I told her

that I had supposed it was for more advanced students, and she said, ' Oh, it is for girls up to twenty ; one supposes a girl is finished by twenty.'

" I asked, as modestly as I could, ' Have you any pupils in Latin and mathematics?' and she said, ' No, it's for girls, you know. Dr. M. hopes we shall have some mathematics next year.' ' And,' I asked, ' some Latin?' ' Yes, Dr. M. hopes we shall have some Latin ; but I confess I believe Latin and mathematics all bosh ; give them modern languages and accomplishments. I suppose your school is for professional women.'

" I told her no ; that the daughters of our wealthiest people demand learning ; that it would scarcely be considered ' good society ' when the women had neither Latin nor mathematics.

" ' Oh, well,' she said, ' they get married here so soon.'

" When I asked her if they had lady teachers, she said ' Oh, no [as if that would ruin the institution] ; nothing but first-class masters.'

" It was clear that the women taught the needle-work."

CHAPTER XI

PAPERS   SCIENCE [1874]   THE DENVER ECLIPSE [1878] —
COLORS OF STARS

"THE dissemination of information in regard to science and to scientific investigations relieves the scientist from the small annoyances of extreme ignorance.

"No one to-day will expect to receive a letter such as reached Sir John Herschel some years ago, asking for the writer's horoscope to be cast; or such as he received at another time, which asked, Shall I marry? and Have I seen *her?*

"Nor can it be long, if the whole population is somewhat educated, that I shall be likely to receive, as I have done, applications for information as to the recovery of stolen goods, or to tell fortunes.

"When crossing the Atlantic, an Irish woman came to me and asked me if I told fortunes; and when I replied in the negative, she asked me if I were not an astronomer. I admitted that I made efforts in that direction. She then asked me what I could tell, if not fortunes. I told her that I could tell when the moon would rise, when the sun would rise, etc. She said, 'Oh,' in a tone which plainly said, 'Is *that* all?'

"Only a few winters since, during a very mild winter, a young lad who was driving a team called out to me on the street, and said he had a question to ask me.

" I stopped; and he asked, ' Shall we lose our ice-crop this winter? '

" It was January, and it was New England. It took very little learning and no alchemy to foretell that the month of February and the neighborhood of Boston would give ice enough; and I told him that the ice-crop would be abundant; but I was honest enough to explain to him that my outlook into the future was no better than his.

" One of the unfavorable results of the attempt to popularize science is this : the reader of popular scientific books is very likely to think that he understands the science itself, when he merely understands what some writer says about science.

" Take, for example, the method of determining the distance of the moon from the earth — one of the easiest problems in physical astronomy. The method can be told in a few sentences; yet it took a hundred years to determine it with any degree of accuracy — and a hundred years, not of the average work of mankind in science, but a hundred years during which able minds were bent to the problem.

" Still, with all the school-masters, and all the teaching, and all the books, the ignorance of the unscientific world is enormous; they are ignorant both ways — they underrate the scientific people and they overrate them. There is, on the one hand, the Irish woman who is disappointed because you cannot tell fortunes, and, on the other hand, the cultivated woman who supposes that you must know *all* science.

" I have a friend who wonders that I do not take

my astronomical clock to pieces. She supposes that because I am an astronomer, I must be able to be a clock-maker, while I do not handle a tool if I can help it! She did not expect to take her piano to pieces because she was musical! She was as careful not to tinker it as I was not to tinker the clock, which only an expert in clock-making was prepared to handle.

" . . . Only a few weeks since I received a letter from a lady who wished to come to make me a visit, and to ' scan the heavens,' as she termed it. Now, just as she wrote, the clock, which I was careful not to meddle with, had been rapidly gaining time, and I was standing before it, watching it from hour to hour, and slightly changing its rate by dropping small weights upon its pendulum. Time is so important an element with the astronomer, that all else is subordinate to it.

" Then, too, the uneducated assume the unvarying exactness of mathematical results; while, in reality, mathematical results are often only approximations. We say the sun is 91,000,000 miles from the earth, plus or minus a probable error; that is, we are right, probably, within, say, 100,000 miles; or, the sun is 91,000,-000 minus 100,000 miles, or it is 91,000,000 plus 100,000 miles off; and this probable error is only a probability.

" If we make one more observation it cannot agree with any one of our determinations, and it changes our probable error.

" This ignorance of the masses leads to a misconception in two ways; the little that a scientist can do, they do not understand, — they suppose him to be godlike in his capacity, and they do not see results; they

BUST OF MARIA MITCHELL.

From Original made by Miss Emma F. Brigham in 1877

overrate him and they underrate him — they underrate his work.

"There is no observatory in this land, nor in any land, probably, of which the question is not asked, 'Are they doing anything? Why don't we hear from them? They should make discoveries, they should publish.'

"The one observation made at Greenwich on the planet Neptune was not published until after a century or more — it was recorded as a star. The observation had to wait a hundred years, about, before the time had come when that evening's work should bear fruit; but it was good, faithful work, and its time came.

"Kepler was years in passing from one of his laws to another, while the school-boy, to-day, rattles off the three as if they were born of one breath.

"The scientist should be free to pursue his investigations. He cannot be a scientist and a school-master. If he pursues his science in all his intervals from his class-work, his classes suffer on account of his engrossments; if he devotes himself to his students, science suffers; and yet we all go on, year after year, trying to work the two fields together, and they need different culture and different implements.

"1878. In the eclipse of this year, the dark shadow fell first on the United States thirty-eight degrees west of Washington, and moved towards the south-east, a circle of darkness one hundred and sixteen miles in diameter; circle overlapping circle of darkness until it could be mapped down like a belt.

"The mapping of the dark shadow, with its limitations of one hundred and sixteen miles, lay across the country from Montana, through Colorado, northern and eastern Texas, and entered the Gulf of Mexico between Galveston and New Orleans. This was the region of total eclipse. Looking along this dark strip on the map, each astronomer selected his bit of darkness on which to locate the light of science.

" But for the distance from the large cities of the country, Colorado seemed to be a most favorable part of the shadow; it was little subject to storms, and reputed to be enjoyable in climate and abundant in hospitality.

" My party chose Denver, Col. I had a friend who lived in Denver, and she was visiting me. I sought her at once, and with fear and trembling asked, ' Have you a bit of land behind your house in Denver where I could put up a *small* telescope?' 'Six hundred miles,' was the laconic reply !

" I felt that the hospitality of the Rocky mountains was at my feet. Space and time are so unconnected ! For an observation which would last two minutes forty seconds, I was offered six hundred miles, after a journey of thousands.

" A journey from Boston to Denver makes one hopeful for the future of our country. We had hour after hour and day after day of railroad travel, over level, unbroken land on which cattle fed unprotected, summer and winter, and which seemed to implore the traveller to stay and to accept its richness. It must be centuries before the now unpeopled land of western Kansas and Colorado can be crowded.

"We started from Boston a party of two; at Cincinnati a third joined us; at Kansas City we came upon a fourth who was ready to fall into our ranks, and at Denver two more awaited us; so we were a party of six — 'All good women and true.'

"All along the road it had been evident that the country was roused to a knowledge of the coming eclipse; we overheard remarks about it; small telescopes travelled with us, and our landlord at Kansas City, when I asked him to take care of a chronometer, said he had taken care of fifty of them in the previous fortnight. Our party had three telescopes and one chronometer.

"We had travelled so comfortably all along the Santa Fe road, from Kansas City to Pueblo, that we had forgotten the possibility of other railroad annoyances than those of heat and dust until we reached Pueblo. At Pueblo all seemed to change. We left the Santa Fe road and entered upon that of the Rio Grande.

"Which road was to blame, it is not for me to say, but there was trouble at once about our 'round-trip ticket.' That settled, we supposed all was right.

"In sending out telescopes so far as from Boston to Denver, I had carefully taken out the glasses, and packed them in my trunks. I carried the chronometer in my hand.

"It was only five hours' travel from Pueblo to Denver, and we went on to that city. The trunks, for some unexplained reason, or for no reason at all, chose to remain at Pueblo.

"One telescope-tube reached Denver when we did;

but a telescope-tube is of no value without glasses. We learned that there was a war between the two railroads which unite at Pueblo, and war, no matter where or when it occurs, means ignorance and stupidity.

"The unit of measure of value which the railroad man believes in is entirely different from that in which the scientist rests his faith.

"A war between two railroads seemed very small compared with two minutes forty seconds of observation of a total eclipse. One was terrestrial, the other cosmic.

"It was Wednesday when we reached Denver. The eclipse was to occur the following Monday.

"We haunted the telegraph-rooms, and sent imploring messages. We placed ourselves at the station, and watched the trains as they tossed out their freight; we listened to every express-wagon which passed our door without stopping, and just as we were trying to find if a telescope could be hired or bought in Denver, the glasses arrived.

"It was now Friday; we must put up tents and telescopes, and test the glasses.

"It rained hard on Friday — nothing could be done. It rained harder on Saturday. It rained hardest of all on Sunday, and hail mingled with the rain. But Monday morning was clear and bright. It was strange enough to find that we might camp anywhere around Denver. Our hostess suggested to us to place ourselves on 'McCullough's Addition.' In New York or Boston, if I were about to camp on private grounds I should certainly ask permission. In the far West you choose your spot of ground, you dig post-holes and you pitch tents, and you set up telescopes and inhabit the land; and then the owner of the land comes to you, and asks if he may not put up a fence for you, to keep off intruders, and the nearest residents come to you and offer aid of any kind.

" Our camping-place was near the house occupied by sisters of charity, and the black-robed, sweet-faced women came out to offer us the refreshing cup of tea and the new-made bread.

" All that we needed was ' space,' and of that there was plenty.

" Our tents being up and the telescopes mounted, we had time to look around at the view. The space had the unlimitedness that we usually connect with sea and sky. Our tents were on the slope of a hill, at the foot of which we were about six thousand feet above the sea. The plain was three times as high as the hills of the Hudson-river region, and there arose on the south, almost from west to east, the peaks upon peaks of the Rocky mountains. One needs to live upon such a plateau for weeks, to take in the grandeur of the panorama.

" It is always difficult to teach the man of the people that natural phenomena belong as much to him as to scientific people. Camping parties who put up telescopes are always supposed to be corporations with particular privileges, and curious lookers-on gather around, and try to enter what they consider a charmed circle. We were remarkably free from specialists of this kind. Camping on the south-west slope of the hill, we were hidden on the north and east, and another party which chose the brow of the hill was much more attractive to the crowd. Our good serving-man was told to send away the few strollers who approached; even our friends from the city were asked to remove beyond the reach of voice.

"There is always some one to be found in every gathering who will not submit to law. At the time of the total eclipse in Iowa, in 1869, there passed in and out among our telescopes and observers an unknown, closely veiled woman. The remembrance of that occasion never comes to my mind without the accompaniment of a fluttering green veil.

"This time it was a man. How he came among us and why he remained, no one can say. Each one supposed that the others knew, and that there was good reason for his presence. If I was under the tent, wiping glasses, he stood beside me; if the photographer wished to make a picture of the party, this man came to the front; and when I asked the servant to send off the half-vagrant boys and girls who stood gazing at us, this man came up and said to me in a confidential tone, 'They do not understand the sacredness of the occasion, and the fineness of the conditions.' There was something regal in his audacity, but he was none the less a tramp.

"Persons who observe an eclipse of the sun always try to do the impossible. They seem to consider it a solemn duty to see the first contact of sun and moon. The moon, when seen in the daytime, looks like a small faint cloud; as it approaches the sun it becomes

wholly unseen; and an observer tries to see when
this unseen object touches the glowing disc of the
sun.

" When we look at any other object than the sun, we
stimulate our vision. A good observer will remain in
the dark for a short time before he makes a delicate
observation on a faint star, and will then throw a cap
over his head to keep out strong lights.

" When we look at the sun, we at once try to deaden
its light. We protect our eyes by dark glasses — the
less of sunlight we can get the better. We calculate
exactly at what point the moon will touch the sun, and
we watch that point only. The exact second by the
chronometer when the figure of the moon touches that
of the sun, is always noted. It is not only valuable for
the determination of longitude, but it is a check on our
knowledge of the moon's motions. Therefore, we try
for the impossible.

" One of our party, a young lady from California, was
placed at the chronometer. She was to count aloud
the seconds, to which the three others were to listen.
Two others, one a young woman from Missouri, who
brought with her a fine telescope, and another from
Ohio, besides myself, stood at the three telescopes. A
fourth, from Illinois, was stationed to watch general
effects, and one special artist, pencil in hand, to sketch
views.

" Absolute silence was imposed upon the whole party
a few minutes before each phenomenon.

" Of course we began full a minute too soon, and the
constrained position was irksome enough, for even time

is relative, and the minute of suspense is longer than
the hour of satisfaction.[1]

"The moon, so white in the sky, becomes densely
black when it is closely ranging with the sun, and it
shows itself as a black notch on the burning disc when
the eclipse begins.

"Each observer made her record in silence, and then
we turned and faced one another, with record in hand
— we differed more than a second; it was a large
difference.

"Between first contact and totality there was more
than an hour, and we had little to do but look at the
beautiful scenery and watch the slow motion of a few
clouds, on a height which was cloud-land to dwellers
by the sea.

"Our photographer begged us to keep our positions
while he made a picture of us. The only value to the
picture is the record that it preserves of the parallelism
of the three telescopes. You would say it was stiff
and unnatural, did you not know that it was the ordering
of Nature herself — they all point to the centre of the
solar system.

"As totality approached, all again took their positions. The corona, which is the 'glory' seen around
the sun, was visible at least thirteen minutes before totality; each of the party took a look at this, and then all
was silent, only the count, on and on, of the young

---

[1] As the computed time for the first contact drew near, the breath of the
counter grew short, and the seconds were almost gasped and threatened to
become inaudible, when Miss Mitchell, without moving her eye from the tube
of the telescope, took up the counting, and continued until the young lady
recovered herself, which she did immediately.

woman at the chronometer. When totality came, even that ceased.

" How still it was !

" As the last rays of sunlight disappeared, the corona burst out all around the sun, so intensely bright near the sun that the eye could scarcely bear it; extending less dazzlingly bright around the sun for the space of about half the sun's diameter, and in some directions sending off streamers for millions of miles.

" It was now quick work. Each observer at the telescopes gave a furtive glance at the un-sunlike sun, moved the dark eye-piece from the instrument, replaced it by a more powerful white glass, and prepared to see all that could be seen in two minutes forty seconds. They must note the shape of the corona, its color, its seeming substance, and they must look all around the sun for the 'interior planet.'

" There was certainly not the beauty of the eclipse of 1869. Then immense radiations shot out in all directions, and threw themselves over half the sky. In 1869, the rosy prominences were so many, so brilliant, so fantastic, so weirdly changing, that the eye must follow them; now, scarcely a protuberance of color, only a roseate light around the sun as the totality ended. But if streamers and prominences were absent, the corona itself was a great glory. Our special artist, who made the sketch for my party, could not bear the light.

" When the two minutes forty seconds were over, each observer left her instrument, turned in silence from the sun, and wrote down brief notes. Happily, some one broke through all rules of order, and shouted out, ' The shadow! the shadow!' And looking toward the south-east we saw the black band of shadow moving from us, a hundred and sixty miles over the plain, and toward the Indian Territory. It was not the flitting of the closer shadow over the hill and dale: it was a picture which the sun threw at our feet of the dignified march of the moon in its orbit.

"And now we looked around. What a strange orange light there was in the north-east! what a spectral hue to the whole landscape! Was it really the same old earth, and not another planet?

"Great is the self-denial of those who follow science. They who look through telescopes at the time of a total eclipse are martyrs; they severely deny themselves. The persons who can say that they have seen a total eclipse of the sun are those who rely upon their eyes. My aids, who touched no glasses, had a season of rare enjoyment. They saw Mercury, with its gleam of white light, and Mars, with its ruddy glow; they saw Regulus come out of the darkening blue on one side of the sun, Venus shimmer and Procyon twinkle near the horizon, and Arcturus shine down from the zenith.

"*We* saw the giant shadow as it *left* us and passed over the lands of the untutored Indian; *they* saw it as it approached from the distant west, as it fell upon the peaks of the mountain-tops, and, in the impressive still-ness, moved directly for our camping-ground.

"The savage, to whom it is the frowning of the Great Spirit, is awe-struck and alarmed; the scholar, to whom it is a token of the inviolability of law, is serious and reverent.

"There is a dialogue in some of the old school-readers, and perhaps in some of the new, between a tutor and his two pupils who had been out for a walk. One pupil complained that the way was long, the road was dusty, and the scenery uninteresting; the other was full of delight at the beauties he had found in the same walk. One had walked with his eyes intellectually closed; the other had opened his eyes wide to all the charms of nature. In some respects we are all, at different times, like each of these boys: we shut our eyes to the enjoyments of nature, or we open them. But we are capable of improving ourselves, even in the use of our eyes — we see most when we are most determined to see. The *will* has a wonderful effect upon the perceptive faculties. When we first look up at the myriads of stars seen in a moonless evening, all is confusion to us; we admire their brilliancy, but we scarcely recognize their grouping. We do not feel the need of knowing much about them.

"A traveller, lost on a desert plain, feels that the recognition of one star, the Pole star, is of itself a great acquisition; and all persons who, like mariners and soldiers, are left much with the companionship of the stars, only learn to know the prominent clusters, even if they do not know the names given to them in books.

"The daily wants of the body do not require that we should say

'Give me the ways of wandering stars to know
The depths of heaven above and earth below.'

But we have a hunger of the mind which asks for

knowledge of all around us, and the more we gain, the
more is our desire; the more we see, the more are we
capable of seeing.

"Besides learning to see, there is another art to be
learned, — *not to see* what is not.

"If we read in to-day's paper that a brilliant comet
was seen last night in New York, we are very likely to
see it to-night in Boston; for we take every long,
fleecy cloud for a splendid comet.

"When the comet of 1680 was expected, a few years
ago, to reappear, some young men in Cambridge told
Professor Bond that they had seen it; but Professor
Bond did not see it.   Continually are amateurs in
astronomy sending notes of new discoveries to Bond,
or some other astronomers, which are no discoveries
at all!

"Astronomers have long supposed the existence of a
planet inferior to Mercury; and M. Leverrier has, by
mathematical calculation, demonstrated that such a
planet exists.   He founded his calculations upon the
supposed discovery of M. Lesbarcault, who declares
that it crossed the sun's disc, and that he saw it and
made drawings.   The internal evidence, from the man's
account, is that he was an honest enthusiast.   I have
no doubt that he followed the path of a solar spot,
and as the sun turned on its axis he mistook the
motion for that of the dark spot; or perhaps the spot
changed and became extinct, and another spot closely
resembling it broke out and he was deceived; his
wishes all the time being 'father to the thought.'

"The eye is as teachable as the hand.   Every one

knows the most prominent constellations, — the Pleiades,
the Great Bear, and Orion.   Many persons can draw the
figures made by the most brilliant stars in these constellations, and very many young people look for the
' lost Pleiad.'   But common observers know these stars
only as bright objects ; they do not perceive that one
star differs from another in glory ; much less do they
perceive that they shine with differently colored rays.

"Those who know Sirius and Betel do not at once
perceive that one shines with a brilliant white light and
the other burns with a glowing red, as different in their
brilliancy as the precious stones on a lapidary's table,
perhaps for the same reason.   And so there is an endless variety of tints of paler colors.

"We may turn our gaze as we turn a kaleidoscope,
and the changes are infinitely more startling, the com-
binations infinitely more beautiful ; no flower garden
presents such a variety and such delicacy of shades.

"But beautiful as this variety is, it is difficult to
measure it ; it has a phantom-like intangibility — we
seem not to be able to bring it under the laws of
science.

"We call the stars garnet and sapphire ; but these
are, at best, vague terms.   Our language has not terms
enough to signify the different delicate shades ; our
factories have not the stuff whose hues might make a
chromatic scale for them.

"In this dilemma, we might make a scale of colors
from the stars themselves.   We might put at the head
of the scale of crimson stars the one known as Hind's,
which is four degrees west of Rigel ; we might make

a scale of orange stars, beginning with Betel as orange
red; then we should have

Betelgeuze,

Aldebaran,

β Ursae Minoris,

. Altair and a Canis,

a Lyrae,

the list gradually growing paler and paler, until we
come to a Lyrae, which might be the leader of a host
of pale yellow stars, gradually fading off into white.

" Most of the stars seen with the naked eye are varieties of red, orange, and yellow. The reds, when seen
with a glass, reach to violet or dark purple. With a
glass, there come out other colors: very decided
greens, very delicate blues, browns, grays, and white.
If these colors are almost intangible at best, they are
rendered more so by the variations of the atmosphere,
of the eye, and of the glass. But after these are all
accounted for, there is still a real difference. Two
stars of the class known as double stars, that is, so
little separated that considerable optical power is necessary to divide them, show these different tints very
nicely in the same field of the telescope.

" Then there comes in the chance that the colors
are complementary; that the eye, fatigued by a brilliant
red in the principal star, gives to the companion the
color which would make up white light. This happens
sometimes; but beyond this the reare innumerable cases
of finely contrasted colors which are not complementary,
but which show a real difference of light in the stars;
resulting, perhaps, from distance, — for some colors

travel farther than others, and all colors differ in their order of march, — perhaps from chemical differences.

" Single blue or green stars are never seen ; they are always given as the smaller companion of a pair.

" Out of several hundred observed by Mr. Bishop, forty-five have small companions of a bluish, or greenish, or purplish color. Almost all of these are stars of the eighth to tenth magnitude; only once are both seen blue, and only in one case is the large one blue. In almost every case the large star is yellow. The color most prevailing is yellow; but the varieties of yellow are very great.

" We may assume, then, that the blue stars are faint ones, and probably distant ones. But as not all faint stars or distant ones are blue, it shows that there is a real difference. In the star called 35 Piscium, the small star shows a peculiar snuffy-brown tinge.

" Of two stars in the constellation Ursa Minoris, not double stars, one is orange and the other is green, both very vivid in color.

" From age to age the colors of some prominent stars have certainly changed. This would seem more likely to be from change of place than of physical constitution.

" Nothing comes out more clearly in astronomical observations than the immense activity of the universe. ' All change, no loss, 'tis revolution all.'

" Observations of this kind are peculiarly adapted to women. Indeed, all astronomical observing seems to be so fitted. The training of a girl fits her for delicate work. The touch of her fingers upon the delicate screws of an astronomical instrument might become

wonderfully accurate in results; a woman's eyes are
trained to nicety of color. The eye that directs a needle
in the delicate meshes of embroidery will equally well
bisect a star with the spider web of the micrometer.
Routine observations, too, dull as they are, are less
dull than the endless repetition of the same pattern in
crochet-work.

"Professor Chauvenet enumerates among 'accidental
errors in observing,' those arising from imperfections
in the senses, as 'the imperfection of the eye in measuring small spaces; of the ear, in estimating small intervals of time; of the touch, in the delicate handling of an
instrument.'

"A girl's eye is trained from early childhood to be
keen. The first stitches of the sewing-work of a little
child are about as good as those of the mature man.
The taking of small stitches, involving minute and
equable measurements of space, is a part of every girl's
training; she becomes skilled, before she is aware of it,
in one of the nicest peculiarities of astronomical observation.

"The ear of a child is less trained, except in the case
of a musical education; but the touch is a delicate sense
given in exquisite degree to a girl, and her training
comes in to its aid. She threads a needle almost as
soon as she speaks; she touches threads as delicate as
the spider-web of a micrometer.

"Then comes in the girl's habit of patient and quiet
work, peculiarly fitted to routine observations. The
girl who can stitch from morning to night would find
two or three hours in the observatory a relief."

CHAPTER XII

RELIGIOUS BELIEFS   COMMENTS ON SERMONS   CONCORD SCHOOL
— WHITTIER   COOKING SCHOOLS   ANECDOTES

PARTLY in consequence of her Quaker training, and
partly from her own indifference towards creeds and
sects, Miss Mitchell was entirely ignorant of the peculiar phrases and customs used by rigid sectarians; so
that she was apt to open her eyes in astonishment at
some of the remarks and sectarian prejudices which
she met after her settlement at Vassar College. She
was a good learner, however, and after a while knew
how to receive in silence that which she did not understand.

" Miss Mitchell," asked one good missionary, " what
is your favorite position in prayer? "   " Flat upon my
back! " the answer came, swift as lightning.

In 1854 she wrote in her diary:

"There is a God, and he is good, I say to myself.
I try to increase my trust in this, my only article of
creed."

Miss Mitchell never joined any church, but for years
before she left Nantucket she attended the Unitarian
church, and her sympathies, as long as she lived, were
with that denomination, especially with the more liber-
ally inclined portion. There were always a few of the
teachers and some of the students who sympathized

with her in her views; but she usually attended the college services on Sunday.

President Taylor, of Vassar College, in his remarks at her funeral, stated that all her life Professor Mitchell had been seeking the truth, — that she was not willing to accept any statement without studying into the matter herself, — " And," he added, " I think she has found the truth she was seeking."

Miss Mitchell never obtruded her views upon others, nor did she oppose their views. She bore in silence what she could not believe, but always insisted upon the right of private judgment.

Miss W., a teacher at Vassar, was fretting at being obliged to attend chapel exercises twice a day when she needed the time for rest and recreation, and applied to Miss Mitchell for help in getting away from it. After some talk Miss Mitchell said: " Oh, well, do as *I* do — sit back folding your arms, and think of something pleasant ! "

" Sunday, Dec. 18, 1866. We heard two sermons: the first in the afternoon, by Rev. Mr. A., Baptist, the second in the evening, by Rev. Mr. B., Congregationalist.

" Rev. Mr. A. took a text from Deuteronomy, about ' Moses; ' Rev. Mr. B. took a text from Exodus, about ' Moses;' and I am told that the sermon on the preceding Sunday was about Moses.

" It seems to me strange that since we have the history of Christ in the New Testament, people continue to preach about Moses.

" Rev. Mr. A. was a man of about forty years of age. He chanted rather than read a hymn. He chanted a sermon. His description of the journey of Moses towards Canaan had some interesting points, but his manner was affected; he cried, or pretended to cry, at the pathetic points. I hope he really cried, for a weakness is better than an affectation of weakness. He said, ' The unbeliever is already condemned.' It seems to me that if anything would make me an infidel, it would be the threats lavished against unbelief.

" Mr. B. is a self-made man, the son of a blacksmith. He brought the anvil, the hammer, and bellows into the pulpit, and he pounded and blew, for he was in earnest. I felt the more respect for him because he was in earnest. But when he snapped his fingers and said, ' I don't care *that* for the religion of a man which does not begin with prayer,' I was provoked at his forgetfulness of the character of his audience.

" 1867. I am more and more disgusted with the preaching that I hear! . . . Why cannot a man act himself, be himself, and think for himself ? It seems to me that naturalness alone is power; that a borrowed word is weaker than our own weakness, however small we may be. If I reach a girl's heart or head, I know I must reach it through my own, and not from bigger hearts and heads than mine.

" March, 1873. There was something so genuine and so sincere in George Macdonald that he took those of us who were *emotional* completely — not by storm so much as by gentle breezes. . . . What he said wasn't profound except as it reached the depths of the heart. . . . He gave us such broad theological lessons! In his sermon he said, ' Don't trouble your-

self about what you *believe*, but *do* the will of God.'
His consciousness of the existence of God and of his
immediate supervision was felt every minute by those who
listened.   .   .   .

"He stayed several days at the college, and the girls
will never get over the good effects of those three days
— the cheerier views of life and death.

".   .   .   Rev. Dr. Peabody preached for us yesterday,
and was lovely.   Every one was charmed in spite of his
old-fashioned ways.   His voice is very bad, but it was
such a simple, common-sense discourse!   Mr. Vassar
said if that was Unitarianism, it was just the right thing.

"Aug. 29, 1875.   Went to a Baptist church, and
heard Rev. Mr. F.   'Christ the way, the only way.'
The sermon was wholly without logic, and yet he said,
near its close, that those who had followed him must
be convinced that this was true.   He said a traveller
whom he met on the cars admitted that we all desired
heaven, but believed that there were as many ways to
it as to Boston.   Mr. F. said that God had prepared
but one way, just as the government in those countries
of the Old World whose cities were upon almost inac-
cessible pinnacles had prepared one way of approach.
(It occurred to me that if those governments possessed
godlike powers, they would have made a great many
ways.)

"Mr. F. was very severe upon those who expect to
be saved by their own deserts.   He said, 'You tender
a farthing, when you owe a million.'   I could not see
what they owed at all!   At this point he might well have
given some attention to 'good works;' and if he must

mention ' debt,' he might well remind them that they sat in an unpaid-for church!

"It was plain that he relied upon his anecdotes for the hold upon his audience, and the anecdotes were attached to the main discourse by a very slender thread of connection. I felt really sad to know that not a listener would lead a better life for that sermon — no man or woman went out cheered, or comforted, or stimulated.

" On the whole, it is strange that people who go to church are no worse than they are!

"Sept. 26, 1880. A clergyman said, in his sermon, ' I do not say with the Frenchman, if there were no God it would be well to invent one, but I say, if there were no future state of rewards and punishments, it would be better to believe in one.' Did he mean to say, ' Better to believe a lie'?

" March 27, 1881. Dr. Lyman Abbott preached. I was surprised to find how liberal Congregational preaching had become, for he said he hoped and expected to see women at the bar and in the pulpit, although he believed they would always be exceptional cases. He preached mainly on the motherhood of God, and his whole sermon was a tribute to womanhood. . . . I rejoice at the ideal womanhood of purity which he put before the girls. I wish some one would preach purity to young men.

"July 1, 1883. I went to hear Rev. Mr. —— at the Universalist church. He enumerated some of the dangers that threaten us: one was ' The doctrines of scientists,' and he named Tyndale, Huxley, and Spencer. I was most surprised at his fear of these men. Can the study of truth do harm?   Does not every true scientist seek only to know the truth?   And in our deep ignorance of what is truth, shall we dread the search for it?

"I hold the simple student of nature in holy reverence; and while there live sensualists, despots, and men who are wholly self-seeking, I cannot bear to have these sincere workers held up in the least degree to reproach.   And let us have truth, even if the truth be the awful denial of the good God.   We must face the light and not bury our heads in the earth.   I am hopeful that scientific investigation, pushed on and on, will reveal new ways in which God works, and bring to us deeper revelations of the wholly unknown.

"The physical and the spiritual seem to be, at present, separated by an impassable gulf; but at any moment that gulf may be overleaped — possibly a new revelation may come.   .   .   .

"April, 1878.   I called on Professor Henry at the Smithsonian Institute.   He must be in his eightieth year; he has been ill and seems feeble, but he is still the majestic old man, unbent in figure and undimmed in eye.

"I always remember, when I see him, the remark of Dorothy Dix, 'He is the truest man that ever lived.'

"We were left alone for a little while, and he introduced the subject of his nearness to death.   He said, 'The National Academy has raised $40,000, the interest of which is for myself and family as long as any of us live [he has daughters only], and in view of my death it is a great comfort to me.'   I ventured to ask him if he feared death at all.   He said, 'Not in the least; I have thought of it a great deal, and have come to feel it a friend. I *cherish* the belief in immortality; I have suffered much, at times, in regard to that matter.' Scientifically considered, only, he thought the probability was on the side of continued existence, as we must believe that spirit existed independent of matter.

"He went to a desk and pulled out from a drawer an old copy of ' Gregory's Astronomy,' and said, ' That book changed my whole life — I read it when I was sixteen years old; I had read, previously, works of the imagination only, and at sixteen, being ill in bed, that book was near me; I read it, and determined to study science.' I asked him if a life of science was a good life, and he said that he felt that it was so.

". . . When I was travelling with Miss S., who was near-sighted and kept her eyes constantly half-shut, it seemed to me that every other young lady I met had wide, staring eyes. Now, after two years sitting by a person who never reasons, it strikes me that every other person whom I meet has been thinking hard, and his logic stands out a prominent characteristic.

" Aug. 27, 1879. Scientific Association met at Saratoga. . . . Professor Peirce, now over seventy years old, was much the same as ever. He went on in the cars with us, and was reading Mallock's ' Is Life Worth Living?' and I asked, ' Is it?' to which Professor Peirce replied, ' Yes, I think it is.' Then I asked, ' If there is no future state, is life worth living?' He replied, ' Indeed it is not; life is a cruel tragedy if there is no immortality.' I asked him if he conceived

of the future life as one of embodiment, and he said
'Yes; I believe with St Paul that there is a spiritual
body. . . .'

"Professor Peirce's paper was on the 'Heat of the
Sun;' he considers the sun fed not by impact of
meteors, but by the compression of meteors. I did not
think it very sound. He said some good things:
'Where the truth demands, accept; what the truth
denies, reject.'

"Concord, Mass., 1879. To establish a school of
philosophy had been the dream of Alcott's life; and there
he sat as I entered the vestry of a church on one of the
hottest days in August. He looked full as young as he
did twenty years ago, when he gave us a 'conversation'
in Lynn. "Elizabeth Peabody came into the room,
and walked up to the seat of the rulers; her white hair
streamed over her shoulders in wild carelessness, and
she was as careless as ever about her whole attire, but
it was beautiful to see the attention shown to her by
Mr. Alcott and Mr. Sanborn.

"Emerson entered, — pale, thin, almost ethereal in
countenance, — followed by his daughter, who sat beside him and watched every word that he uttered. On
the whole, it was the same Emerson — he stumbled at
a quotation as he always did; but his thoughts were
such as only Emerson could have thought, and the
sentences had the Emersonian pithiness. He made his
frequent sentences very emphatic. It was impossible
to see any thread of connection; but it always was so —
the oracular sentences made the charm. The subject
was 'Memory.' He said, 'We remember the selfish-

ness or the wrong act that we have committed for years. It is as it should be — Memory is the police-officer of the universe.' 'Architects say that the arch never rests, and so the past never rests.' (Was it, never sleeps?) 'When I talk with my friend who is a genealogist, I feel that I am talking with a ghost.'

"The little vestry, fitted perhaps for a hundred people, was packed with two hundred, — all people of an intellectual cast of face, — and the attention was intense. The thermometer was ninety in the shade!

"I did not speak to Mr. Emerson; I felt that I must not give him a bit of extra fatigue.

"July 12, 1880. The school of philosophy has built a shanty for its meetings, but it is a shanty to be proud of, for it is exactly adapted to its needs. It is a long but not low building, entirely without finish, but water-tight. A porch for entrance, and a recess similar at the opposite end, which makes the place for the speakers. There was a small table upon the platform on which were pond lilies, some shelves around, and a few busts — one of Socrates, I think.

"I went in the evening to hear Dr. Harris on 'Philosophy.' The rain began to come down soon after I entered, and my philosophy was not sufficient to keep me from the knowledge that I had neither overshoes nor umbrella; I remembered, too, that it was but a narrow foot-path through the wet grass to the omnibus. But I listened to Dr. Harris, and enjoyed it. He lauded Fichte as the most accurate philosopher following Kant — he said not of the greatest *breadth*, but the most acute.

"After Dr. Harris' address, Mr. Alcott made a few remarks that were excellent, and said that when we had studied philosophy for fifteen years, as the lecturer had done, we might know something; but as it was, he had pulled.us to pieces and then put us together again.

"The audience numbered sixty persons.

"May, 1880. I have just finished Miss Peabody's account of Channing. I have been more interested in Miss Peabody than in Channing, and have felt how valuable she must have been to him. How many of Channing's sermons were instigated by her questions! . . . Miss Peabody must have been very remarkable as a young woman to ask the questions which she asked at twenty.

"April, 1881. The waste of flowers on Easter Sunday distressed me. Something is due to the flowers themselves. They are massed together like a bushel of corn, and look like red and white sugar-plums as seen in a confectioner's window.

"A pillow of flowers is a monstrosity. A calla lily in a vase is a beautiful creation; so is a single rose. But when the rose is crushed by a pink on each side of it, and daisies crush the pinks, and azaleas surround the daisies, there is no beauty and no fitness.

"The cathedral had no flowers.

"Aug. 22, 1882. We visited Whittier; we found him at lunch, but he soon came into the parlor. He was very chatty, and seemed glad to see us. Mrs. L. was with me, and Whittier was very ready to write in the album which she brought with her, belonging to her adopted son. We drifted upon theological subjects, and I asked Mr. Whittier if he thought that we fell from a state of innocence; he replied that he thought we were better than Adam and Eve, and if they fell, they 'fell up.'

"His faith seems to be unbounded in the goodness of God, and his belief in moral accountability. He said, 'I am a good deal of a Quaker in my conviction that a light comes to me to dictate to me what is right.' We stayed about an hour, and we were afraid it would be too much for him; but Miss Johnson, his cousin, who lives with him, assured us that it was good for him; and he himself said that he was sorry to have us go.

"One thing that he said, I noted: that his fancy was for farm-work, but he was not strong enough; he had as a young man some literary ambition, but never thought of attaining the reputation which had come to him.

"July 31, 1883. I have had two or three rich days! On Friday last I went to Holderness, N.H., to the Asquam House; I had been asked by Mrs. T. to join her party. There were at this house Mr. Whittier, Mr. and Mrs. Cartland, Professor and Mrs. Johnson, of Yale, Mr. Williams, the Chinese scholar, his brother, an Episcopal clergyman, and several others. The house seemed full of fine, cultivated people. We stayed two days and a half.

"And first of the scenery. The road up to the house is a steep hill, and at the foot of the hill it winds and turns around two lakes. The panorama is complete one hundred and eighty degrees. Beyond the lakes lie the mountains. We do not see Mt. Washington. The house has a piazza nearly all around it. We had a room on the first floor — large, and with two windows opening to the floor.

"The programme of the day's work was delightfully monotonous. For an hour or so after breakfast we sat in the ladies' parlor, we sewed, and we told anecdotes. Whittier talked beautifully, almost always on the future state and his confidence in it. Occasionally he touched upon persons. He seems to have loved Lydia Maria Child greatly.

"When the cool of the morning was over, we went out upon the piazza, and later on we went under the trees, where, it is said, Whittier spends most of the time.

"There was little of the old-time theology in his views; his faith has been always very firm. Mr. Cartland asked me one day if I really felt there was any doubt of the immortality of the soul. I told him that on the whole I believed it more than I doubted it, but I could not say that I felt no doubt. Whittier asked me if there were no immortality if I should be distressed by it, and I told him that I should be exceedingly distressed; that it was the only thing that I craved. He said that 'annihilation was better for the wicked than everlasting punishment,' and to that I assented. He said that he thought there might be persons so depraved as not to be worth saving. I asked him if God made such. Nobody seemed ready to reply. Besides myself there was another of the party to whom a dying friend had promised to return, if possible, but had not come.

"Whittier believed that they did sometimes come. He said that of all whom he had lost, no one would be so welcome to him as Lydia Maria Child.

"We held a little service in the parlor of the hotel, and Mrs. C. read the fourteenth chapter of John. Rev. Mr. W. read a sermon from 'The pure in heart shall see God,' written by Parkhurst, of New York. He thought the child should be told that in heaven he should have his hobby-horse. After the service, when we talked it over, I objected to telling the child this. Whittier did not object; he said that Luther told his little boy that he should have a little dog with a golden tail in heaven.

"Aug. 26, 1886. I have been to see an exhibition of a cooking school. I found sixteen girls in the basement of a school-house. They had long tables, across which stretched a line of gas-stoves and jets of gas. Some of the girls were using saucepans; they set them upon the stove, and then sat down where they could see a clock while the boiling process went on.

"At one table a girl was cutting out doughnuts; at another a girl was making a pudding — a layer of bits of bread followed by a layer of fruit. Each girl had her rolling-pin, and moulding-board or saucepan.

"The chief peculiarity of these processes was the cleanliness. The rolling-pins were clean, the knives were clean, the aprons were clean, the hands were clean. Not a drop was spilled, not a crumb was dropped.

"If into the kitchen of the crowded mother there

could come the utensils, the commodities, the clean towels, the ample *time*, there would come, without the lessons, a touch of the millennium.

"I am always afraid of manual-labor schools. I am not afraid that these girls could not read, for every American girl reads, and to read is much more important than to cook; but I *am* afraid that not all can *write* — some of them were not more than twelve years old.

"And what of the boys? Must a common cook always be a girl? and must a boy not cook unless on the top of the ladder, with the pay of the president of Harvard College?

"I am jealous for the schools; I have heard a gentleman who stands high in science declare that the cooking schools would eventually kill out every literary college in the land — for women. But why not for men? If the food for the body is more important than the food for the mind, let us destroy the latter and accept the former, but let us not continue to do what has been tried for fifteen hundred years, — to keep one half of the world to the starvation of the mind, in order to feed better the physical condition of the other half.

"Let us have cooks; but let us leave it a matter of choice, as we leave the dressmaking and the shoe-making, the millinery and the carpentry, — free to be chosen!

"There are cultivated and educated women who enjoy cooking; so there are cultivated men who enjoy Kensington embroidery. Who objects? But take care that some rousing of the intellect comes first, — that it may be an enlightened choice, — and do not so fill the

day with bread and butter and stitches that no time is
left for the appreciation of Whittier, letting at least the
simple songs of daily life and the influence of rhythm
beautify the dreary round of the three meals a day."

Miss Mitchell had a stock of conundrums on hand,
and was a good guesser. She told her stories at all
times when they happened to come into her mind. She
would arrive at her sister's house, just from Poughkeepsie
on a vacation, and after the threshold was crossed and
she had said " Good morning," in a clear voice to be
heard by all within her sight, she would, perhaps, say,
" Well, I have a capital story which I must tell before I
take my bonnet off, or I shall forget it!" And there
went with her telling an action, voice, and manner which
added greater point to the story, but which cannot be
described. One of her associates at Vassar, in recalling
some of her anecdotes, writes: " Professor Mitchell was
quite likely to stand and deliver herself of a bright little
speech before taking her seat at breakfast. It was as
though the short walk from the observatory had been
an inspiration to thought."

She was quick at repartee. On one occasion Char-
lotte Cushman and her friend Miss Stebbins were visiting
Miss Mitchell at Vassar. Miss Mitchell took them out
for a drive, and pointed out the different objects of
interest as they drove along the banks of the Hudson.
" What is that fine building on the hill?" asked Miss
Cushman. — " That," said Miss Mitchell, " was a boys'
school, originally, but it is now used as a hotel, where
they charge five dollars a day!" — " Five dollars a day?"
exclaimed Miss Cushman; "Jupiter Ammon!" — "No,"

said Miss Stebbins, " Jupiter Mammon ! " — " Not at all,"
said Miss Mitchell, " Jupiter *gammon!*"

" Farewell, Maria," said an old Friend, " I hope the
Lord will be with thee."

"Good-by," she replied, " I *know* he will be with you."

A characteristic trait in Miss Mitchell was her aver-
sion to receiving unsolicited advice in regard to her
private affairs. " A suggestion is an impertinence," she
would often say. The following anecdote shows how
she received such counsel :

A literary man of more than national reputation said
to one of her admirers, " I, for one, cannot endure your
Maria Mitchell." At her solicitation he explained why ;
and his reason was, as she had anticipated, founded on
personal pique. It seems he had gone up from New
York to Poughkeepsie especially to call upon Professor
Mitchell. During the course of conversation, with that
patronizing condescension which some self-important
men extend to all women indiscriminately, he proceeded
to inform her that her manner of living was not in
accordance with his ideas of expediency. " Now," he
said, " instead of going for each one of your meals all
the way from your living-rooms in the observatory
over to the dining-hall in the college building, I should
think it would be far more convenient and sensible for
you to get your breakfast, at least, right in your own
apartments. In the morning you could make a cup of
coffee and boil an egg with almost no trouble." At
which Professor Mitchell drew herself up with the air of
a tragic queen, saying, " And is my time worth no more
than to boil eggs ? "

CHAPTER XIII

MISS MITCHELL was a voluminous letter writer and an excellent correspondent, but her letters are not essays, and not at all in the approved style of the "Complete Letter Writer." If she had any particular thing to communicate, she rushed into the subject in the first line. In writing to her own family and intimate friends, she rarely signed her full name; sometimes she left it out altogether, but ordinarily " M. M." was appended abruptly when she had expressed all that she had to say. She wrote as she talked, with directness and promptness. No one, in watching her while she was writing a letter, ever saw her pause to think what she should say next or how she should express the thought. When she came to that point, the " M. M." was instantly added. She had no secretiveness, and in looking over her letters it has been almost impossible to find one which did not contain too much that was personal, either about herself or others, to make it proper; especially as she herself would be very unwilling to make the affairs of others public.

"Oct. 22, 1860. I have spent $100 on dress this year. I have a very pretty new felt bonnet of the

fashionable shape, trimmed with velvet; it cost only
$7, which, of course, was pitifully cheap for Broadway.
If thou thinks after $100 it wouldn't be extravagant for
me to have a waterproof cloak and a linsey-woolsey
morning dress, please to send me patterns of the latter
material and a description of waterproofs of various
prices. They are so ugly, and I am so ditto, that I feel
if a few dollars, more or less, would make me look
better, even in a storm, I must not mind it."

"My orthodoxy is settled beyond dispute, I trust, by
the following circumstance: The editor of a New York
magazine has written to me to furnish an article for the
Christmas number on 'The Star in the East.' I have
ventured, in my note of declination, to mention that if I
investigated that subject I might decide that there was
no star in the case, and then what would become of
me, and *where should I go?* Since that he has not
written, so I may have hung myself!

"1879. April 25. I have 'done' New York very
much as we did it thirty years ago. On Saturday I
went to Miss Booth's reception, and it was like Miss
Lynch's, only larger than Miss Lynch's was when I was
there. . . . Miss Booth and a friend live on Fifty-
ninth street, and have lived together for years. Miss
Booth is a nice-looking woman. She says she has
often been told that she looked like me; she has gray
hair and black eyes, but is fair and well-cut in feature.
I had a very nice time.

"On Sunday I went to hear Frothingham, and he was
at his very best. The subject was 'Aspirations of
Man,' and the sermon was rich in thought and in word.

. . . Frothingham's discourse was more cheery than usual; he talked about the wonderful idea of personal immortality, and he said if it be a dream of the imagination let us worship the imagination. He spoke of Mrs. Child's book on ' Aspirations,' and I shall order it at once. The only satire was such a sentence as this: on speaking of a piece of Egyptian sculpture he said, ' The gates of heaven opened to the good, not to the orthodox.'

" To-day, Monday, I have been to a public school (a primary) and to Stewart's mansion. I asked the major-domo to take us through the rooms on the lower floor, which he did. I know of no palace which comes up to it. The palaces always have a look as if at some point they needed refurbishing up. I suppose that Mrs. Stewart uses that dining-room, but it did not look as if it was made to eat in. I still like Gerôme's ' Chariot Race' better than anything else of his. The ' Horse Fair ' was too high up for me to enjoy it, and a little too mixed up.

" 1873. St. Petersburg is another planet, and, strange to say, is an agreeable planet. Some of these Europeans are far ahead of us in many things. I think we are in advance only in one universal democracy of freedom. But then, that is everything.

" Nov. 17, 1875. I think you are right to decide to make your home pleasant at any sacrifice which involves *only* silence. And you are so all over a radical, that it won't hurt you to be toned down a little, and in a few years, as the world moves, your family will have moved one way and you the other a little, and you will suddenly find yourself on the same plane. It is much the way that has been between Miss —— and myself. To-day she is more of a women's rights woman than I was when I first knew her, while I begin to think that the girls would better dress at tea-time, though I think on that subject we thought alike at first, so I'll take another example.

"I have learned to think that a *young* girl would better not walk to town alone, even in the daytime. When I came to Vassar I should have allowed a child to do it. But I never knew *much* of the world — never shall — nor will you. And as we were both born a little deficient in worldly caution and worldly policy, let us receive from others those lessons, — *do as well as we can*, and keep our *heart* unworldly if our manners take on something of those ways.

"Oct. 25, 1875. . . . I have scarcely got over the *tire* of the congress[1] yet, although it is a week since I returned. I feel as if a great burden was lifted from my soul. You will see my ' speech' in the 'Woman's Journal,' but in the last sentence it should be ' eastward ' and not ' *earth*ward.' It was a grand affair, and babies came in arms. School-boys stood close to the platform, and school-girls came, books in hand. The hall was a beautiful opera-house, and could hold at least one thousand seven hundred. It was packed and jammed, and rough men stood in the aisles. When I had to speak to announce a paper I stood *very still* until they became quiet. Once, as I stood in that way, a man at the

---

[1] The annual meeting of the Association for the Advancement of Women, of which Miss Mitchell was president. It was held at Syracuse, N.Y., in 1875.

extreme rear, before I had spoken a word, shouted out,
'Louder!' We all burst into a laugh. Then, of course,
I had to make them quiet again. I lifted the little
mallet, but I did not strike it, and they all became still.
I was surprised at the good breeding of such a crowd.
In the evening about half was made up of men. I
could not have believed that such a crowd would keep
still when I asked them to.

"They say I did well. Think of my developing as
a president of a social science society in my old age!"

Miss Mitchell took no prominent part in the woman
suffrage movement, but she believed in it firmly, and
its leaders were some of her most highly valued friends.

"Sept. 7, 1875. Went to a picnic for woman suffrage at a beautiful grove at Medfield, Mass. It was a
gathering of about seventy-five persons (mostly from
Needham), whose president seemed to be vigorous and
good-spirited.

"The main purpose of the meeting was to try to
affect public sentiment to such an extent as to lead to
the defeat of a man who, when the subject of woman
suffrage was before the Legislature, said that the women
had all they wanted now — that they could get anything
with 'their eyes as bright as the buttons on an angel's
coat.' Lucy Stone, Mr. Blackwell, Rev. Mr. Bush, Miss
Eastman, and William Lloyd Garrison spoke.

"Garrison did not look a day older than when I first
saw him, forty years ago; he spoke well — they said
with less fire than he used in his younger days. Garrison said what every one says — that the struggle for
women was the old anti-slavery struggle over again;

that as he looked around at the audience beneath the trees, it seemed to be the same scene that he had known before.

". . . We had a very good bit of missionary work done at our table (at Vassar) to-day. A man whom we all despise began to talk against voting by women. I felt almost inclined to pay him something for his remarks.

"A group from the Washington Women Suffrage Association stopped here to-day. . . . I liked Susan B. Anthony very much. She seemed much worn, but was all alive. She is eighteen months younger than I, but seems much more alert. I suppose brickbats are livelier than logarithms!"

Miss Mitchell was a member of several learned societies.

She was the first woman elected to membership of the American Academy of Arts and Sciences, whose headquarters are at Boston.

In 1869 she was chosen a member of the American Philosophical Society, a society founded by Benjamin Franklin, in Philadelphia.

The American Association for the Advancement of Science made her a member in the early part of its existence. Miss Mitchell was one of the earliest members of the American Association for the Advancement of Women. At one period she was president of the association, and for many years served as chairman of the committee on science. In this latter capacity she reached, through circulars and letters, women studying science in all parts of the country; and the reports, as shown from year to year, show a wonderful increase in the number of such women. She was a member, also, of the New England Women's Club, of Boston, and after her annual visit at Christmas she entertained her students at Vassar with descriptions of the receptions and meeting of that body. She was also a member of the New York Sorosis. She received the degree of Ph.D. from Rutgers Female College in 1870, her first degree of LL.D. from Hanover College in 1832, and her last LL.D. from Columbia College in 1887.

Miss Mitchell had no ambition to appear in print, and most of her published articles were in response to applications from publishers.

A paper entitled " Mary Somerville " appeared in the " Atlantic Monthly " for May, 1860. There were several articles in " Silliman's Journal," — mostly results of observations on Jupiter and Saturn, — a few popular science papers in " Hours at Home," and one on the " Herschels," printed in " The Century " just after her death.

Miss Mitchell also read a few lectures to small societies, and to one or two girls' schools; but she never allowed such outside work to interfere with her duties at Vassar College, to which she devoted herself heart and soul.

When the failure of her health became apparent to the members of her family, it was with the utmost difficulty that Miss Mitchell could be prevailed upon to resign her position. She had fondly hoped to remain at Vassar until she should be seventy years old, of which she lacked about six months. It was hoped that complete rest might lead to several years more of happy life for her; but it was not to be so — she died in Lynn, June 28, 1889.

It was one of Miss Mitchell's boasts that she had earned a salary for over fifty years, without any intermission. She also boasted that in July, 1883, when she slipped and fell, spraining herself so that she was obliged to remain in the house a day or two, it was the first time in her memory when she had remained in the house a day. In fact, she made a point of walking out every day, no matter what the weather might be. A serious fall, during her illness in Lynn, stopped forever her daily walks.

She had resigned her position in January, 1888. The resignation was laid on the table until the following June, at which time the trustees made her Professor Emeritus, and offered her a home for life at the observatory. This offer she did not accept, preferring to live with her family in Lynn. The following extracts from letters which she received at this time show with what reverence and love she was regarded by faculty and students.

" Jan. 9, 1888. . . . You may be sure that we shall be glad to do all we can to honor one whose faithful service and honesty of heart and life have been among the chief inspirations of Vassar College throughout its history. Of public reputation you have doubtless had enough, but I am sure you cannot have too much of the affection and esteem which we feel toward you, who have had the privilege of working with you."

" Jan. 10, 1888. You will consent, you *must* consent, to having your home here, and letting the work go. It is not astronomy that is wanted and needed, it is Maria Mitchell. . . . The richest part of my life here is connected with you. . . . I cannot picture Vassar without you. There's nothing to point to! "

" May 5, 1889. In all the great wonder of life, you have given me more of what I have wanted than any other creature ever gave me. I hoped I should amount to something for your sake."

Dr. Eliza M. Mosher, at one time resident physician at the college, said of her: " She was quick to withdraw objections when she was convinced of error in her judgment. I well remember her opposition to the ground I took in my ' maiden speech ' in faculty meeting, and how, at supper, she stood, before sitting down, to say, 'You were right this afternoon. I have thought the matter over, and, while I do not like to believe it, I think it is true.' "

Of her rooms at the observatory, Miss Grace Anna Lewis, who had been a guest, wrote thus : " Her furniture was plain and simple, and there was a frank simplicity corresponding therewith which made me believe she chose to have it so. It looked natural for her. I think I should have been disappointed had I found her rooms fitted up with undue elegance."

" Professor Mitchell's position at Vassar gave astronomy a prominence there that it has never had in any other college for women, and in but few for men. I suppose it would have made no difference what she had taught. Doubtless she never suspected how many students endured the mathematical work of junior Astronomy in order to be within range of her magnetic personality." (From "Wide Awake," September, 1889.)

A graduate writes: "Her personality was so strong that it was felt all over the college, even by those who were not in her department, and who only admired her from a distance."

Extract from a letter written after her death by a former pupil: "I count Maria Mitchell's services to Vassar and her pupils infinitely valuable, and her character and attainments great beyond anything that has yet been told. . . . I was one of the pupils upon whom her freedom from all the shams and self-deceptions made an impression that elevated my whole standard, mental and moral. . . . The influence of her own personal character sustains its supreme test in the evidence constantly accumulating, that it strengthens rather than weakens with the lapse of time. Her influence upon her pupils who were her daily companions has been permanent, character-moulding, and unceasingly progressive."

President Taylor, in his address at her funeral, said: "If I were to select for comment the one most striking trait of her character, I should name her *genuineness*. There was no false note in Maria Mitchell's thinking or utterance. . . .

"One who has known her kindness to little children, who has watched her little evidences of thoughtful care for her associates and friends, who has seen her put aside her own long-cherished rights that she might make the way of a new and untried officer easier, cannot forget the tenderer side of her character. . . .

"But it would be vain for me to try to tell just what it was in Miss Mitchell that attracted us who loved her. It was this combination of great strength and independence, of deep affection and tenderness, breathed through and through with the sentiment of a perfectly genuine life, which has made for us one of the pilgrim-shrines of life the study in the observatory of Vassar College where we have known her *at home*, surrounded by the evidences of her honorable professional career. She has been an impressive figure in our time, and one whose influence lives."

INTRODUCTORY NOTE

On the 17th of December, 1831, a gold medal of the value of twenty ducats was founded, at the suggestion of Professor Schumacher, of Altona, by his Majesty Frederic VI., at that time king of Denmark, to be awarded to any person who should first discover a telescopic comet. This foundation and the conditions on which the medal would be awarded were announced to the public in the "Astronomische Nachrichten" for the 20th of March, 1832. The regulations underwent a revision after a few years, and in April, 1840 ("Astronomische Nachrichten," No. 400), were republished as follows:

" 1. The medal will be given to the first discoverer of any comet, which, at the time of its discovery, is invisible to the naked eye, and whose periodic time is unknown.

" 2. The discoverer, if a resident of any part of Europe except Great Britain, is to make known his discovery to Mr. Schumacher at Altona. If a resident in Great Britain, or any other quarter of the globe except the continent of Europe, he is to make his discovery known directly to Mr. Francis Baily, London. [Since Mr. Baily's decease, G. B. Airy, Esq., Astronomer Royal, has been substituted in this and in the 7th and 8th articles of the regulations.]

" 3. This communication must be made by the *first post* after the discovery. If there is no regular mail at the place of discovery, the first opportunity of any other kind must be made use of, without waiting for other observations. Exact compliance with this condition is indispensable. If this condition is not complied with, and only one person discovers the comet, no medal will be given for the discovery. Otherwise, the medal will be assigned to the discoverer who earliest complies with the condition.

" 4. The communication must not only state as exactly as possible the time of the discovery, in order to settle the question between rival claims, but also as near as may be the place of the comet, and the direction in which it is moving, as far as these points can be determined from the observations of one night.

" 5. If the observations of one night are not sufficient to settle these points, the enunciation of the discovery must still be made, in compliance with the third article. As soon as a second observation is made, it must be communicated in like manner with the first, and with it the longitude of the place where the discovery is made, unless it take place at some known observatory. The expectation of obtaining a second observation will never be received as a satisfactory reason for postponing the communication of the first.

" 6. The medal will be assigned twelve months after the discovery of the comet, and no claim will be admitted after that period.

" 7. Messrs. Baily and Schumacher are to decide if a discovery has been made. If they differ, Mr. Gauss, of Gottingen, is to decide.

" 8. Messrs. Baily and Schumacher have agreed to communicate mutually to each other every announcement of a discovery.

"Altona, April, 1840."

On the 1st of October, 1847, at half-past ten o'clock, P.M., a telescopic comet was discovered by Miss Maria Mitchell, of Nantucket, nearly vertical above Polaris about five degrees. The further progress and history of the discovery will sufficiently appear from the following correspondence. On the 3d of October the same comet was seen at half-past seven, P.M., at Rome, by Father de Vico, and information of the fact was immediately communicated by him to Professor Schumacher at Altona. On the 7th of October, at twenty minutes past nine, P.M., it was observed by Mr. W. R. Dawes, at Camden Lodge, Cranbrook, Kent, in England, and on the 11th it was seen by Madame Rümker, the wife of the director of the observatory at Hamburg. Mr. Schumacher, in announcing this last discovery, observes : [1] " Madame Rümker has for several years been on the lookout for comets, and her persevering industry seemed at last about to be rewarded, when a letter was received from Father de Vico, addressed to the editor of this journal, from which it appeared that the same comet had been observed by him on the 3d instant at Rome."

Not deeming it probable that his daughter had anticipated the observers of this country and Europe in the discovery of this comet, no steps were taken by Mr. Mitchell with a view to obtaining the king of Denmark's medal. Prompt information, however, of the discovery was transmitted by Mr. Mitchell to his friend, William C. Bond, Esq., director of the observatory at Cambridge. The observations of the Messrs. Bond upon the comet commenced on the 7th of October ; and on the 30th were transmitted by me to Mr. Schumacher, for publication in the "Astronomische Nachrichten." It was stated in the memorandum of the Messrs. Bond that the comet was seen by Miss Mitchell on the 1st instant. This notice appeared in the "Nachrichten" of Dec. 9, 1847, and the priority of Miss Mitchell's discovery was immediately admitted throughout Europe.

My attention had been drawn to the subject of the king of

---

[1] " Astronomische Nachrichten," No. 616.

Denmark's comet medal by some allusion to it in my correspondence with Professor Schumacher, in reference to the discovery of telescopic comets by Mr. George P. Bond, of the
observatory at Cambridge. Having learned some weeks after
Miss Mitchell's discovery that no communication had been
made on her behalf to the trustees of the medal, and aware
that the regulations in this respect were enforced with strictness, I was apprehensive that it might be too late to supply
the omission. Still, however, as the spirit of the regulations
had been complied with by Mr. Mitchell's letter to Mr. Bond
of the 3d of October, it seemed worth while at least to
make the attempt to procure the medal for his daughter. Although the attempt might be unsuccessful, it would at any rate
cause the priority of her discovery to be more authentically
established than it might otherwise have been.

I accordingly wrote to Mr. Mitchell for information on the
subject, and applied for, and obtained from Mr. Bond, Mr.
Mitchell's original letter to him of the 3d of October, with the
Nantucket postmark. These papers were transmitted to Professor Schumacher, with a letter dated 15th and 24th January.

On the 8th of February I wrote a letter to my much esteemed friend, Captain W. H. Smyth, R.N., formerly president of the Astronomical Society at London, requesting him
to interest himself with Professor Schumacher to obtain the
medal for Miss Mitchell. Captain Smyth entered with great
readiness into the matter, and addressed a note on the subject
to Mr. Airy, the Astronomer Royal, at Greenwich. Mr. Airy
kindly wrote to Professor Schumacher without loss of time;
but it was their united opinion that a compliance with the
condition relative to immediate notice of a discovery was indispensable, and that it was consequently out of their power to
award the medal to Miss Mitchell. Mr. Schumacher suggested,
as the only means by which this difficulty could be overcome,

an application to the Danish government, through the American legation at Copenhagen.

Conceiving that the correspondence could be carried on more promptly through the Danish legation at Washington, I addressed a letter on the 20th of April to Mr. Steene-Billé, Charge d'Affaires of the king of Denmark in this country, and sent with it copies of the documents which had been forwarded to Professor Schumacher. Mr. Steene-Billé, however, was of opinion that the application, if made at all, should be made through the American legation at Copenhagen ; but he expressed at the same time a confident opinion that, owing to the condition and political relations of Denmark, the application would necessarily prove unavailing.

It was at this time that the difficulties in Schleswig-Holstein were at their height, and it seemed hopeless at such a moment, and in face of the opinion of the official representative of the Danish government in this country, to engage its attention to an affair of this kind. No further attempt was accordingly made by me, for some weeks, to pursue the matter. In fact, a report reached the United States that the medal had actually been awarded to Father de Vico. Although this was believed by me to be an unfounded rumor, the regulations allowing one year for the presentation of claims, there was reason to apprehend that it proceeded from some quarter well informed as to what would probably take place at the expiration of the twelvemonth.

On the 5th of August, Father de Vico, who had left Rome in the spring in consequence of the troubles there, made a visit to Cambridge, in company with the Right Rev. Bishop Fitzpatrick, of Boston, and on this occasion informed me that he had received an intimation from Professor Schumacher that the comet-medal would be awarded to Miss Mitchell. I was disposed to think that Father de Vico labored under some misapprehension as to the purport of Professor Schumacher's communications, as afterwards appeared to be the case. I felt encouraged, however, by his statement not only to renew my correspondence on the subject with Professor Schumacher, but I determined, on the 8th of August, to address a letter to R. P. Fleniken, Esq., Chargé d'Affaires of the United States at Copenhagen. This letter was accompanied with copies of the original papers.

Mr. Fleniken entered with great zeal and interest into the subject. He lost no time in bringing it before the Danish government by means of a letter to the Count de Knuth, the Minister at that time for Foreign Affairs, and of another to the king of Denmark himself. His Majesty, with the most obliging promptness, ordered a reference of the case to Professor Schumacher, with directions to report thereon without delay. Mr. Schumacher had been for a long time in possession of the documents establishing Miss Mitchell's priority, which was, indeed, admitted throughout scientific Europe. Professor Schumacher immediately made his report in favor of granting the medal to Miss Mitchell, and this report was accepted by the king. The result was forthwith communicated by the Count de Knuth to Mr. Fleniken, with the gratifying intelligence that the king had ordered the medal to be awarded to Miss Mitchell, and that it would be delivered to him for transmission as soon as it could be struck off. This has since been done.

It must be regarded as a striking proof of an enlightened interest for the promotion of science, not less than of a kind regard for the rights and feelings of the individual most concerned in this decision, that the king of Denmark should have bestowed his attention upon this subject, at a period of so much difficulty and alarm for Europe in general and his own kingdom in particular. It would not have been possible to act more promptly in a season of the profoundest tranquillity. His Majesty has on this occasion shown that he is animated by the same generous zeal for the encouragement of astronomical research which led his predecessor to found the medal; while he has performed an act of gracious courtesy toward a stranger in a distant land which must ever be warmly appreciated by her friends and countrymen.

Nor ought the obliging agency of the Count de Knuth, the Minister of Foreign Affairs, to be passed without notice. The slightest indifference on his part, even the usual delays of office, would have prevented the application from reaching the king before the expiration of the twelvemonth within which all claims must, by the regulations, be presented. No one can reflect upon the pressure of business which must have existed in the foreign office at Copenhagen during the past year, without feeling that the Count de Knuth must largely share his sovereign's zeal for science, as well as his love of justice. Nothing else will account for the attention bestowed at such a political crisis on an affair of this kind. The same attention appears to have been given to the subject by his successor, Count Moltka.

It was quite fortunate for the success of the application that the office of chargé d'affaires of the United States at Copenhagen happened to be filled by a gentleman disposed to give it his prompt and persevering support. A matter of this kind, of course, lay without the province of his official duties. But no subject officially committed to him by the instructions of his government could have been more zealously pursued. On the very day on which my communication of the 8th of August reached him, Mr. Fleniken addressed his letters to the minister of foreign affairs and to the king, and he continued to give his attention to the subject till the object was happily effected, and the medal placed in his hands.

The event itself, however insignificant in the great world of politics and business, is one of pleasing interest to the friends of American science, and it has been thought proper that the following record of it should be preserved in a permanent form. I have regretted the frequent recurrence of my own name in the correspondence, and have suppressed several letters of my own which could be spared, without rendering less intelligible the communications of the other parties, to whom the interest and merit of the transaction belong.

EDWARD EVERETT.

CAMBRIDGE, 1st February, 1849.

CORRESPONDENCE

HON. WILLIAM MITCHELL TO WILLIAM C. BOND, ESQ., CAMBRIDGE.

"Nantucket, 10 mo. 3d, 1847.

"MY DEAR FRIEND: I write now merely to say that Maria discovered a telescopic comet at half-past ten on the evening of the first instant, at that hour nearly vertical above Polaris five degrees. Last evening it had advanced westwardly; this evening still further, and nearing the pole. It does not bear illumination, but Maria has obtained its right ascension and declination, and will not suffer me to announce it. Pray tell me whether it is one of George's; if not, whether it has been seen by anybody. Maria supposes it may be an old story. If quite convenient, just drop a line to her; it will oblige me much. I expect to leave home in a day or two, and shall be in Boston next week, and I would like to have her hear from you before I can meet you. I hope it will not give thee much trouble amidst thy close engagements.

"Our regards are to all of you, most truly,

"WILLIAM MITCHELL."

HON. EDWARD EVERETT TO HON. WILLIAM MITCHELL.

"Cambridge, 10th January, 1848.

"DEAR SIR: I take the liberty to inquire of you whether any steps have been taken by you, on behalf of your danghter, by way of claiming the medal of the king of Denmark for the

(275)

first discovery of a telescopic comet. The regulations require that information of the discovery should be transmitted by the next mail to Mr. Airy, the Astronomer Royal, if the discovery is made elsewhere than on the continent of Europe. If made in the United States, I understand from Mr. Schumacher that information may be sent to the Danish minister at Washington, who will forward it to Mr. Airy, — but it must be sent by next mail.

"In consequence of non-compliance with these regulations, Mr. George Bond has on one occasion lost the medal. I trust this may not be the case with Miss Mitchell.

"I am, dear sir, with much respect, faithfully yours,

"EDWARD EVERETT."

EXTRACT FROM A LETTER OF THE HON. WILLIAM MITCHELL TO HON. EDWARD EVERETT.

"Nantucket, 1st mo. 15th, 1848.

"ESTEEMED FRIEND: Thy kind letter of the 10th instant reached me duly. No steps were taken by my daughter in claim of the medal of the Danish king. On the night of the discovery, I was fully satisfied that it was a comet from its location, though its real motion at this time was so nearly opposite to that of the earth (the two bodies approaching each other) that its apparent motion was scarcely appreciable. I urged very strongly that it should be published immediately, but she resisted it as strongly, though she could but acknowledge her conviction that it was a comet. She remarked to me, 'If it is a new comet, our friends, the Bonds, have seen it. It may be an old one, so far as relates to the discovery, and one which we have not followed.' She consented, however, that I should write to William C. Bond, which I did by the first mail that left the island after the discovery. This letter did not reach my friend till the 6th or 7th, having been somewhat delayed here and also in the post-office at Cambridge.

" Referring to my journal I find these words: ' Maria will not consent to have me announce it as an original discovery.'

" The stipulations of His Majesty have, therefore, not been complied with, and the peculiar circumstances of the case, her sex, and isolated position, may not be sufficient to justify a suspension of the rules. Nevertheless, it would gratify me that the generous monarch should know that there is a love of science even in this to him remote corner of the earth.

" I am thine, my dear friend, most truly,

" WILLIAM MITCHELL."

HON. EDWARD EVERETT TO PROFESSOR SCHUMACHER, AT ALTONA.

" Cambridge, 15th January, 1848.

" DEAR SIR : Your letter of the 27th October, accompanying the ' Planeten-Circular,' reached me but a few days since. If you would be so good as to forward to the care of John Miller, Esq., 26 Henrietta street, Covent Garden, London, any letter you may do me the favor to write to me, it would reach me promptly.

" The regulations relative to the king of Denmark's medal have not hitherto been understood in this country. I shall take care to give publicity to them. Not only has Mr. Bond lost the medal to which you think he would have been entitled,[1] but I fear the same has happened to Miss Mitchell, of Nantucket, who discovered the comet of last October on

---

[1] Mr. Schumacher had remarked to me, in his letter of the 27th of October, that Mr. George P. Bond would have received the medal for the comet first seen by him as a nebulous object on the 18th of February, 1846, if his observation made at that time had been communicated, according to the regulations, to the trustees of the medal.

the first day of that month. I think it was not seen in Europe till the third.

"I remain, dear sir, with great respect, faithfully yours,

"EDWARD EVERETT."

———

HON. EDWARD EVERETT TO HON. WILLIAM MITCHELL.

"Cambridge, 18th January, 1848.

"DEAR SIR: I have your esteemed favor of the 15th, which reached me this day. I am fearful that the rigor deemed necessary in enforcing the regulations relative to the king of Denmark's prize may prevent your daughter from receiving it. I learn from Mr. Schumacher's letter, that, besides Mr. George Bond, Dr. Bremeker lost the medal because he allowed a single post-day to pass before he announced his discovery. There could, in his case, be no difficulty in establishing the fact of his priority, nor any doubt of the good faith with which it was asserted. But inasmuch as Miss Mitchell's discovery was actually made known to Mr. Bond by the next mail which left your island, it is possible — barely possible — that this may be considered as a substantial compliance with the regulation. At any rate, it is worth trying; and if we can do no more we can establish the lady's claim to all the credit of the prior discovery. I shall therefore apply to Mr. Bond for the letter which you wrote, and if it contains nothing improper to be seen by others we will forward it to the Danish minister at Washington with a certified extract from your journal. I will have a certified copy of all these papers prepared and sent to Mr. Schumacher; and if any departure from the letter of the regulations is admissible, this would seem to be a case for it. I trust Miss Mitchell's retiring disposition will not lead her to oppose the taking of these steps.

"I am, dear sir, with great respect, faithfully yours,

[Signed]   "EDWARD EVERETT."

POSTSCRIPT TO MR. EVERETT'S LETTER TO PROFESSOR
SCHUMACHER OF THE 15TH JANUARY, 1848.

" P.S. — The foregoing was written to go by the steamer of the 15th, but was a few hours too late. I have since received some information in reference to the comet of October which leads me to hope that you may feel it in your power to award the medal to Miss Maria Mitchell. Miss Mitchell saw the comet at half-past ten o'clock on the evening of October 1st. Her father, a skilful astronomer, made an entry in his journal to that effect. On the third day of October he wrote a letter to Mr. Bond, the director of our observatory, announcing the discovery. This letter was despatched the following day, being the first post-day after the discovery of the comet. This letter I transmit to you, together with letters from Mr. Mitchell and Mr. Bond to myself. Nantucket, as you are probably aware, is a small, secluded island, lying off the extreme point of the coast of Massachusetts. Mr. Mitchell is a member of the executive council of Massachusetts and a most respectable person.

" As the claimant is a young lady of great diffidence, the place a retired island, remote from all the high-roads of communication ; as the conditions have not been well understood in this country ; and especially as there was a substantial compliance with them — I hope His Majesty may think Miss Maria Mitchell entitled to the medal.

" Cambridge, 24th January, 1848.

EXTRACT FROM A LETTER FROM MR. EVERETT TO CAPTAIN W. H. SMYTH, R.N., LATE PRESIDENT OF THE ROYAL ASTRONOMICAL SOCIETY, LONDON, DATED CAMBRIDGE, 8TH FEBRUARY, 1848.

"I have lately been making interest with Mr. Schumacher to cause the king of Denmark's medal to be given to Miss Mitchell for the discovery of the comet to which her name has been given, if I mistake not, in the journal of your society as well as in the 'Nachrichten.' She unquestionably discovered it at half-past ten on the evening of the 1st of October; it was not, I think, seen in Europe till the 3d. Her father, on the 3d, wrote a letter to Mr. Bond, the director of our observatory, informing him of this discovery; and this letter was sent by the first mail that left the little out-of-the-way island (Nantucket) after the discovery. The *spirit* of the regulations was therefore complied with. But as the *letter* requires that the notice should be given either to the Danish minister resident in the country or to Mr. Airy, if the discovery is made elsewhere than on the continent of Europe, it is possible that some demur may be made. The precise terms of the regulations have not been sufficiently made known in this country. As the claim in this case is really a just one, the claimant a lady, industrious, vigilant, a good astronomer and mathematician, I cannot but hope she will succeed; and if you have the influence with Schumacher which you ought to have, I would take it kindly if you would use it in her favor."

CAPTAIN SMYTH TO MR. EVERETT.

"3 Cheyne Walk, Chelsea, 10th March, 1848.

"MY DEAR SIR: On the receipt of your last letter, I forthwith wrote to the astronomer royal, urging the claims of Miss Mitchell, of Nantucket, and he immediately replied, saying that he would lose no time in consulting his official colleague, Mr. Schumacher, on the subject. I have just received the accompanying letter from Greenwich, by which you will perceive how the matter stands at present; I say at present, because, however the claim may be considered as to the technical form of application, there is no doubt whatever of her fully meriting the award.

" I am, my dear sir, very faithfully yours,

[Signed]   " W. H. SMYTH."

G. B. AIRY, ESQ., TO CAPTAIN SMYTH.

" Royal Observatory, Greenwich, 10th March, 1848.

" MY DEAR SIR : I have received Mr. Schumacher's answer in regard to Miss Mitchell's supposed claims for the king of Denmark's medal. We agree, without the smallest hesitation, that we cannot award the medal. We have in all cases acted strictly in conformity with the published rules ; and I am convinced, and I believe that Mr. Schumacher is convinced, that it is absolutely necessary that we do not depart from them.

" Mr. Schumacher suggests, as the only way in which Miss Mitchell's claim in equity could be urged, that application might be made on her part, through the American legation, to the king of Denmark ; and the king can, if he pleases, make exception to the usual rules.

" I am, my dear sir, yours most truly,

[Signed]   " G. B. AIRY."

HON. EDWARD EVERETT TO R. P. FLENIKEN.

" Cambridge, Mass., 8th August, 1848.

" DEAR SIR : Without the honor of your personal acquaintance, I take the liberty of addressing you on a subject which I am confident will interest you as a friend of American science.

"You are doubtless aware that by the liberality of one of the kings of Denmark, the father, I believe, of his late Majesty, a foundation was made for a gold medal to be given to the first discoverer of a telescopic comet. Mr. Schumacher, of Altona, and Mr. Baily, of London (and since his decease Mr. Airy, Astronomer Royal at Greenwich), were made the trustees of this foundation. Among the regulations established for awarding the medal was this : that the discoverer should, by the first mail which leaves the place of his residence after the discovery, give notice thereof to Mr. Schumacher if the discovery is made on the continent of Europe, and to Mr. Airy if made in any other part of the world ; provided that, if the discovery be made in America, the notice may be given to the Danish minister at Washington. It has been deemed necessary to adhere with great strictness to this regulation, in order to prevent fraudulent claims.

"On the first day of October last, at about half-past ten o'clock in the evening, a telescopic comet was discovered, in the island of Nantucket, by Miss Maria Mitchell, daughter of Hon. W. Mitchell, one of the executive council of this State. Mr. Mitchell made an entry of the discovery at the time in his journal. In consequence of Miss Mitchell's diffidence, she would not allow any publicity to be given to her discovery till its reality was ascertained. Her father, however, by the first mail that left Nantucket for the mainland, addressed a letter to Mr. W. C. Bond, director of the observatory in this place, acquainting him with his daughter's discovery. A copy of this letter I herewith transmit to you. The comet was not discovered in Europe till the 3d of October, when it was seen by Father de Vico, the celebrated astronomer at Rome.

"You perceive from this statement that, if Mr. Mitchell had addressed his letter to the Danish minister at Washington instead of Mr. Bond, his daughter would have been entitled to the medal, under the strict terms of the regulations. But these regulations have not been generally understood in this country; and as the fact of Miss Mitchell's prior discovery is undoubted, and recognized throughout Europe, it would be a pity that she should lose the medal on a mere technical punctilio. The comet is constantly called 'Miss Mitchell's comet' in the monthly journal of the Royal Astronomical Society at London, and in the 'Astronomische Nachrichten,' the well-known astronomical journal, edited by Mr. Schumacher himself, at Altona. Father de Vico (who, with his brothers of the Society of Jesuits, has left Rome since the revolution there) was at this place (Cambridge) three days ago, and spoke of Miss Mitchell's priority as an undoubted fact.

"Last winter I addressed a letter to Mr. Schumacher, acquainting him with the foregoing facts relative to the discovery, and transmitting to him the *original* letter of Mr. Mitchell to Mr. Bond, dated 3d October, bearing the original Nantucket postmark of the 4th. I also wrote to Capt. W. H. Smyth, late president of the Royal Astronomical Society of England, desiring him to speak to Mr. Airy on the subject. He did so, and Mr. Airy wrote immediately to Mr. Schumacher. Mr. Schumacher in his reply expressed the opinion, in which Mr. Airy concurs, that *under the regulations* it is not in their power to award the medal to Miss Mitchell. They suggest, however, that an application should be made, through the American legation at the Danish court, to His Majesty the King of Denmark, for authority, under the present circumstances, to dispense with the literal fulfilment of the conditions.

"It is on this subject that I take the liberty to ask your good offices. I accompany my letter with copies of a portion of the correspondence which has been had on the subject, and I venture to request you to address a note to the proper

department of the Danish government, to the end that
authority should be given to Messrs. Schumacher and Airy to
award the medal to Miss Mitchell, *provided they are satisfied
that she first discovered the comet.*

"I will only add that, should you succeed in effecting this
object, you will render a very acceptable service to all the
friends of science in America.

"I remain, dear sir, with high consideration, your obedient,
faithful servant,

    [Signed]   "EDWARD EVERETT.

"To R. P. FLENIKEN, ESQ., Charge d'Affaires of the United
    States of America at Copenhagen."

R. P. FLENIKEN, ESQ., TO THE COUNT DE KNUTH.

"Legation des Etats Unis d'Amerique, ⎱
a Copenhague, le 6 Septembre, 1848. ⎰

"MONSIEUR LE MINISTRE: J'ai l'honneur de remettre sous
ce pli a votre Excellence une lettre que j'ai reçue d'un de mes
concitoyens les plus distingués, avec une correspondance
touchant une matiere a laquelle il me semble que le Danemark ne soit guère moins intéressé que ne le sont les Etats
Unis; le premier y ayant contribué le digne motif, l'autre en
ayant heureusement accompli l'objet.

"Je recommande ces documents a l'examination attentive
de votre Excellence, sachant bien l'interet profond qu'elle ne
manque jamais de prendre a de tels sujets, et la réputation
éminente de cultivateur des sciences et de la littérature, dont
elle jouit avec tant de justice. J'y ai joint une lettre de
moi-meme, addressee a sa Majesté le Roi de Danemark.

"La matiere dont il est question, Monsieur, sera d'autant
plus intéressante a votre Excellence, qu'on peut la regarder
comme une voix de réponse addressée a l'ancienne Scandi-

navie, proclaimant les prodiges merveilleux de la science moderne, des bords mêmes du Vinland des Vikinger hardis et entreprenants du dixième et de l'onzième siècles.

"Je prie votre Excellence de vouloir bien soumettre tous les documents ci-joints a l'œil de sa Majesté, et dans le cas heureux ou vous seriez d'avis que ma compatriote, Mlle. Mitchell, puisse avec justice revendiquer la récompense génereuse instituée par le Roi Fredéric VI., alors, Monsieur, je prie votre Excellence de vouloir bien appuyer de ses propres estimables et puissantes recommandations l'application des amis de la jeune demoiselle.

"Je m'empresse a cette occasion, Monsieur, de renouveler a votre Excellence l'assurance de ma considération tres distinguée.

"R. P. FLENIKEN.

"A Son Excellence M. LE COMTE DE KNUTH, Ministre d'Etat, et Chef du Département des Affaires Etrangeres.

TRANSLATION.[1]

"Legation of the United States of America, ⎱
City of Copenhagen, September 6th, 1848. ⎰

"SIR : I have the honor to communicate to you a letter from a distinguished citizen of my own country, together with a correspondence relating to a subject in which Denmark and the United States appear somewhat equally interested, the former in furnishing a laudable motive, and the latter as happily achieving the object.

"I commend these papers to your careful examination, being well aware of the deep interest you take in all such subjects, and of the eminent reputation you so justly enjoy

---

[1] This and the other translations of the French letters are printed as received in this country.

as a gentleman of science and of literature.   They are accompanied by a letter from myself addressed to His Majesty the
King of Denmark.

"This subject will not be the less interesting to you, sir,
as it would appear to be a returning voice addressed to ancient
Scandinavia, speaking of the wonderful achievements of modern science, from the ' Vinland ' of the hardy and enterprising
' Northmen ' of the tenth and the eleventh centuries.

" I beg, therefore, that you will obligingly lay them all
before His Majesty, and should they happily impress you that
my countrywoman, Miss Mitchell, is fairly entitled to the
generous offering of King Frederic VI., be pleased, sir, to
accompany the application of her friends in her behalf by
your own very valuable and potent recommendation.

" I avail myself of this occasion to renew to your Excellency
the assurance of my most distinguished consideration.

[Signed]   " R. P. FLENIKEN.

"To His Excellency THE COUNT DE KNUTH, Minister of
State and Chief of the Department of Foreign Affairs.

R. P. FLENIKEN, ESQ., TO THE KING OF DENMARK.

" Legation des Etats Unis d'Amerique, ⎱
a Copenhague, le 6 Septembre, 1848. ⎰

"SIRE: Le soussigné a l'honneur, par l'intermédiaire de
M. votre ministre d'etat et chef du departement des affaires
étrangeres, de soumettre a votre Majesté une lettre d'un
citoyen tres distingue des Etats Unis, accompagnée de la
copie d'une correspondance concernant une matiere a laquelle
votre Majesté, soverain également distingué par la libéralité
génereuse qu'elle fait voir dans ses rapports sociaux et
politiques, et par l'admiration ardente qu'elle manifeste envers

la science et la littérature, ne peut manquer de prendre un vif intérêt.

" Le soussigné se félicite beaucoup d'etre l'intermédiaire par les mains duquel ces documents arrivent sous l'œil de votre Majesté, étant persuadé que la lecture en fournira a votre Majesté l'occasion de recourir avec une grande satisfaction patriotique, comme protecteur éminent des sciences, a l'institution d'un de ses illustres prédécesseurs ; et ce souvenir de la haute position a laquelle le Danemark s'est élevé dans les arts et les sciences, ne lui sera peut-etre pas moins doux quand elle songe que c'est justement sur cette même cote, où déja au dixieme siecle l'intrépidité et l'esprit hardi de ses ancetres Scandinaves les avaient amenés a la découverte du grand continent occidental et a la fondation d'une colonie, que vient de s'accomplir cette conquete de la science, dont parlent les dits papiers.

" Le soussigné ose donc espérer, qu'a la suite d'une examination attentive des lettres ci-jointes, et desquelles il paraîtrait etre généralement reconnu qu'a Mlle. Mitchell des Etats Unis est du l'honneur d'avoir la premiere découvert la comete télescopique qui aujourd'hui porte son nom, que votre Majesté ne trouvera point dans la réserve louable qui empecha cette jeune demoiselle de se précipiter a la poursuite d'une renommee publique, une cause suffisante de lui refuser le prix de sa brillante découverte ; mais qu'au contraire elle donnera l'ordre de lui expédier la médaille, autant comme une récompense due a ses éminents talents scientifiques, que pour témoigner combien votre Majesté sait apprécier cette modestie charmante qui s'opposa a ce que Mlle. Mitchell recherchat une célébrité publique et scientifique, avec le seul but de remplir une forme tout-a-fait technique.

" Le soussigné, chargé d'affaires des Etats Unis de l'Amérique, saisit avec empressement cette occasion d'offrir a votre Majesté l'expression de sa considération la plus haute et la plus distinguée.

"R. P. Fleniken.

"À Sa Majesté Frederic VII., Roi de Danemark, Duc de Slesvig et de Holstein."

TRANSLATION.

"Legation of the United States of America, }
City of Copenhagen, September 4th, 1848. }

"Sire: The undersigned has the honor, through your Majesty's minister of state and chief of the department of foreign affairs, to communicate to you a letter from a very distinguished citizen of the United States, together with copies of a correspondence relating to a subject in which your Majesty, alike distinguished for generous liberality in social and political affairs as a sovereign, as well as an ardent admirer of science and of literature, will doubtless feel a lively interest.

"The undersigned is happy to be the medium through which those papers reach the eye of your Majesty, feeling sensible that their perusal will furnish occasion to your Majesty to recur with much national pleasure to the act of one of your illustrious predecessors as a distinguished patron of science; and this recurrence to the eminent position that Denmark has attained in the arts and the sciences may perhaps not be the less pleasurable from the fact that the trophy of science to which the papers allude was achieved on the very coast where, as far back as the tenth century, the intrepidity and enterprise of your Majesty's Scandinavian ancestors first discovered and planted a colony upon the great western continent.

"The undersigned therefore hopes that, after a careful examination of the accompanying papers, from which it would seem to be admitted that Miss Mitchell, of the United States, is entitled to the honor of first discovering the telescopic comet bearing her name, your Majesty will not be able to perceive in that commendable delicacy which forbade her hastily seeking public notoriety a sufficient motive for withholding from her the reward of her eminent discovery; but, on the contrary, will direct the medal to be awarded to her, not only as a suitable encouragement to her distinguished scientific attainments, but also as evincing your Majesty's appreciation of that beautiful virtue which withheld her from rushing into public and scientific renown merely to comply with a purely technical condition.

"The undersigned, American chargé d'affaires, gladly improves this very pleasant occasion to tender to your Majesty the expression of his high and most distinguished consideration.

[Signed]   "R. P. FLENIKEN.

"To his Majesty FREDERIC VII., King of Denmark, Duke of Schleswig and Holstein."

THE COUNT DE KNUTH TO MR. FLENIKEN.

"Copenhague, ce 6 Octobre, 1848.

"MONSIEUR: J'ai eu l'honneur de recevoir votre office du 6 du passe, par lequel vous avez exprimé le desir que la medaille instituée par feu le Roi Frederic VI., en recompense de la decouverte de cometes telescopiques, fut accordee a Mlle. Maria Mitchell, de Nantucket dans les Etats Unis d'Amerique.

"Apres avoir examine les pieces justificatives que vous avez bien voulu me communiquer relativement a cette reclamation, je ne saurais que partager votre avis, Monsieur, qu'il paraît hors de doute que la découverte de la comete en question est effectivement due aux savantes recherches de Mlle. Mitchell; et que ce n'est que faute de n'avoir pas observe les formalités prescrites, qu'elle n'a point jusqu'ici recu une marque de distinction a laquelle elle paraît avoir de si justes titres.

"Le savant astronome, le Professeur Schumacher, ayant egalement recommandé Mlle. Mitchell a la faveur qu'elle sollicite maintenant, je me suis empressé de referer cette question au roi, mon auguste maître, en mettant en meme temps sous les yeux de sa Majesté la lettre que vous lui avez addressee a ce sujet; et c'est avec bien du plaisir que je me vois aujourd'hui a meme de vous faire part, Monsieur, que sa Majesté n'a point hesité a satisfaire a votre demande, en accordant a Mlle. Mitchell la médaille qu'elle ambitionne.

"Aussitot que cette médaille sera frappée, je m'empresserai de vous la faire parvenir.

"En attendant je saisis avec bien du plaisir cette occasion pour vous renouveler, Monsieur, les assurances de ma considération très distinguée.

"F. W. KNUTH.

"À MONSIEUR FLENIKEN, Chargé d'Affaires des Etats Unis d'Amérique."

————

TRANSLATION.

"Copenhagen, 6th October, 1848.

"SIR: I have had the honor to receive your communication of the 6th ultimo, in which you express the desire that the medal instituted by his late Majesty, Frederic VI., as a reward for the discovery of telescopic comets, should be granted to Miss Maria Mitchell, of Nantucket, in the United States of America.

"On examination of the justificatory pieces which you have been good enough to forward me, relating to her claim, I cannot do otherwise than participate in your opinion, sir, that it would appear to admit of no doubt that the discovery of the comet in question was really due to Miss Mitchell's learned researches; and that her not having as yet received a mark of distinction to which she seems to have such a just claim was entirely owing to her not having observed the prescribed forms.

"The learned astronomer, Professor Schumacher, having likewise recommended Miss Mitchell to the favor which she now solicits, I hasten to refer this question to the king, my august master, at the same time laying before His Majesty the letter which you have addressed to him on this subject; and I have much pleasure in being now enabled to inform you, sir, that His Majesty has not hesitated to grant your request by awarding to Miss Mitchell the medal which she desires.

"As soon as this medal is struck, I will have it forwarded to you, and meanwhile have much pleasure in availing myself of this occasion to renew to you, sir, the assurances of my most distinguished consideration.

[Signed] "F. W. KNUTH.

"To MR. FLENIKEN, Chargé d'Affaires of the United States of America."

MR. FLENIKEN TO THE COUNT DE KNUTH.

"Legation des Etats Unis d'Amerique, ⎱
a Copenhague, le 7 Octobre, 1848. ⎰

"MONSIEUR: Le soussigné a eu l'honneur de recevoir l'office que votre Excellence lui a addressé en date d'hier pour lui faire part de la nouvelle heureuse que sa Majesté, apres avoir examiné les documents que vous avez bien voulu lui soumettre, ayant pour objet d'établir le fait que Mlle. Mitchell ait la première decouvert la comete télescopique d'Octobre de l'an dernier, a bien voulu trouver ces preuves suffisantes, et a ordonné qu'on frappe une médaille, afin de la lui faire présenter comme une marque de distinction que sa Majesté croit qu'elle mérite en effet, quoiqu'elle n'ait pas rigoureusement observé les formalités prescrites par le Roi Frédéric VI., fondateur de ce don.

" Le soussigné s'empresse donc d'assurer votre Excellence et en meme temps de vous prier, Monsieur, de vouloir bien faire parvenir cette assurance a sa Majesté, que cet acte signalé de liberalité ne peut manquer d'etre dignement et hautement apprécié par les institutions scientifiques des Etats Unis, par Mlle. Mitchell qui est l'objet de cette distinction génereuse, et par les nombreux amis scientifiques de cette dame ; enfin, par tous ceux qui prennent de l'intéret a la réussite heureuse des recherches astronomiques.

" Le soussigné ne peut terminer cette communication sans exprimer a votre Excellence (en la priant de porter aussi ses sentiments a la connaissance de sa Majesté) sa vive appréciation de ce noble et éclatant acte de justice, si promptement et si génereusement rendu a sa jeune compatriote par le roi de Danemark, et il saisit avec empressement cette occasion de renouveler a votre Excellence les assurances de sa considération très distinguée.

" R. P. FLENIKEN.

"À Son Excellence M. LE COMTE DE KNUTH, Ministre d'Etat et Chef du Départment des Affaires Etrangeres."

TRANSLATION.

" Legation of the United States, 1
Copenhagen, October 7th, 1848. J

"SIR : The undersigned has the honor to acknowledge the receipt of your Excellency's communication of yesterday's date, conveying to him the gratifying intelligence that His Majesty, from an examination of the evidence which you obligingly laid before him, tending to establish the fact of Miss Mitchell's having discovered the telescopic comet of October, last, has been pleased to consider it quite satisfactory, and has ordered a medal to be struck for her as a mark of distinction to which his Majesty deems her entitled, notwithstanding her omission to comply with the prescribed conditions of Frederic VI., who instituted the donation.

"The undersigned, therefore, begs to express to you, sir, and through you to His Majesty, the assurance that this eminent act of liberality cannot fail to be duly and highly appreciated by the scientific institutions of his own country, by Miss Mitchell herself, who is the object of this generous distinction, and by her numerous scientific friends, as well as by all who feel an interest in successful astronomical achievements.

" The undersigned cannot close this communication without expressing to you and to the king his own unaffected appreciation of this noble and distinguished act of justice, so promptly and so generously bestowed upon his unobtrusive countrywoman by the king of Denmark, and avails himself of the occasion to renew to your Excellency the assurance of his most distinguished consideration.

[Signed] . "R. P. FLENIKEN.

"To His Excellency THE COUNT DE KNUTH, Minister of State, etc., etc., etc."

RETURN TO: CIRCULATION DEPARTMENT
198 Main Stacks

LOAN PERIOD 1	2	.	3
Home Use			
4	5		6

ALL BOOKS MAY BE RECALLED AFTER 7 DAYS.
Renewals and Recharges may be made 4 days prior to the due date.
Books may be renewed by calling 642-3405.

DUE AS STAMPED BELOW.

JUN 0 3 2003

APR 2 5 2005

FORM NO. DD6
50M 5-02

UNIVERSITY OF CALIFORNIA, BERKELEY
Berkeley, California 94720–6000

69800365R00175

Made in the USA
Middletown, DE
09 April 2018